BOATHOUSE ROW

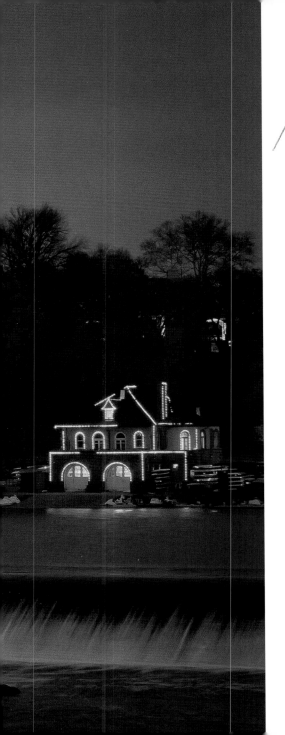

BOATHOUSE ROW

WAVES OF CHANGE IN THE BIRTHPLACE OF AMERICAN ROWING

DOTTY BROWN

TEMPLE UNIVERSITY PRESS

PHILADELPHIA   ROME   TOKYO

TEMPLE UNIVERSITY PRESS

Philadelphia, Pennsylvania 19122

www.temple.edu/tempress

Published 2017

All reasonable attempts were made to locate the copyright holders for
the illustrations published in this book. If you believe you may be one of
them, please contact Temple University Press, and the publisher
will include appropriate acknowledgment in
subsequent editions of the book.

Author photograph by April Saul

Design by Steve Kress

Library of Congress Cataloging-in-Publication Data

Names: Brown, Dotty, 1945–, author.
Title: Boathouse row : waves of change in the birthplace
of American rowing / Dotty Brown.
Description: Philadelphia : Temple University Press, [2016] |
Includes bibliographical references and index.
Identifiers: LCCN 2016022123 | ISBN 9781439912829 (cloth : alk.paper)
Subjects: LCSH: Rowing—Pennsylvania—Philadelphia—History. | Rowing—United States—History. |
Architecture, Victorian—Pennsylvania—Philadelphia.
Classification: LCC GV796 .B77 2016 | DDC 797.12/30974811—dc23 LC record available at
https://lccn.loc.gov/2016022123

♾ The paper used in this publication meets the requirements of
the American National Standard for Information Sciences—Permanence of
Paper for Printed Library Materials, ANSI Z39.48-1992

Printed in the United States of America

9 8 7 6 5 4 3 2 1

BOATHOUSE ROW

Waves of Change in the Birthplace of American Rowing

was supported by a generous donation from

H. F. (Gerry) Lenfest

To My husband, Larry, and our daughters,
Jordi, Becca, and Naomi,
for having always allowed me
the freedom to follow my dreams

CONTENTS

PREFACE

Life's currents sometimes sweep you in unexpected directions. That is what happened to me when Micah Kleit, executive editor of Temple University Press, suggested I write a book on the history of Boathouse Row. I was a member of the Vesper Boat Club and had recently left my newspaper career at the *Philadelphia Inquirer*. But I was hesitant. A book as ambitious as what Micah envisioned could take several years. I knew that the research would have to both fascinate and challenge me if I were to go the distance, not to mention create a work that would surprise and intrigue the public.

So I tested the waters. Immersing myself in fragile club archives of the 1800s, I began unearthing untold stories of wealth, intrigue, gambling, and pageantry from an era when rowing was *the* spectator sport of its time. Talking to long-time club members, I was enthralled by their memories of battles fought and victories won, not just on the water, but in the boathouses, as the clubs grappled with many of the same economic and social pressures that touched the nation.

I quickly realized that the picture postcard image of Boathouse Row, so charmingly Victorian in daytime and arrestingly lit at night, was as superficial as the Broadway marquee of a prize-winning play. I wanted to take the reader inside, behind the stage set, to meet the people who had played dramatic roles on Boathouse Row: the artist Thomas Eakins, himself a rower; the eccentric architect Frank Furness, whose imagination burnished the Row; the rags-to-riches Irish Catholic Kelly dynasty, who put Boathouse Row in klieg lights internationally; Ernestine Bayer and so many other Philadelphia women who fought for women's right to row. (Yes, it really was a fight, and it took generations.)

Beyond these well-known figures were many others whose fame has dimmed over time. Huge in his day was billionaire Edward T. Stotesbury, remembered only for his smallest gesture—donating a silver cup for what is now the largest high school regatta in the world. Other forgotten stars are Jersey farm boy Joe Burk, whose zeal and ethic led him to become one of the greatest rowers and collegiate coaches of all time; and Tom "the Bear" Curran, a larger-than-life character whose wit and wiles brought waves of victories to his initiates.

Then there's the surprising story of how an odd, ornery, unlikely group of men, drawn to Boathouse Row by their one shared passion and coached by a German and a Jew, stunned the world. Through the stories of these people and others, I have sought to chart some of the social undercurrents that have swirled through Boathouse Row, as struggles of class, race, and gender played out over more than 150 years.

Underlying the dynamism, the energy, and the continuing evolution of Boathouse Row is, of course, the sport of rowing. From single scull to heavyweight eight, its technical challenges and physical demands attract some of the most disciplined and competitive athletes in the nation, in numbers that continue to soar despite the absence of financial incentives.

My thanks to the many athletes, historians, and archivists who have helped me bring to life the story of Boathouse Row.

BOATHOUSE ROW

CHAPTERONE

BEFORE BOATHOUSE ROW

First There Was a Dam

On an Indian summer day in 1835, thousands of Philadelphians closed up shop and made their way by foot and by horseback, by wagon and by carriage, to witness the very first full-scale regatta on the Schuylkill River. Many of the spectators were elegantly dressed—the men in frock coats and top hats; the women in long dresses, shawls, and plumed chapeaux. At least, that is how the Italian painter Nicolino Calyo, who was passing through Philadelphia that fall, depicted them in the era before photography.

The crowd that November 12, more than 175 years ago, was the single largest gathering ever assembled on the river, all for a race. Big awards were at stake. The seven crews competing in the eight-oared category vied for a boat known as *The Prize*. Second place in the three-mile contest was a silver cup. Another race featured four smaller barges, each with four oars.

The oarsmen sported eye-catching costumes, often matching the colors of their boat. Those rowing the eight-oared *Imp* wore white trousers, red-and-white striped shirts, and red Greek fishermen's caps to complement their boat's broad red stripe. By contrast the Blue Devils, dressed in white pantaloons, blue-and-white striped shirts, and round blue hats, rowed a blue shell with a long gold stripe.

1835: The First Regatta

In a painting that depicts the first known large regatta on the Schuylkill River, seven 8-oared barges compete on November 12, 1835. They are the *Falcon*, *Sylph*, *Blue Devil*, *Metamora*, *Aurora*, *Imp*, and victorious *Cleopatra*. This unsigned gouache is the work of Italian painter Nicolino Calyo, who was passing through Philadelphia that fall. The artist (who does not show the huge crowds that witnessed the race) positions himself on the west bank of the Schuylkill, across from where the lighthouse now stands, looking upriver. The estate on the right is the former Sedgeley mansion, which stood near Lemon Hill. The painting came into the possession of the Undine Barge Club following the death of Captain Benjamin McMackin (1804–1867), described in a 1904 account by founding member John B. Thayer as a "celebrated Delaware River steamboat captain of seventy years ago."

Gouache, Nicolino Calyo, 1835. Courtesy of the Undine Barge Club.

Such was the pageant of what was fast becoming the most popular spectator sport in the United States. The excitement over rowing and the demand of crews for riverfront access would soon prompt Philadelphia to dedicate a short, bucolic stretch of its Schuylkill River, now known as Boathouse Row, to aficionados of the sport.

From that cradle of clubs and competition would emerge a credo of amateurism—the first such rules in the nation. A relentless spirit of athleticism and rivalry would take Philadelphia rowers to the heights of international competition, even as some of the city's most noteworthy architects vied to design structures, one more distinctive than the next.

Less visible but no less important were the social undercurrents that would roil and transform the Row over the following 175 years, much as they changed America.

Immigrants and tradesmen seeking an avenue to success would find their way into clubs, which were largely dependent on the wealthy to shoulder the cost of boats, boathouses, equipment, and travel.

Women would fight tradition and territoriality for access and equality, as they did in everything else.

And doors would open or close to young rowers, depending on the resources of their school or its patronage.

All that was yet to come. Back in 1835, Philadelphia was just entering the fray.

While men had competed against one another on water for as long as testosterone and floating craft had existed, historians date the roots of modern-day rowing races to England in 1716, when an actor, Thomas Doggett, offered a purse of an orange coat and a silver badge to the fastest of the Thames watermen, who ordinarily transported people and goods across the river. The annual spectacle inspired unruly crowds, gambling, and a professional rowing class. By the 19th century, Britain's upper crust, which at first had been happy to place bets on the watermen, began to regard the big-stakes races as ruinous to an exercise that so perfectly married supreme physical conditioning with balance, concentration, and teamwork. Soon the amateur "gentleman rowers" of Oxford and Cambridge universities, along with the rowing clubs of the Thames, would fight to claim the sport as their own and force out the professional rowers, often from the laboring classes, whose races invited foul play.

The sport's first big hurrah in the United States occurred in 1824, when at least 50,000 spectators—the largest gathering of Americans ever at a sporting event—crowded around New York Harbor to watch four New York watermen take on four sailors from a visiting British warship. Both crews competed in similar

24-foot Whitehall boats, a streamlined rowboat or wherry, named for the Battery's Whitehall Street. Happily, the *American Star* defeated the *Certain Death* for what at the time was an astounding $1,000 purse (about $25,000 today).

In this era before the invention of basketball, baseball, or football; before radio or TV; before cameras or cars, the sport of rowing quickly spread to other American cities perched on rivers—from Boston to Detroit, Pittsburgh to New Orleans, Poughkeepsie to San Francisco.

On the Schuylkill River, the western border of colonial Philadelphia, ferrymen rowing heavy barges dominated transport until 1805, when the first bridge was built at High Street (now Market). While they may have raced one another for fun or wager, it was only after the construction of a dam in 1821, then the longest in the country, that the suddenly calmed river became an ideal venue for the sport of rowing.

The dam was part of an ingenious solution to the difficulty of delivering clean water to the city after the first effort, using tons of wood to power unreliable steam engines, proved too costly. Visionary engineer Frederick Graff devised a hydraulic system, powered by the river and waterwheels, to pump the city's water supply from the Schuylkill up to a reservoir on Fair Mount, the highest point in the city. From this plateau, where the Philadelphia Museum of Art now stands, cast-iron pipes would transport water through the city.

Disguised by handsome, white neoclassical buildings surrounded by gracious gardens, the technological marvel quickly became one of the most visited sites in the country. Some said that coming to Philadelphia without seeing the Fairmount Water Works was akin to visiting London without viewing Westminster Abbey.

The water above the dam, once a tidal river that had challenged ferrymen with rapids and falls, was instantly calmed. A "lake," the rowers called it. Soon groups of young men, sufficiently well off to afford leisure time, were pooling money to build simple boat sheds along the riverbank above the dam and to buy boats for racing and for steamy summer outings to the taverns that opened up at the Falls of Schuylkill (now East Falls), famously serving catfish and waffles.

Small rowing clubs such as the Imps and the Blue Devils came and went. Among the first was the Falcon Barge Club, organized on April 19, 1834, largely by city merchants and professionals. Its constitution reveals its commitment to rules and discipline, typical of the clubs. Members had to be at least 20 years old and wear the club uniform within three months of admission. Rowing on Sunday was not allowed, nor were members to speak ill of one another: "No personal reflections or animadversions on the conduct of members shall be

FAIRMOUNT WATER-WORKS.

FROM THE WEST SIDE.

Publ. by C.G.Childs & R.H.Hobson, Philad.ᵃ 1829.

G.Lehman Fecit.

A Canal to Bypass the Dam

A bargeman on a keelboat carrying freight blows a trumpet to announce his approach to the lockkeeper of the Fairmount Dam Canal Lock (the channel is barely visible on the left). The canal allowed shipping to bypass the dam, which was added in 1821 as part of an overhaul of the Fairmount Water Works. The city had built its first water system in 1801 after yellow fever killed 5,000 residents. It used tons of wood to fuel steam engines that pumped clean water to the city, but proved costly and unreliable. The new system, using water wheels, was celebrated as the most efficient water system in the country.

Fairmount Water-Works from the West Side, lithograph based on a painting by George Lehman, published 1829 by C. G. Childs and R. H. Hobson, Philadelphia. The Library Company of Philadelphia.

allowed in the club." Admission was $10 (about $270 today); monthly dues, 25 cents (nearly $7). Fines for a plethora of potential infractions consumed two and half pages of the document.

The river, as paintings of the time show, was still rustic, bordered by a few large hilltop mansions with sweeping grounds. But soon businesses crept in, including the breweries, which utilized river water to make beer and gave rise to Brewerytown. By mid-century, industries upriver were using the Schuylkill as a "convenient sewer." River traffic was increasing as well. A canal along the west bank, near where the Schuylkill Expressway now runs parallel to the river, ferried coal from the anthracite lodes near Pottsville, about 100 miles upriver to the northwest. Steamboats, too, frequented the river, often creating dangerous wakes for smaller craft.

Philadelphia's planners, alarmed by the growing chaos and pollution, decided something had to be done to protect the city's water supply. At the same time, they wanted to ensure the beauty of the riverfront for a public desirous of green spaces for walking, picnics, and carriage rides. In 1844, the city took its first step toward the creation of Fairmount Park. It bought Lemon Hill, just upstream from the Water Works. By 1859, inspired in part by Frederick Law Olmsted's vision of meandering paths and carriageways for Central Park in New York, the city signed on to a plan for a park extending upriver almost a mile to just above Girard Ave.

It gave permission for several stone structures to be built—a double boathouse along the riverbank nearest the dam and Water Works (Pacific Barge Club); the Philadelphia Skating Club and Humane Society at the other end, just before a bend in the river; and the Bachelors Barge Club in the middle. Nine years later, in 1867, the new Fairmount Park Commission ordered all other boathouses torn down, including some made of brick. Any house constructed without regard to "architectural adornment" had to go. The Commission would allow only picturesque boathouses made of stone and designed in an ornamental style to be built on the stretch of waterfront above the Water Works. Each blueprint would have to pass muster.

Onto this stage set would now step the people: men and women of energy, enthusiasm, ambition, artistry, passion, determination—even obsession. Their dreams, dares, disappointments, and desires—hidden from view behind gabled dormers, ornamental woodwork, hipped roofs, Gothic Revival arches, and Tudor balconies— became the pulse of Boathouse Row. It would be these people who shaped the course of the Row, who made it so much more than a 19th-century postcard.

Drawn by T.Birch   Engraved by R.Campbell

The Beginnings of Fairmount Park

In 1824, decades before Boathouse Row, a steamboat with two paddle wheels approaches the Fairmount Dam Canal Lock. In the background are several estates, including the 45-acre Lemon Hill, which Philadelphia bought in 1844 to protect its water supply from industrial pollution. Within two years of establishing Fairmount Park in 1855, the city began enlarging it by purchasing 33 acres adjacent to Lemon Hill and the nearby Sedgeley estate. Tourists flocked to Philadelphia to view the technological marvel of the Water Works and the dam, the longest in the country when it was built. A walkway, 253 feet long and 26 feet wide, no longer exists. The canal was demolished in the 1950s with the construction of Martin Luther King Drive and the Schuylkill Expressway.

View of the Dam and Water Works at Fairmount, Philadelphia, engraving by Robert Campbell, 1824, from an original drawing by Thomas Birch. The Library Company of Philadelphia.

CHAPTERTWO

THOMAS EAKINS

In the Heyday of Rowing, a Young Artist Paints His Friends

On July 11, 1861, two weeks shy of his 17th birthday, Thomas Eakins graduated from Central High School in Philadelphia into a world that was dramatically changing.

Most immediate and concerning for the aspiring artist was war. Eleven states had seceded from the Union, and President Lincoln, newly inaugurated, had just won congressional authorization for 500,000 volunteer troops. Many from the city, including classmates, were looking to enlist.

Another revolution was also underway. Creating turmoil was the Industrial Age, in full throttle in Philadelphia, the second-largest city in the country after New York and possibly the fourth largest in the world. Railways, iron works, shipping, banking, and the world's largest textile industry, with 260 factories, were fueling employment, wealth, and a growing middle class, as well as construction, congestion, and social dislocation. The city, a hub of invention and innovation, had pioneered steam locomotives and ways to use anthracite coal. Medicine and science were breaking through old boundaries; even women now had their own medical school, opened in 1850. Immigrants, from Ireland, Germany, and England, seeing opportunity here, had helped to catapult the city's population by 58 percent in the 1840s and another 38 percent in the decade of the 1850s. More were pouring in.

Thomas Eakins, a rower himself, knew well the enormous physical and mental effort of competitive sculling. He paints himself into the background of *The Champion Single Sculls* and signs and dates the painting on his boat, as if to acknowledge the challenge that he too faces as an aspiring artist. Although in three years Eakins moves on to other subjects, his 24 rowing sketches and paintings endure as a vivid portrayal of the historical prominence of Boathouse Row in the sport of rowing.

Thomas Eakins, *The Champion Single Sculls (Max Schmitt in a Single Scull)* (detail), 1871. The Metropolitan Museum of Art. Image source: Art Resource, New York.

But for Thomas Eakins, fascinated by light, mood, and motion, the changes transforming a small stretch of the Schuylkill River, a 20-minute walk from his home, would most influence his early life and art.

Eakins, who lived at 1729 Mt. Vernon Street, had grown up during a period of dramatic change for the stretch of the Schuylkill River above the Fairmount Water Works. Once an unsightly and dangerous hodge-podge of steamships, barges, railroads, carriages, tow canals, iron foundries, taverns, breweries, and marauding gangs of thieves known as the "Schuylkill Rangers," the river in 1861 was on the verge of becoming one of the country's preeminent venues for sport and recreation. Soon it would also become an architectural icon of the city, with a name: *Boathouse Row*.

Eakins' growing up had coincided with the Row's going up, and it is no surprise that in his first major artistic challenge, Eakins would try to capture on canvas what he loved and knew so well. He was the right man in the right place at the right time to immortalize the play of light and energy on the river and portray the balance, concentration, and athleticism of its rowers. While he would later move on to other subjects, his rowing paintings evoke the spirit of Philadelphia's Boathouse Row as no one else's have. He painted his river, his friends, and the country's most popular sport from the perspective of an insider.

Thomas Eakins was born in Philadelphia in 1844. That same year, the city made a decision critical to the enjoyment of its citizens: it purchased the 45-acre Lemon Hill, a prominent knoll that looked down on the neoclassical buildings of the Fairmount Water Works, built two decades earlier. The initial impetus to acquiring this estate was to stymie further upstream industrialization that was threatening to pollute the city's water supply.

At first, the city did not do much with Lemon Hill, leasing it to a beer hall. But gaining philosophical ground among urban planners was the notion of parks open to all citizens as a "pastoral counterpoint" to the pressure cooker of urban life and as a way to "promote peaceful coexistence among the city's increasingly diverse constituencies."

New York State in 1853 had set aside more than 750 acres for what would become New York City's Central Park. The citizens of Philadelphia, with growing income and leisure time, were demanding places to play as well.

Among them was Thomas Eakins' father, Benjamin Eakins, a member of the city's respected artisan class. In the Census of 1850, Benjamin Eakins modestly describes himself as a "teacher of penmanship." Really, he was a master calligrapher who held prestigious posts. He taught for nearly 50 years at one of the city's private academies, the Quaker-run Friends Central School, then at 4th and Cherry Streets. He also penned diplomas

Cresent
Philadelphia

Malta
Undine

Bachelors
University
West Phila.

Quaker City
Vesper

Pennsylvania
College

GENTLEMEN'S

LADIE'S

1854
A.D.
University Barge Club

**Skating on the
Schuylkill**

During the freezing winters of the 1800s, thousands take to the ice at Boathouse Row, where a scattering of early boathouses line the shoreline below Lemon Hill. The Philadelphia Skating Club (now the Philadelphia Girls' Rowing Club) is at the bottom of the hill. This engraving, which commemorates the founding of the University Barge Club in 1854, was likely executed in the 1870s, given the clubs named at the top.

Rendition of an engraving by Hugo Sebald, originally created in 1862 as an advertisement for skate makers Clarenbach and Herder. Courtesy of the University Barge Club.

for the University of Pennsylvania and Jefferson Medical College. Benjamin Eakins' craft plus smart investments earned him enough to indulge in the many sports he loved—hunting, swimming, sailing, rowing, and spending time at his "fishing house" on the Cohansey Creek in South Jersey.

Ice-skating was a particular passion. In 1849, when his eldest, Thomas, was five years old, Benjamin Eakins signed "B. Eakins" on the founding papers of the Skater's Club of the City and County of Philadelphia, the first figure-skating club in the nation. Skating was hugely popular during the bone-chilling winters of the mid-1800s, when the Schuylkill regularly froze over. One January day in 1856, when Thomas was 11, the Skater's Club reported 20,000 Philadelphians out on the river and policemen stationed at Poplar Street "to oversee people walking the planks onto the ice."

In a letter written from Paris years later, Thomas would think back on the skating lessons his father had given him and how the same tips might benefit his younger sister, Margaret. "If you get a chance on the river," he wrote his father, "get Maggie to roll over the very rough ice as you did me when I was little. That makes a fellow steady."

In summer, too, Philadelphians in growing numbers were enjoying the river. At a time when the Jersey shore was many hours away, a popular hot day's outing was to row up to the Falls of Schuylkill, where the Falls Bridge now stands. There the men, sometimes accompanied by their girlfriends, would dine on fried catfish, waffles, and mint juleps at one of several inns, such as Bobby Arnold's, before rowing home, often a romantic ride under the stars.

Racing, though, offered more challenge, more thrill for rowers—and for spectators.

In the 1850s, an era before the rise of baseball in the 1860s, football in the 1870s, and the invention of basketball in 1891, rowing was *the* sport. Young men of means were pooling their resources to buy boats and oars and build places to store them, forming more substantial rowing clubs than those that had sprung up in rowing's first blush in the 1830s. Spectators crowded the riverbanks, anxious to reap the rewards of their bets.

In 1853, four years after the founding of the Skater's Club, a group of well-to-do young men "desirous of promoting our mutual enjoyment . . . in the manly art of rowing" organized as the Bachelors Barge Club, so named because it was intended for bachelors; once married, men would lose voting rights.

The next year, ten underclassmen at the University of Pennsylvania, tired of renting boats from Charlie's Boathouse, bought the four-oared barge the *Hesperus* from the Bachelors Club and launched the University Barge Club.

With a menu of catfish, mint juleps, and waffles, the taverns of the Falls of Schuylkill (now East Falls) were the place to go on a hot summer's day in the 1800s. Young oarsmen would often strip off their club uniforms and take a cooling swim in the river before rowing home to Boathouse Row under the stars. Popular in 1845 was Bobby Evan's Hotel, which had become Tissots Park Hotel by 1897, the time of this watercolor.

Bobby Evan's Hotel, Falls of Schuylkill, 1845. David J. Kennedy. Historical Society of Pennsylvania.

In 1856, a group of men, older than the Penn students, established the Undine Barge Club "with the object of healthful exercise, relaxation from business, friendly intercourse, and pleasure."

By 1858, so many clubs were out competing—and clashing—that nine of them united to create the first amateur governing body for sports in the United States. The Schuylkill Navy would represent the clubs before the city, arbitrate interclub disputes, set rules for navigating the river, and organize regattas. Most critically, it would lead the way in setting national standards for amateur sport.

While the Schuylkill Navy was overseeing the water, city officials, intent on beautifying its shoreline, were becoming increasingly alarmed by the haphazard emergence of the boat shelters, often crudely built of brick or wood. In 1859, when Eakins was 15, the city ordered them torn down. The city gave permission for several

structures to be built on a narrow stretch of its prime riverfront land in a picturesque style, harmonious with the natural landscape. These were a double boathouse built by the Pacific Barge Club near the Water Works and a stone house built by the Bachelors Barge Club a bit farther upstream.

Also granted permission was the newly merged Philadelphia Skating Club and Humane Society, with a dual mission of rescue and sport. Its Italianate stone building (now home to Philadelphia Girls' Rowing Club) was two stories tall, with arched windows and a balcony facing the river. Its completion in April 1861, at a point farthest away from the Water Works, was a keystone moment in the history of Boathouse Row. Not only would the Skating Club become the architectural anchor for the Row, but it remains today the oldest of the original houses still intact. (Only a portion of the Pacific Barge Club remains.)

1873: A Stereoscopic View

Boathouse Row was in the midst of a building boom in 1873, depicted in this pair of slightly different images, which creates a three-dimensional effect when seen through a stereoscopic viewer. From left: Skating Club (1860), Vesper/Malta (1873), University (1870–1871), Bachelors (1860), Crescent/Pennsylvania Barge (1869–1871), Pacific (1860, now Fairmount). Yet to be built in the open stretch: University of Pennsylvania's College Boat House (1874–1875), West Philadelphia (1878, later Penn AC), and Undine (1883).

James Cremer, *Scenery in Fairmount Park*, circa 1873. Courtesy of James Hill.

Scenery in Fairmount Park.

Eakins was celebrating a milestone that year: his high school graduation. It had taken both luck and intelligence for him to gain admission to Central High School, the first and only public high school in the city for most of the 19th century, aside from its sister school, the Philadelphia High School for Girls. Then, as now, admission was based on merit; its purpose was to give a demanding college-prep education to talented lower- and middle-class students whose families could not afford the only alternative at the time—the private high schools, such as William Penn Charter, Friends Central, and Episcopal Academy.

At Central High School, Eakins had enjoyed a rigorous classical training, especially in the arts, where the curriculum, heavily weighted to science and mathematics, emphasized perspective and mechanical drawing. He graduated with a 92.8 grade point average (GPA) and delivered one of eight addresses—the "Tom C. Eakins Fourth Honor," or scientific address. It presaged his dual interest in art and science—especially anatomy and the mechanics of motion.

Entering into a nation at war, he soon saw several of his 11 classmates enlist. Among them was one of Eakins' closest friends—Billy Sartain, who graduated "meritorious" in the class, with a 94 GPA. Billy's father, John Sartain, was a skilled engraver who, in 1855, was named a director of the Pennsylvania Academy of the Fine Arts (PAFA), a position he would hold for 22 years. Billy's sister, Emily Sartain, herself an artist, exchanged deeply philosophical letters with Eakins and for a while appeared to be his intended.

Another close friend and classmate who went off to war was the champion rower Max Schmitt. The future lawyer, born in Bavaria, had also bested Eakins academically, graduating with a 95.7 GPA.

While Eakins' views about the war are not known, what is clear is that he did not volunteer. Instead, he began to study "life drawing," with nude models, at the PAFA, then on Chestnut Street between 10th and 11th Streets. He also studied anatomy there at a time when Dr. Samuel Gross—the trauma surgeon he would later portray in his graphic and controversial masterpiece *The Gross Clinic*—was also drawing at the academy.

On the river, meanwhile, with so many men off to battle the Confederacy, the rowing clubs were struggling, as they would during every war and every recession that followed. The Schuylkill Navy suspended its annual regatta, although Boston held its Fourth of July race throughout the war. Professional scullers, in the newly popular one-man sculls, continued their high-stakes meets, accompanied by a frenzy of public gambling.

For instance, in 1862, the Schuylkill was chosen as neutral turf for a two-day standoff between Josh Ward of Newburgh, New York—the national champion undefeated in 15 races—and his challenger, James Hamill of Pittsburgh, then largely unknown. In a major upset, Hamill won the $500 purse (about $11,600 today) in the three-mile race, winning in 22 minutes, 22 seconds. He also won the five-mile race the next day.

Eakins was not an official member of any of the clubs, and his signature does not appear in any of the surviving boat club logbooks, in which rowers, to this day, record their mileage. But letters and diaries—his and others—prove that he got onto the river during the war years. His connections, his "club," was the intellectual, artistic-scientific community that straddled such institutions as Central High School, Jefferson Medical College, and the PAFA. There is reason to believe that he rowed out of the Undine Barge Club with Joseph Boggs Beale, a Central High student who graduated six months after Eakins. Also an artist, Beale joined Undine in 1861.

At Undine, Eakins may have rowed with his high school chemistry teacher, Dr. Benjamin H. Rand, who was club president from 1859 to 1865 and whose portrait was among the first that Eakins would paint. (Rand's father, a calligrapher, would later succeed Eakins' father, penning diplomas for Jefferson Medical College.)

Central High,
Class of 1861

Several men important in the life and work of Thomas Eakins (on right with pocket square) were also members of his Central High School Class of 1861. He traveled in Europe with William Sartain (top) and courted William's sister, Emily, who later headed what is now the Moore College of Art. (Their father, engraver John Sartain, was a director of the Pennsylvania Academy of the Fine Arts, where Eakins later taught.) William J. Crowell (bottom right) married Eakins' sister, Frances, and Eakins was engaged to Crowell's sister before her death. Max Schmitt (between Eakins and Crowell) became the champion rower Eakins famously painted in 1871.

O. H. Willard, *Central High School Class*, June 1861. William Sartain Scrapbooks, vol. 2. Courtesy of the Pennsylvania Academy of the Fine Arts, Philadelphia. Charles Bregler's Thomas Eakins Collection, purchased with the partial support of the Pew Memorial Trust.

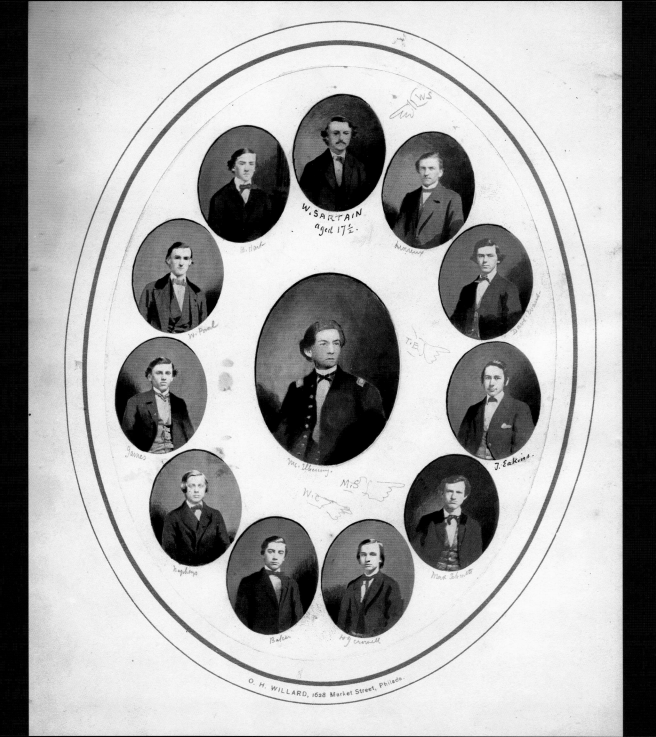

Benjamin Rand, Teacher and Rower

Thomas Eakins' portrait of Benjamin Howard Rand underscores the nexus of Philadelphia's artistic, scientific, and rowing communities of the 1870s. Rand, who was Eakins' chemistry professor at Central High and later taught at Jefferson Medical College, was president of the Undine Barge Club from 1859 to 1865. This portrait of Rand was prominently displayed at the 1876 Centennial's art exhibition, which was headed by engraver John Sartain, the father of Eakins' classmate William Sartain. Like Eakins' father, Rand's father was a calligrapher, and he succeeded the senior Eakins in his job penning diplomas for Jefferson graduates. In 1877, Eakins donated this portrait to Jefferson, which sold it for about $20 million to the Crystal Bridges Museum, in Arkansas in 2007.

Thomas Eakins, *Portrait of Professor Benjamin Howard Rand*, oil on canvas, 1874. Crystal Bridges Museum of American Art, Bentonville, AR. Courtesy of the Philadelphia Museum of Art.

Most likely, Eakins rowed with the Pennsylvania Barge Club, organized in 1861, where his good friend Max Schmitt was a member. Chris Doyle, a club member who has studied its history, says that Eakins' name does not appear in club records because only those of competitors were recorded. He points out that one of Eakins' paintings, *Oarsmen on the Schuylkill*, is also known as *Pennsylvania Barge Club Four*. "I think he liked these guys. They were his friends. They palled around. They drank upstairs. It was his social life. I think that's more the narrative."

On August 26, 1864, a month after Eakins turned 20—an age when the federal conscription act of 1863 required that he register for the draft—he tried to dodge that possibility and paid $25 to the city's New Bounty Fund of the 15th Ward, a mechanism for enticing others to serve in his place.

Did the young artist then take off for Montreal, escaping Philadelphia in the last year of war? Perhaps, wonders Eakins scholar Elizabeth Milroy. No records prove a Canadian sojourn, but Milroy finds it curious that Eakins was not listed in the Philadelphia City Directory in 1865 and later wrote about Montreal. Wherever he spent the final days of the Civil War, Eakins' painting master at the Pennsylvania Academy in 1866 pronounced him ready for the École des Beaux Arts in Paris, the premier destination for aspiring artists. On September 22, Eakins boarded a steamer in New York. Seeing him off were his father, Benjamin, as well as Academy of Fine Arts Director John Sartain and his daughter, Eakins' girlfriend, Emily.

During the Atlantic crossing, Eakins dreamed about Max Schmitt and water—the river water he knew so well and the ocean water he was now experiencing. In a letter home to his mother, he wrote, "I had been rowing with Max and I was drinking some cool beer . . . but while I was drinking someone put salt in it, and I was still forced to drink it."

There is no evidence that Eakins got the chance to row in Paris, but his letters reveal that he often broke from his art studies for other sporting adventures, including hiking in the Alps, swimming, and wrestling and lifting weights in a local gym.

In the winter of 1867, the 22-year-old showed off his ice-skating skills, honed in childhood with coaching from his father, to onlookers at the Bois de Boulogne. In a letter home, he complains about the quality of the skate rentals and then writes, "I made up my mind to go it a little modestly at first & skated straight forward round & round till I got a little accustomed to the things. By remembering to keep skating always on the front part of the skates, that is on my toes, I found myself rapidly improving and in ten minutes I concluded there was no more danger of falling so I went back to the middle of the pond and showed them some touches I guess they never dreamed of."

"I go to the Gymnasium 3 times a week," he writes his family later that year. "It is not to be compared with [the Philadelphia gym] Hildebrand & Lewis's. . . . It's on the ground which is covered with a half foot of tan [tree bark]. There is no heavy weight practice but a good deal of somersaulting & swinging on trapezes and wrestling. Wrestling is great fun but it fills our ears eyes nose & hair with tan & we look like pigs when we are done & it's another hour's work to get clean again."

His passion for sports was very much of his time. With the Industrial Revolution had come sedentary jobs, and many people now craved exercise, not only for pleasure but also for its health benefits. If they were not health conscious already or needed to learn technique, numerous how-to books and magazine articles were being published, especially in England, to educate them. Their initial audience was upper-class British gentlemen, but the idea quickly caught on across the Pond among Americans with newfound leisure time.

Among the first major treatises on exercise was Donald Walker's *British Manly Exercises; In Which Rowing and Sailing Are Now First Described*, published in 1834 in England and in 1836 in Philadelphia. Its 264 pages

A Rowing Machine, 1885

An ad for a rowing machine, made by J. M. Lifeline of New York City, touts rowing as "the most beneficial of exercises, because it calls into play every muscle in the body and gives to each one a full and equal share of work." This "perfect parlor rowing apparatus" sold in 1885 for $10 (about $245 today). It had a counter that compared the rower's stroke rate with that of Canadian champion Ned Hanlan's rate of 32 per minute.

Reproduced from Frederick William Janssen, *History of American Amateur Athletics* (New York: Charles R. Bourne, 1885), 84.

EAKINS SEES
HIS FIRST "VELOCIPEDE"

The earliest pedal-powered bicycles were being produced in France just when Eakins was studying there. In the fall of 1867, Eakins caught sight of one such two-wheeled "velocipede." It is "beautiful in its simplicity," Eakins writes, drawing a sketch of it in a letter to his father. "The rider makes it go by working his feet on two little cranks setting out from the front wheel."

Bicycling would, a decade or so later, be all the rage in Philadelphia. In 1881, the Vesper Boat Club, facing financial problems, debated changing its name to the "Vesper Boat and Bicycle Club" but voted the idea down. By the early 1890s, the city would have 29 cycling clubs. Sedgeley, formed in 1897 by a group of women who also wanted a place to exercise, initially named itself the "Bicycle, Barge and Canoe Club."

Letter from Thomas Eakins to his father, Benjamin Eakins, Paris, November 9, 1867. Pennsylvania Academy of the Fine Arts, Philadelphia. Archives.

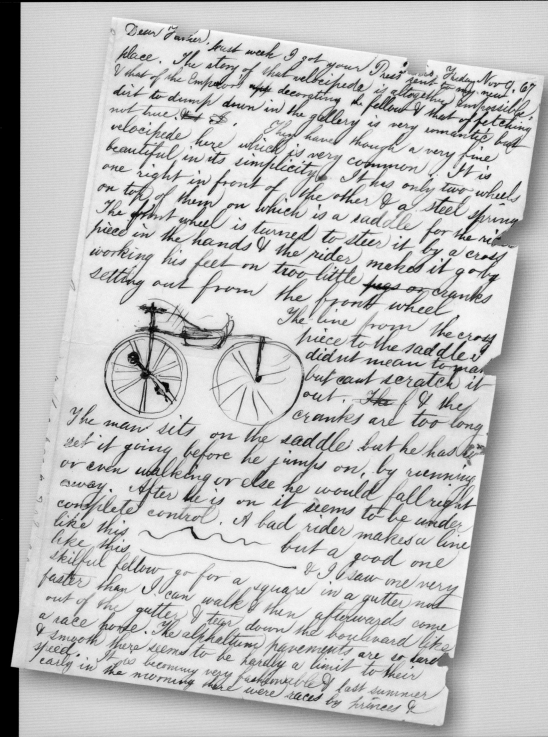

are filled with the tips one might get from a trainer today, including advice on nutrition, hydration, proper respiration, and whole body training. Walker also gives step-by-step instructions on the proper way to perform all the sports of the era: walking, running, weightlifting, skating, riding, hunting—and rowing. He endorses strength building using periods of rest between reps: "In active exertion, the member exercised swells with the more frequent and more copious flow of blood, and heat is developed in it with greater abundance; and if we repeat the same motions many times after intervals of repose, all the muscles exercised become permanently developed." The respiration resulting from vigorous exercise, he says, not only "promotes the expulsion of injurious agents" but "produces a fresh colour in persons who may have become pale through a sedentary life."

Exercise also had a moral imperative. Walker, like the Victorians who followed, saw inactivity as leading to "vice" and to gambling. On the other hand, "well-regulated exercises excite ambition to excel and energy in the performance of every duty."

Dozens of other exercise manuals followed, increasingly focused on rowing as it became the most popular sport of the time. In Philadelphia, the Undine Barge Club, for one, authorized spending club money on several of these books to be "kept in the rooms of the club for perusal of members." They included the 1863 *Manual of British Rural Sports* by "Stonehenge," the pseudonym of John Henry Walsh, a fellow of the Royal College of Surgeons, and in 1866, *The Art of Rowing and Training* by "Argonaut," the pen name of Edward Dampier Brickwood, a stellar British rower.

Of course, almost all of this discourse on exercise was directed at men. Rowing, in particular, was seen as far too rigorous a sport for frail Victorian women. Besides, how could they do it in skirts? Instead of rowing, they rode as passengers in "ladies boats" with the men seated next to them doing the exertion. Thus, in his 1871 book, *A History of Rowing in America*, Robert Johnson could get away with saying, "Health to be won, must be like maidens fair, and stately dames, diligently sought."

Eakins saw rowing not only as healthful but also as mental therapy: when his sister Fanny wrote saying she was discouraged about her piano playing, he suggested that she "take a walk to Fairmount or a row up the river."

With so much interest in exercise, gyms and sports clubs proliferated in Philadelphia. In 1859, a Philadelphia physician, Paul B. Goddad, opened a predecessor to the soon-to-follow athletic clubs. He called his establishment "The Natatorium and Institute for Scientific Instruction in the Improvement of Physical Powers." Its mission was to apply scientific principles to swimming and exercise "to improve one's health and physical condition."

Also springing up were gun clubs, horse clubs, hunting clubs, riding clubs, tennis clubs, and fishing clubs. Cricket was particularly popular among all Philadelphians, and in 1860 there were even three African American cricket clubs "which played the game among themselves."

Going well beyond sports, Philadelphians were joining all kinds of fraternal organizations as old social patterns frayed in a city swelling with immigrants from Ireland, Germany, and Great Britain. Rich or poor, artistic or athletic, musical or political, religious or socially concerned, people in the ever more diverse and splintered city wanted to feel as if they belonged somewhere. In droves, they sought the familiarity and camaraderie of a club, where they could make friends, share interests, and in some cases garner prestige. Even those from "the meanest boy's gang . . . sought a sense of social place and community in club life." By the 1870s, the city had 24 different singing societies, 91 German secret societies, and 800 private social service organizations, not to mention such rarified groups as the Philadelphia Club and the Union League.

From this culture, boat clubs also emerged. At least two of them sprang from the city's independent fire companies, which had a history of competition to the point of mayhem. By mid-century, Philadelphia was taking steps to consolidate and modernize firefighting into a citywide force. The neighborhood companies, each one with its own clubhouse, uniforms, social makeup, and status, began seeking other ways to maintain their brotherhood.

Some fire companies turned their energy and fellowship to the river, bringing with them their love of costume and ritual, and a nicknaming tradition. They were not necessarily made up of working-class men. The social status of volunteer firemen typically mirrored the neighborhood they served.

The Bachelors Barge Club, the oldest club in continual existence on the Row, was started by members of the Phoenix Hose Company. It covered the Center City neighborhood around 7th and 8th Streets, among the wealthiest neighborhoods in town at the time. Many of the volunteer firemen were also members of the Yes, Oui, Si Chess Club, which met in the Athenaeum Building.

One of Bachelors' founders and its president was Israel W. Morris, whose family dated back to the Revolution. Club minutes from the 1850s reveal that Bachelors held its monthly meetings at his family mansion just off Washington Square.

Return to Roots

Some members of the University Barge Club (below) also had a fire company tradition, as echoed in this photo of rowers in costume, marking the club's 70th anniversary in 1924.

Courtesy of the University Barge Club.

From Fireman to Oarsman

Until Philadelphia launched a professional citywide fire department in 1870, volunteer neighborhood fire companies manned the front lines, each with its own neighborhood turf. They were tightly knit social groups with uniforms, nicknames, and other traditions that carried through when a few of them turned their energy and camaraderie to the river as early boat clubs. Members of the Phoenix Hose Company (above), made up of residents of prosperous eastern Center City, formed the Bachelors Barge Club in 1853.

Phoenix Hose Company. Reproduced from Walter H. Pflaumer et al., eds., *150 Years: History of the Bachelors Barge Club, 1853–2003* (Philadelphia: Bachelors Barge Club, 2006), 17.

Bachelors Minute Book, 1853

First Minute Book of the Bachelors Barge Club, 1853.

Courtesy of the Bachelors Barge Club.

A Rarefied Reunion, 1903

Members of Philadelphia's upper crust—or those hoping to arrive there—regarded membership in the Bachelors Barge Club as a stepping-stone. Some did not even row but would dine regularly at the club's upriver house, the Button, which opened in 1883. Among those present at the club's 50th anniversary in 1903 are J. B. Lippincott (publisher), Clarkson Clothier (department store executive), and W. Atlee Burpee (founder of Burpee Seeds).

50th Reunion, 1903. Courtesy of the Bachelors Barge Club.

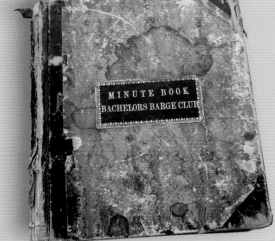

this is your invitation to the
naming party
at
the button
wednesday, feb. 13, 1929

victims
william w. wood ··· w. c. mcadoo jr.

godfathers
"brush" "rich" "chow" "tan"

Naming Night

The guest books at the Bachelors' upriver dining club, the Button, are filled with witty poems, toasts, invitations to black tie dinners, and elegant sketches penned by club members. Among the celebrations were "naming parties," in which new members were anointed with a one-syllable nickname. A logbook of these monikers, still assigned today, assures that none is repeated. Also continuing is a tradition at the start of every dinner, where members hold their forks and knives (like oars) upright on the table and then let them fall to rowing commands: "Are you ready, men? Settle! Eyes in the boat! Handle your oars! Toss! Let Fall."

Logbook, the Button, 1929. Courtesy of the Bachelors Barge Club.

A firehouse tradition that the Bachelors men continued was a naming ceremony. Each new member was given a single-syllable nickname recorded in a book, never to be used again, a practice still in place today. Thus, Israel Morris, who became a wealthy iron merchant, was "Brother Tubes." Publisher J. B. Lippincott, who joined in 1882, was "Brother Type." Maxwell Wyeth, a member of the family that invented a press to make pills, was initiated in 1889 as "Brother Drugs." Clarkson Clothier, of the Strawbridge & Clothier department store family, was "Brother Silk."

With the passage of time, recruiting the most competitive rowers became an ever greater imperative, and the naming tradition took on a new purpose as club membership became more ethnically, religiously, and economically diverse. "The names were for camaraderie, but also it was a way to check rank at the door," explained Henry Hauptfuhrer, a Bachelors member who has studied the club's history. By the 1920s, Olympic medalist Ken Myers—a fireman whose day job was shoveling coal on a Reading Railroad locomotive—would have sat down to dinner with one of the wealthiest men in America, club president Edward T. Stotesbury, a partner in Drexel & Company.

The University Barge Club also had a firehouse tradition. Its University of Pennsylvania members would "run with the Independence Fire Engine." The club's first uniform was similar to its fire company outfit, consisting in part of a red shirt and varnished leather helmet. The uniform, which had to be worn whenever a member stepped into a club boat, quickly morphed to a "white shirt with a wide turn-down collar, pantaloons of white duck, tight in the seat and wide in the ankles, a broad leather belt having upon it in large metal letters UBC, and a stiff brimmed straw hat, with a wide ribbon containing the word 'University,' upon the ends of which again appeared the initials."

The students almost immediately extended invitations to Penn alumni to help defray costs, and soon joining the undergraduates were older men of stature. Among them were such old-line Philadelphia names as Pepper, Biddle, Emlen, Van Pelt, Wister, Sinkler, and Penrose, as well as a few DuPonts. (Inviting some confusion, UBC at #7 Boathouse Row was never the racing club of the University of Pennsylvania, whose rowing home is the College Boat Club at #11.)

"Gentlemen" was a word used often in describing club membership in those days. John B. Thayer, a founding member of University, wrote that Bachelors "was comprised of gentlemen, almost all of them well known to the students, but much older in point of years." Many of those joining the boat clubs craved competition; others joined instead for the status and connections that membership brought, but never actually lifted an oar.

Bachelors Barge Club, the Crew
That Rowed the Linda.

Courtesy of the Bachelors Barge Club.

THE *LINDA* TAKES NEW YORK

On May 16, 1859, "tired of the monotony of boating on our favorite Schuylkill River" and "seeking notoriety," a crew of six men and a coxswain of the Bachelors Barge Club embarked on a 130-mile voyage from Philadelphia to New York City. They were, according to their one-syllable monikers: "Bullion," "Shaver," "May," "Box," "Flag," and "Admiral."

Leaving at 6.30 A.M., they rowed their boat, the *Linda*, through the canal locks that then circumvented the Fairmount Dam, down the Schuylkill to its juncture with the Delaware River, and by 11:00 A.M. had come north to Dock Street. The heavy thole-pin barge did not have yet-to-be-invented sliding seats. So the men tried to boost their leg power by greasing leather pads sewn on their pants. That night, after rowing 49 miles, they reached Trenton. The next day, they rowed the Delaware and Raritan Canal to New Brunswick, where they were greeted by 3,000 people, creating "quite a sensation." Though urged to stay the night, the crew rowed on in darkness, increasingly concerned about finding lodging in the "vast wilderness."

Pulling alongside a steamer, they were told Perth Amboy lay but a few miles away. Bad directions! It was midnight when they finally tumbled out of their boat to reconnoiter. At 2 A.M., after an hour's search for a hotel, "we laid ourselves down to sleep, having pulled a distance of 53 miles."

Hauling five hours the next morning, they reached Castle Garden in New York Harbor "having accomplished the whole journey of one hundred and thirty miles in twenty-six and one-half hours."

Thomas Eakins

This photo of Thomas Eakins at age 35 was taken in 1879 by Frederick Gutekunst , a noted photographer and member of the Undine Barge Club.

While in Paris studying art, Thomas Eakins often writes home, asking about the successes of his friend and classmate Max Schmitt, who is trouncing competitors in his single scull. Eakins returns to Philadelphia in time to watch Schmitt race on the afternoon of October 5, 1870, and win a "champion belt and pair of silver mounted sculls," as the *Evening Bulletin* reported. Eakins would spend his life in Philadelphia, one of the few great American artists to do so. His love of the city resonates in this painting— from the Quakers in their outmoded rowboat to the bridges and mansions of the Schuylkill River. Eakins' world is also one of trains and steamboats, but their technological power does not come close to matching the sheer physicality of his rowers.

Thomas Eakins, *The Champion Single Sculls (Max Schmitt in a Single Scull)*, 1871. The Metropolitan Museum of Art. Image source: Art Resource, New York.

Eakins returned to Philadelphia in July 1870 as rowing was enjoying a revival following the Civil War, when so many young men had been engaged in battle. That year, the Rowing Association of American Colleges was formed—the first collegiate athletic organization in the United States, though the University of Pennsylvania would be slow to join. Within a few years, rowing became a national phenomenon, with 364 rowing clubs around the country.

New technology was making the boats lighter and faster. Some were made of layers of paper, varnished to keep the water out. The sliding seat, also invented in 1870, was just beginning to replace the jerry-rigged method of getting leg power in the stroke by applying grease to rowers' leather-covered bottoms. And a swivel oarlock set on outriggers that extended well beyond the sides of the boats gave the arms more range and power.

Eakins, 27, anxious to finally prove his artistic acumen after years of study and practice, turned to the subject he knew and loved. During his years in Paris, he had eagerly followed the rowing career of his friend Max Schmitt, who was winning race after race. Knowing Schmitt was about to compete in an important single scull championship, Eakins, on July 2, 1869, had asked his sister Fanny about the results.

"I'm looking out for news of Max's race which will come in your letter Sunday day after tomorrow. I will be real sorry if he don't win this time for it will break his heart if he don't, and it is an ambition that don't wrong others." Finally hearing from her the news of Max's victory, he replied, "I am glad he beat & you give him my congratulations next time you see him."

On October 5, 1870, Eakins surely stood among the thousands who watched Schmitt race against three other single scullers, all from the Pennsylvania Barge Club, on the three-mile course from Turtle Rock (where the lighthouse now stands) to Columbia Bridge and back. His varnished paper boat, built by the Long Island boat builder Judge Elliot, was 33½ feet long, 13 inches wide, and weighed just 40 pounds. Turning around the stake at the halfway point, Schmitt, a lean 135 pounds for his 5-foot 11-inch frame "had no trouble in maintaining the advantage," reported the *Spirit of the Times*. Schmitt wrapped up the race in a fast-paced 20 minutes, three lengths ahead of his nearest rival.

Schmitt's victory would be the subject of Eakins' first major painting, the one that now comes to mind when America thinks of rowing. Eakins called it *The Champion Single Sculls*, but it is also known as *Max Schmitt in a Single Scull*.

The work was a test of everything that Eakins had learned and loved, a perfect confluence of his skills and passions. In the foreground, Max Schmitt sits in his lightweight shell, the *Josie*, the oars balanced in his left

The Pair-Oared Shell, 1872

The Biglin brothers, professional racers from New York whom Eakins befriended and painted numerous times, are shown practicing for a much anticipated pair-oared race to take place May 20, 1872. Here, in the early evening light, they pass under the old Columbia Railroad Bridge.

Thomas Eakins, *The Pair-Oared Shell*, 1872. Philadelphia Museum of Art. Gift of Mrs. Thomas Eakins and Miss Mary Adeline Williams, 1929.

hand in a moment of repose for a champion rower. Schmitt wears a flimsy T-shirt, his muscled arms are bare—an opportunity for Eakins to show a bit of body to his prudish Philadelphia audience and to apply his anatomy studies at Jefferson and the life-drawing skills he had honed in Paris.

Very small, in the distance, is a steamboat, vapor puffing against the yellowed foliage of a late autumn afternoon. There is also a train, crossing a railroad bridge. They are hints of the industrial backdrop of the times, which recedes from the rower who is focused on his race and the natural beauty of the river. It is an out-of-the-city experience that today's rowers also enjoy, as only the hum of the Schuylkill Expressway intrudes on the dipping of the oars and the sightings of turtles, geese, blue herons, and cormorants.

**The Biglin Brothers
Racing, 1872**

About 30,000 spectators
stand on steamboats, the
riverbanks, and the Fair
Mount (now the site of the
Art Museum) to watch John
and Barney Biglin race two
Pittsburgh oarsmen, Henry
Coulter and Lewis Cavitt. All
are professional rowers,
racing for a purse of $2,000
(nearly $40,000 today). The
contest, on May 20, 1872,
is also the first American
pair-oared race—two men
rowing sweep, each with one
oar. Tension is high. The
Pittsburgh men pull at a
lung-screaming 41 strokes a
minute and immediately take
the lead, but bad steering
through the Columbia Bridge
has them faltering over the
five-mile course. The Biglins,
rowing at 40, win by a minute
and are declared world
champions. John and Barney
Biglin are grist for several
works by Eakins, who breaks
artistic ground by painting
athletes in motion.

Thomas Eakins, *Biglin Brothers
Racing*, 1872. National Gallery of
Art, Washington, DC, Gallery
Archives.

The composition is a graceful application of Eakins' meticulous training in perspective at Central High. At the same time, art critics say, so exacting is his use of color and light—particularly in the reflections of the boats, bridges, and trees on the water—that one can pinpoint the time: 5:00 P.M.

Who is the person in the single scull behind Schmitt, rowing so hard? It is the young Eakins himself, who has signed his name to his own boat. Is this Eakins, the artist, striving for recognition? Or is this Eakins simply putting himself on the river because, after all, he is Schmitt's friend, a fellow rower, and this is his river, too?

Whatever joy and satisfaction Eakins might have had with this painting was tempered by the situation at home. His mother, mentally ill, was once again back from the hospital. Since returning to Philadelphia, a family friend wrote, "he has never spent an evening from home as it worried his Mother & . . . they never leave her a minute."

In May 1872, another landmark of rowing history took place on the Schuylkill: the nation's first pair-oared race—two people sculling a boat in tandem, each with two oars.

By then, Fairmount Park was a major destination for Philadelphians, encompassing nearly 3,000 acres, up to City Avenue, and was visited that year by 750,000 pedestrians, nearly 400,000 vehicles, and 26,500 equestrians. By then, too, the Schuylkill Navy had grown to arguably the largest rowing organization in the world, with 10 clubs, 67 boats, 471 members, and boats and houses valued at $100,000 (about $2 million today.)

The famed professional rowers John and Barney Biglin were a huge draw, and some 30,000 excited spectators crowded the shores and gathered on the plateau where the Art Museum now stands, to see them compete in a five-mile race against two men from Pittsburgh.

But even before Eakins could paint the victorious Biglin brothers, his mother, Carolyn Cowperthwait Eakins, died on June 24. Her death certificate reads, "exhaustion from mania."

Eakins continued his series of rowing paintings—he would execute 24 oils, watercolors, and sketches between 1870 and 1874—as Centennial excitement mounted. In 1871, Congress had approved Philadelphia as the national site for the celebration, with fairgrounds to be built on the west side of the river, upstream from Boathouse Row, near the nation's first zoo, which opened in 1874. Between May and November 1876, nearly 10 million people entered the fairgrounds, with 250 buildings surrounded by a three-mile-long fence. Three dozen foreign countries had exhibits, as did individual states, with elaborate structures built by some of America's best architects. Richard Wagner was commissioned to write the opening day "Centennial Inauguration March." America's technology was on display with such innovations as Heinz Ketchup and Alexander Graham Bell's telephone shown to the public for the first time.

In a sports highlight of the fair, Philadelphia hosted America's first International Regatta. Canadian oarsman Edward "Ned" Hanlan, rowing as an amateur, won the singles championship and then went on to global fame as a professional. Crews from England, Ireland, and Canada also competed. The London Rowing Crew left irate after a judge claimed that the men of its four-oared boat had fouled. The *Times* of London carped that in America, "amateur was an elastic term and included coal-whippers, glass-blowers, hewers of wood and drawers of water."

The complexion of some of the American rowing clubs was beginning to change as winning began to trump socializing as the clubs' mission, though perhaps not as dramatically as the *Times* portrayed it. The

America's First International Regatta

The nation's Centennial celebration, held from May to November 1876 in Philadelphia, draws nearly 10 million people to its more than 200 buildings and exhibition halls. The city's focus had already gravitated to the Schuylkill River, with the gracious gardens of its much-expanded Fairmount Park and its new zoo, the country's first—its gate and elephant house designed by architect Frank Furness. Eakins exhibits several paintings at the fair's International Exhibition of Arts, though, to his dismay, his ambitious but shocking canvas of a bloody surgery. *The Gross Clinic*, is relegated to the medical building.

In late August, rowers from Ireland, England, and Canada compete in the nation's first International Rowing Competition. The London crew defeats a Canadian boat, but a foul is called against Canada. Rejecting the judge's verdict, the miffed Canadians leave behind their second place prize of $1,000. In photo above, London (foreground) is shown winning the sixth heat.

The photo below shows the Centennial's sprawling skyline, with the Railroad Bridge built by the Pennsylvania Railroad in the foreground and a glimpse of the Girard Avenue Bridge to the left.

London Crew, Centennial, 1876. Courtesy of the Bill Miller Collection.

Railroad Bridge across the Schuylkill, 1876. Special Collections Research Center, Temple University Libraries, Philadelphia.

In a photo taken some time between 1900 and 1915, Philadelphians, shading themselves with boater hats and parasols, stroll along Boathouse Row. Visible on the left is the Pennsylvania Barge Club (with porch).

Boathouses on Schuylkill, from the Drive, Fairmount Park, Philadelphia. Library of Congress, Prints and Photographs Division.

increased diversity, at least in class, is reflected in the occupations of men seeking entry into the clubs. In the first decades of rowing, club minutes would typically record only the applicant's name and address. By the end of the 19th century, their ages and jobs were also cited.

Those seeking to join the Vesper Boat Club in the 1890s, its minutes show, included artists, bookkeepers, clerks, machinists, engineers, builders, a publisher, a stockbroker, a geologist, a coal merchant, students, salesmen, draftsmen, plumbers, and sign writers. Those who presumably did not have to work for a living were listed as "gentleman."

Although club secretaries did not record an applicant's ethnic background or religion, some of the boat clubs began taking in more German and Irish immigrants, most of whom were also Catholic—a group that in Philadelphia still faced significant discrimination. No doubt some of them were eager to prove themselves in a sports arena as the first modern Olympic Games, set for 1896, approached.

Whatever the income level of their members, the clubs struggled, then as now, to get those in arrears to pay their dues. Every boat club at every meeting announced the names of the deadbeats and debated who should be warned and who should be suspended. Standard procedure was to post the men's names prominently in the boathouse in the hopes that shame or embarrassment might open their pockets.

Even as the rowing clubs were changing, so Eakins' art was evolving. More than almost any artist before him, Eakins was intent on capturing motion and athleticism. The public did not appreciate his realism. Shortly after its completion in April 1871, *The Champion Single Sculls* was displayed at the Union League of Philadelphia to mixed reviews. The most positive was by a critic writing in the *Philadelphia Inquirer*, who said, "Despite a somewhat scattered effect, gives promise of a conspicuous future. A walnut frame would greatly improve the present work." Eakins gave it to Max Schmitt to hang in his living room.

Hoping to establish a national reputation at the Centennial's art exhibit, which millions of people would visit, in 1875 Eakins took on another cutting-edge subject: If Max Schmitt and the Biglin brothers were at the apex of the world of sport, Dr. Samuel Gross, chief of surgery at Jefferson Medical College, was equally at the vanguard of medicine. Eakins' monumental canvas, 8 feet tall and 6½ feet wide, *The Gross Clinic*, graphically depicts an operation on a serious leg infection. The surgical instruments and the doctors' bloody hands stand out against the dark shrouding of the patient. Nearby, an anguished woman, possibly the subject's mother, hides her eyes from the scene, something a lot of Philadelphians wanted to do as well. Although family friend John Sartain was chief of the arts section of the Centennial, *The Gross Clinic* was rejected for the main art exhibit in Memorial Hall (now the Please Touch Museum). Instead, it was relegated to the fair's remote Army Post Hospital. Two years later, the Jefferson Alumni Association bought it for a "paltry sum of $200" (about $4,700 today).

Eakins would achieve more notoriety than fame, even though he had the backing of Fairman Rogers, a prominent Philadelphian who served on the boards of both Jefferson Medical College and the PAFA. In 1879, Rogers gave the struggling Eakins one of his few commissions. In *A May Morning in the Park* (also known as *The Fairman Rogers Four-in-Hand*), Eakins explored horses in motion, a work now at the Philadelphia Museum of Art.

But even Rogers, who hired Eakins to teach at the PAFA, could not help him when, in 1886, Eakins was fired from his post for, among other indiscretions, removing the loin cloth from a male model before a co-ed drawing class.

Eakins died in 1916, having sold but a handful of paintings; some portraits were so repugnant to their subjects that they destroyed them. He would not live to see New York's Metropolitan Museum of Art call him "America's greatest, most uncompromising realist." Nor would he witness the city of Philadelphia wage a furious campaign to raise $68 million in 2008 to prevent *The Gross Clinic* from leaving town. It was perhaps the least Philadelphia

could do for its most celebrated artist, who, by *not* leaving town, immortalized Boathouse Row and his home city.

"I envy you your drive along the Wissahickon among those beautiful hills with which are connected some of my most pleasant reminiscences," Eakins had written Emily Sartain from Paris. "You say you had a slight sensation somewhat resembling pride in your native city. I feel like scolding you for such a weak avowal of your real sentiments. You should hear me tell the Frenchmen about Philadelphia. I feel 6 ft & 6 inches high whenever I only say I am an American, but seriously speaking, Emily, Philadelphia is certainly a city to be proud of."

New York's Metropolitan Museum of Art, which owns Eakins' *The Champion Single Sculls (Max Schmitt in a Single Scull)* has touted the work as among the "key pictures in American art history." It hangs in its galleries, a timeless tribute to Philadelphia's rowing scene.

CHAPTER THREE

FRANK FURNESS

Architectural One-upmanship
Remakes the Row

The sight of 25-year-old Frank Furness upon his return from the Civil War was startling—his eyes blazed with confidence, his red mutton chops sprouted extravagantly from his cheeks. He had served in Rush's Lancers, actually carrying a lance on horseback in the early years of battle, like some medieval knight. Later, he would charge across a field to enemy lines to tie a life-saving tourniquet around the bleeding leg of a Confederate soldier, saying, "I can't see him suffer." In another daring escapade that won him the Medal of Honor, he raced through volleys of bullets to deliver ammunition to his men.

The war years had emboldened him, burnished him, etched more deeply a love of action, purpose, and a streak of recklessness that would come to characterize the 600 homes, rail stations, banks, churches, country houses, and landmark civic buildings, which he would design over the next four decades in Philadelphia and its suburbs, invigorating the landscape.

Though not a rower, Furness would set a new high bar for Boathouse Row with his idiosyncratic design for the Undine Barge Club. Its boathouse, fantastical yet functional, escalated a competition of architectural one-upmanship along

Frank Furness

With his eclectic vision and a large dose of daring, Frank Furness returns from the Civil War to excite the cityscape of Philadelphia. Among his first commissions, in 1871, is to design the new home of the Pennsylvania Academy of the Fine Arts on Broad Street. It startles the city, pulsating with an imaginative play of geometric forms, strong lines, and colors. A decade later, he designs the Undine Barge Club boathouse, a masculine building that captures the energy of its occupants and sets in motion architectural innovation on Boathouse Row.

Frank Furness. Reproduced from James F. O'Gorman, *The Architecture of Frank Furness* (Philadelphia: Philadelphia Museum of Art, 1973), cover.

the Row even as it added to Furness' bold portfolio, which presaged the era of modern architecture. Yet here, his imprint remains.

The arresting gingerbread ribbon of late 19th-century buildings—charming in daylight and now strikingly lit at night—is among Philadelphia's most dramatic and iconic sights.

Philadelphia was on the cusp of a post-war boom in late 1864, when Frank Furness took off his Union uniform after four years of service and plunged back into his passion. Architects were in demand as the ever more industrial city was evolving into a "workshop of the world," as the city called itself—a national hub for manufacturing, textiles, shipping, and railroads. A raft of religious groups, spurred by the city's reputation for tolerance and a wave of immigration, were raising houses of worship. And the city's pioneering cultural and scientific institutions were expanding into second-generation structures.

Down along the Schuylkill River, Philadelphia was executing a grand plan to create a pastoral refuge from urban life. In their winning design of 1859 for an expansive Fairmount Park, landscape architects James C. Sidney and Andrew Adams laid out their vision:

> *A Public Park, having for its object the recreation of the citizens, should present the greatest possible contrast to the artificiality of the city, with its straight and closely built up streets. . . . Rural enjoyment is most effectively obtained by simplicity, both in general design and embellishment.*

In this pastoral Victorian landscape, they saw no place for the wooden shacks and brick boatsheds that the new aficionados of the sport of rowing were erecting on park land next to the Fairmount Water Works. The boathouses, wrote Sidney and Adams, "should be remodeled and improved, so as to be in keeping with the surroundings, and we are assured by several of the boat clubs, that this will be cheerfully done, by the young gentlemen composing these clubs at their own expense."

The Undine Barge Club was among the early rowing organizations that found itself scrambling for a new home. The club, named for a sea nymph who falls in love with a prince, to a tragic end, had formed in May 1856. Boats and buildings cost money, and this club of rowers, most age 30 and older, had come up with it: $80 to buy a four-oared barge in New York City and $100 to build a rudimentary boathouse 50 feet long and 8 feet wide in which to store it (a total of about $5,000 today.) Members were also expected to purchase a

The Row, From Then to Now

The evolution of Boathouse Row begins with the city's 1859 and 1860 edicts that the simple, unsightly boathouses be replaced by ones built of stone to complement its vision for a picturesque Fairmount Park. The few initial houses soon joined by others, are ever larger and richer in architectural detail. With time, the swaths of green between the regularly spaced houses are eaten up by 20th-century additions built to accommodate more and more rowers. Today, a growing island of accumulated silt adjacent to the dam partially obscures the view of Boathouse Row from the Fairmount Water Works.

1860s

By the late 1860s, the earliest stone houses of Boathouse Row can be seen behind the walkway of the Fairmount dam and a docked steamboat. The wakes of large power boats played havoc with the smaller oared craft.

Steamboat Wharf, Fairmount Park, Philadelphia. Courtesy of James Hill.

1876

By the Centennial Exposition of 1876, with rowing the nation's most popular spectator sport, the Row has achieved an elegant Victorian look. Rising behind the Row on Lemon Hill is the Observation Tower, which offered views of the city from 1876 through the end of the century.

International Exhibition, 1876. Courtesy of James Hill.

2016

The Row today is a lively though crowded potpourri of styles after a century of additions to accommodate ever-growing numbers of high school, collegiate, women, and masters rowers.

**The First
Undine Barge Club**

The Undine Barge Club's first utilitarian boathouse is ordered demolished by Fairmount Park, along with others built in the 1850s on the banks of the Schuylkill River near the Fairmount Water Works.

The First Boat House, from Louis Heiland, *The Undine Barge Club of Philadelphia*. Historical Society of Pennsylvania.

distinctive club uniform: a red shirt trimmed with blue, with white anchors on the collar; black pants; white belt; and a straw hat for summer.

The demolition order from the city, dated November 7, 1859, sent Undine into limbo. It read:

> *Dear Sir: We find that it will be necessary to remove the two boathouses at Fairmount this fall, and shall feel obliged if you will make arrangement to remove yours at your earliest convenience. Respectfully yours, Sidney & Adams.*

Undine spent that winter like a homeless relative, begging berth for its barge, from boathouse to boathouse as each in turn was ordered demolished. Even the purchase of the Keystone Club's house in 1860 was no solution, as the city soon ordered that it too be taken down; Undine sold it for scrap for $10.

Nonetheless, that December, the president of Undine, Dr. Benjamin Howard Rand (then Thomas Eakins' chemistry teacher at Central High School) adjourned the rootless club to its annual Christmas feast: "a good array of chicken salad, huge fried oysters, ale and whiskey, and other viands. . . . The whole company gave up to mirth and festivity. Truly the Undine Barge Club was in its glory."

On March 4, 1861, the day of Abraham Lincoln's inauguration, and with the nation on the brink of war, Undine held its monthly meeting with yet another dislocation. Now the six-oared barge that they had bought from the Keystone Club would have to be moved out of the Bachelors Barge Club boathouse, where it had spent the winter, as Bachelors too was demolishing its house.

But there was good news—possible refuge in the just completed Philadelphia Skating Club, one of the first stone structures to be built under the new city rules, which required boathouses to be "architecturally neat and attractive." The picturesque two-story building, made of irregularly cut stone and capped by a wooden cupola, was designed by park architect James C. Sidney in the Italianate style, popular at the time for country

ANNUAL REPORT

OF THE

SECRETARY

OF THE

UNDINE BARGE CLUB

OF PHILADELPHIA.

1867.

PHILADELPHIA:
HENRY B. ASHMEAD, BOOK AND JOB PRINTER,
1102 and 1104 Sansom Street.
1868.

Undine at the Skating Club

Having lost its own boat-house, Undine in 1861 moves into the just completed home of the Philadelphia Skating Club and Humane Society, one of the Row's first permanent structures. Undine remains a renter there for two decades before turning to Frank Furness, who dreams up the most distinctive boathouse on the Row.

Annual Report of the Secretary of the Undine Barge Club of Philadelphia, 1867 Historical Society of Pennsylvania.

sites on the edge of cities. It had cost Skating Club members $4,990, the equivalent of about $142,000 today. The entrance faced the park; a porch built over two boat bays looked to the river. In winter, it would house the Philadelphia Skating Club, which had merged with the Rescue and Humane Society, an organization that saved skaters who fell through the ice. In summer, the house had space for a rowing club or two.

Besides Undine, the University Barge Club (UBC) was also eager to move in. Since shortly after its founding in 1854, UBC had been rowing out of a small "one-story brick building, covered with a plain board roof and divided into two compartments," shared with the Philadelphia Barge Club, "an association of gentlemen of the same type as those who comprise our own club," UBC founder John B. Thayer wrote on its 50th anniversary. Rowers could not wait for a new location; exiting their dock was a dangerous maneuver around old pilings in the river left over from an abandoned coal wharf.

Both clubs found a haven at the Skating Club. Undine members had voted to bid up to $300 a year in rent but landed the larger boat bay and use of the upstairs in summer for just $225. Just months later, in September 1861, war began sapping the club's membership, and even their well-negotiated rent (about $6,000 today) was unaffordable. In a letter to the Skating Club, Undine wrote, "Much to our disappointment we have added but one name to our active roll and one to our contributing list, while two of our members have joined the army and two others have resigned. Of course, too, those of us who are left suffer from the hard times and under these circumstances we have felt justified in asking for a reduction of our rent."

Of the more than a dozen rowing clubs that had raced to engage in the most popular sport in the country before the Civil War, few remained afterward. By the late 1860s, most of the early members of the Schuylkill Navy, including the Falcon, American, Chebucto, Atlantic, Union, Excelsior, Independent, and Keystone— were history. Among the survivors were Bachelors, Undine, and UBC.

———

By the time Captain Frank Furness (pronounced *furnace*) returned to town, the riverfront had begun its transformation. The shacks were gone, and a few stone houses had gone up—the earliest building blocks of what would become Boathouse Row. The Skating Club (now Philadelphia Girls' Rowing Club) stood grandly at one end. A smaller double boathouse, built by the Pacific Barge Club, anchored the other end closest to the Fairmount Water Works. Bachelors Barge Club, in a stone building with a peaked roof and a tiny balcony above three boat bays, was in the middle.

Public Boathouses of the 1870s

With interest high in boating on the Schuylkill in the early 1870s, operators of floating boathouses rent boats to the public. George Popps' facility is in the foreground. The adjacent boathouse offers rentals of "skeletons" and "outriggers." Seen between them is the 1860–1861 stone boathouse shared by the Pacific and Quaker boat clubs. A public boathouse (Plaisted Hall at #1 Boathouse Row) existed until the 1990s, when it was demolished.

Boat House, Fairmount, detail of undated stereoscopic, R. Newell, publisher. Courtesy of James Hill.

Mundane is what Frank Furness would have said about the new houses. Individuality, courage, and dissent were the lessons he had learned growing up. His father, William Henry Furness, minister of the liberal First Unitarian Church of Philadelphia, was arguably the city's most outspoken clergyman against slavery. In 1859, when the body of white abolitionist John Brown, hanged in Virginia, came by train through Philadelphia en route to burial in New York, the Rev. Furness and his eldest son, Horace, spent the night with the coffin in a secret location, protecting it from pro-slavery mobs.

A frequent visitor to the Furness home was Ralph Waldo Emerson, a childhood friend and Harvard classmate of the senior Furness. Emerson shared his love of nature and art with Frank, who as a teenager seemed little interested in his studies or in attending Harvard, as his father so wished him to do. Frank's infatuation with architecture may have been prompted by a gift from Emerson—a stereoscopic viewer. In a letter, his father told Emerson of Frank's fascination with the gadget, through which each eye sees a slightly different version of a scene that the brain fuses into a 3-D image.

Instead of Harvard, the 16-year-old Furness began to study architecture and soon moved to New York to work under the Paris-trained Richard Morris Hunt. Hunt demanded that his students "so thoroughly" memorize, indeed internalize, every form of architecture—Greek, Roman, Gothic, Moorish, Italianate—that "you acquire a certain idea or instinct of proportion that will never leave you," Furness would later write.

Having learned the rules of architecture, Furness came back from war hell-bent on breaking them. As anyone starting out might do, he turned to his father's circle of prominent liberals and intellectuals for his first commissions.

It did not hurt that Furness' brother, the Shakespearean scholar Horace Howard Furness, had married Helen Kate Rogers, the sister of one of Philadelphia's Renaissance men. Fairman Rogers' day job was teaching civil engineering at the University of Pennsylvania, but his interests and influence ranged far wider. He was a founding member of the National Academy of Sciences, on the board of Jefferson Medical College, a founder of the Union League, and an expert on coachmanship. (Rogers also mentored Thomas Eakins, commissioning him to paint *The Fairman Rogers Four-in-Hand*, now in the Philadelphia Museum of Art.)

Most fortuitously for Furness, Rogers chaired the building committee of the nation's first art school, the Pennsylvania Academy of the Fine Arts, when it voted in 1871 to move uptown from Chestnut Street, between 10th and 11th, to Broad and Cherry. Also on the PAFA building committee and backing Furness was engraver John Sartain, a member of the Rev. Furness' congregation.

Furness' design for the new Academy of Fine Arts both shocked and delighted the staid Quaker city filled with colonial architecture and marble-stooped row homes. The building "percolated" with the architectural elements he had internalized—French Second Empire, Venetian Gothic, Islamic, and the romantic Byzantine influenced "Neo-Grec." With a divided entrance, a stairway that fragments into smaller flights, and compressed pillars that explode with energy, Furness alternately "disconcerted" visitors, "rerouted them or startled them," wrote architectural historian Michael Lewis. "He stamped, thrust, extruded the parts of his buildings as if they were something alive."

At the same time, Boathouse Row was undergoing an upheaval of its own, its second in a decade. The Fairmount Park Commission, established in 1867, had ratcheted up standards for any structures on parkland. Beyond building in stone, its new Committee on Plans and Improvements now demanded that any boathouse built "without regard to architectural adornment" had to come down as well.

Almost immediately, the six-year-old Pennsylvania Boat House (now Pennsylvania Barge Club), together with the Crescent Boat Club, which had just formed from the merger of two other clubs, won approval to construct "very ornamental" attached houses at what is now #4 and #5 Boathouse Row. The park committee plotted the new double boathouse halfway between the Pacific Club house (by then shared with the Quaker City Barge Club) and Bachelors, setting a rhythm of regular spacing. One Crescent innovation was to position a door off center, seen as an idiosyncratic and picturesque departure. More practically, it also boasted such touches as a locker for each member and oiled and varnished wooden floors.

The University Barge Club, which had been sparring with its boathouse mate, Undine, in their shared quarters at the Skating Club, moved out in 1871 into a new double boathouse with the Philadelphia Barge Club. The boathouse is characterized by an unusual greenish stone called "serpentine," quarried some 35 miles away in West Chester. The intention might have been to echo College Hall on the University of Pennsylvania's campus, also built of this porous and now disintegrating stone. (UBC today occupies both halves of the structure at #7–8 Boathouse Row.)

The Malta and Vesper boat clubs in 1873 joined forces to build connected boathouses (#9 and #10) in an ornamental style. And the next year the newly formed College Boat Club, the racing organization of the University of Pennsylvania, upped the ante with the kind of second-floor space for relaxing and socializing that soon all the clubs would demand.

"The house is all that could be desired by the most exacting, containing all the conveniences and appliances necessary for a complete boat house, and for the comfort of the members," the University Magazine reported. "It has the largest boat room on the river and surpasses in its conveniences many of the houses, while in beauty of finish and symmetry of form it is unsurpassed."

No longer were the houses simply functional structures to store boats and change clothes, but social venues in a much fuller sense, with parlor rooms decorated by Gimbel Brothers and appropriate for entertaining ladies, not to mention smoking cigars and drinking beer and whiskey—practices that many of the clubs had previously barred inside their boathouses in the 1850s and 1860s, along with rowing on Sunday.

Fred Duling, who joined the Malta Boat Club in 1959 at age 15, was astonished to learn from club records that in 1900, Malta had spent over $550 in today's dollars for two months' worth of cigars, or about $3,300 a year. Looking more deeply, he learned that some clubs branded their own cigars. "They'd have a manufacturer in New York put on their own wrapper brand," he said. "They spent the equivalent of the cost of a new single [scull]. I couldn't believe it. Look, this wasn't a rowing club," he joked. "This was a cigar club with a rowing problem."

The initial double boathouse of the Malta and Vesper clubs (left) is a functional building, designed simply to house their boats. Soon the clubs turn to some of Philadelphia's best architects to add more social elements, including upstairs parlors for entertaining and balconies facing the river, and then balconies facing the park, so members can see passersby and be seen. Along with those changes come increasingly distinct architectural flourishes.

James Cremer, *Scenery in Fairmount Park*, crop of Malta-Vesper boathouse from stereoscopic photograph, 1873. Courtesy of James Hill.

The Malta-Vesper boathouses (right), after nearly 150 years of expansions and renovations.

View of Boathouse "Vesper," Looking East from West Bank of Schuylkill River, Library of Congress Prints and Photographs Division.

1873

2016

Boathouse Row was a male domain. Inviting women into the boathouses could prove dicey. In 1878, the Captain of the Fairmount Park Guard, which patrolled the Row for decorum as well as crime, reported to the Vesper Boat Club that a member had made "frequent use of the Boathouse for immoral purposes." The member resigned.

That summer, the West Philadelphia Boat Club dealt with a similar scandal. On August 3, quite a party apparently took place in the clubhouse after several members reportedly picked up three "girls" on the carriage road outside the boathouse (now Kelly Drive). At a special meeting a few days later, club officers interrogated the men as to whether they had brought prostitutes into the club. A report of the grilling went on for ten pages in its minute book and resulted in the expulsion of one member and the suspension of two others.

The men of the Undine Barge Club also desired a better venue for socializing, especially with one another. The Skating Club was still adequate for its boats, now that UBC had moved into its own building. But for gatherings and special dinners, what better spot could there be than the Falls of Schuylkill? For decades, the clubs had been rowing three miles upriver to what is now East Falls. Sometimes, when it was just the men, the crews would stop north of the Columbia Bridge "and there strip off our uniforms and spend half an hour or more in a delicious bath in the cool, pure, uncontaminated waters of the river." Continuing upriver to the taverns at the Falls, they would dine on catfish and waffles, followed by "moderate libations of mint juleps, rum punches and the like, seat ourselves in the summer-house overlooking the river, enjoy our cigars and pipes until the shades of night had fallen."

Other times the outings were coed, in wider "ladies boats," with dates sitting in flouncy dresses beside the men who rowed, showing off their quads and biceps.

On a steamy August 7, 1875, as the oarsmen sweltered, with no respite from yet-to-be-invented electric fans, let alone air conditioning, the Undine Barge Club voted to build an upriver social house at a cost of "not more than twelve hundred dollars exclusive of the ground."

Exactly how Undine approached the up-and-coming architect Frank Furness to design it is not known, nor how much he was paid. Furness' personal records have long disappeared, and the minutes of the Undine Barge Club do not tell the tale. But Philadelphia, which even today can feel like a small town, was much smaller in the summer of 1875. Undine's former president, Benjamin Howard Rand, taught chemistry at Jefferson Medical College, where Furness' influential brother-in-law, Fairman Rogers, was on the board.

Although Undine was only interested in a modest cottage, Furness would not have scoffed at the commission. He needed the work. The Panic of 1873, with a run on the banks, had hurt business. He had been forced to lay off his latest hire—the enormously talented Louis Sullivan, then 16, who would come to be known as the "father of skyscrapers" and mentor to Frank Lloyd Wright. "Sullivan, I'm sorry—the jig is up," the young architect remembered Furness telling him that September. "The office now is running dry. You've done well, mighty well. I like you. I wish you might stay."

Another likely appeal for Furness was a chance to be part of Philadelphia's focus—indeed, the nation's focus—the upcoming Centennial International Exhibition of 1876. Some 200 buildings and pavilions were being erected on the west side of the Schuylkill River, just upriver from Boathouse Row. Furness had won the commission for the fair's Brazilian Pavilion. Nearby, at the Zoological Society of Philadelphia—the nation's first zoo, which opened in 1874—Furness had designed the Elephant House (later torn down) and its gates (still there).

Members of the Undine Barge
Club enjoy a summer evening
on the porch of Castle
Ringstetten, located on Kelly
Drive just above the Falls
Bridge. For nearly 150 years,
Undine has enjoyed dinners
and dances at its upriver
home, designed in 1875 by
Frank Furness. Some men
who were not rowers joined
for the social aspects of the
upriver homes of Boathouse
Row, of which one other
remains in use—the "Button"
of the Bachelors Barge Club.
In 1909, the "Clubs and
Clubmen" column of the
Philadelphia Inquirer wrote,
"The upriver houses of
the most important boat
clubs . . . are snug little
houses where old customs
and hilarity reign supreme
and the culinary is the most
important department."

Courtesy of Ray Del Bianco.

For Castle Ringstetten, named for the prince's palace in the Legend of Undine, Furness did not dig deeply into his architectural grab bag. For its time, it was simplicity itself. "It shows Furness making a cottage-type clubhouse on a low budget," said Lewis. "Furness wasn't always eccentric." The upriver club, 20 feet wide by 45 feet deep, largely consists of a main room, a kitchen, and an expansive wrap-around porch looking toward the river, where Undine members still enjoy the camaraderie of monthly dinners despite the steady buzz of cars on Kelly Drive. On the oak mantle over the fireplace are inscribed these words, taken from the historic Beefsteak Club in London:

Let no one bear beyond this threshold hence,
Words uttered here in friendly confidence.

Simplicity aside, Furness insisted that the builder use the best materials. The original work orders state that the building be "properly framed and put together in the strongest and most substantial manner . . . the flooring to be of California pine tongue & grooved one-inch thick," windows to be hung with "best sash cord," wood on the walls and ceilings to be "free from bark and other imperfections," windows to be glazed with "best American glass."

Undine financed the ultimate cost of $1,700 (about $36,000 today) by selling bonds, which it later paid off, and by assessing members the equivalent of $430 a year over two years.

Other upriver clubs soon followed. Just a couple doors down from Castle Ringstetten along Kelly Drive, Bachelors built the "Button" (as in the flower). Like the Castle, it survives today as a social venue for the club. Between the two, the Philadelphia Barge Club built the Anchorage (now gone); and across the river, UBC leased the Lilacs from Fairmount Park, a location that became impractical after the Schuylkill Expressway blocked access from the river in 1956. For some men more interested in socializing and networking than exercising, the upriver clubs were their sole reason for membership.

But most Undine men had joined to row. So many that in 1875, a locker crisis emerged. Club officers were shocked, shocked to learn that there was price gouging going on for a scarce commodity. "One or two parties," the minutes state, had obtained "as many closets . . . as possible, for the purpose of making a 'corner' in said closets, whereby an income may be created by the rental of same at exorbitant rates to such unfortunate members who do not own one . . . bringing disrepute on the club."

CASTLE
RINGSTETTEN

Poking Fun at Himself

Frank Furness, who loved drawing pithy cartoons, turns his wit and whimsy even on himself in this self-portrait.

Undine ordered its officers to "use every effort in their power to prevent such speculation" and also that the annual locker rental not exceed "more than a 10 percent return on accepted value of closet—say $5." More lockers were built. Still, they were not enough.

Beyond the crowded conditions, after two decades Undine's relationship with its host, the Skating Club, had frayed. In a reminiscence of those years, John Frederick Lewis described the "friction" from the Skating Club's perspective.

Objection [by Skating Club] would be made to renovating furniture in the Club House because the furniture was used by the tenant; to defraying expenses for repairing the gas-making machine, because the tenant burned the gas; to even repairing the house, because the boating season was nine months, and the skating season a short three; and in thousands of other little ways, some pleasant, others not, this porcupine and snake affection was manifested.

There were generational issues as well: the younger barge club members "were looked upon by many of the old skaters with more or less suspicion." In 1881, after the Skating Club won an ugly electoral battle over control of the clubhouse, Undine applied to the Fairmount Park Commission for permission to build a boathouse of its own.

They were almost too late to the party. Little room was left on the Row. Even the struggling West Philadelphia Boat Club (which in 1924 became the Pennsylvania Athletic Club) had finally managed to wrangle a spot. Made up of men from the West Philadelphia neighborhood, the club had been rowing from below the dam, at Grays Ferry. They dearly wanted the convenience and status of being in the same neighborhood as their rivals. But club minutes show a near-constant state of financial woe. In January 1874, during the hard economic times following the Panic of 1873, West Philadelphia took the dire step of briefly doubling its monthly dues to $4 (about $80 today) to pay its bills. The next year, its delegate to the Schuylkill Navy enviously reported back that the College Boat Club had been admitted, with $2,000 worth of boats and a new boathouse costing $8,500 furnished (a total of about $225,000 today).

West Philadelphia was hoping to build for well under half that. But how to raise the money? In 1876, someone came up with the idea of growing the number of affluent members through a mailing to the homes of "all

Furness Raises the Bar

By the time Furness designs Undine's boathouse in 1882, most of the other boathouses are built. But Furness' dynamic use of differing geometric shapes, breaking free of the Victorian Gothic mold, influences subsequent renovations along Boathouse Row. Furness "favored a bigness of the parts, boldness of projection, a forthrightness in the openings that implied confidence in virility," writes architectural historian Michael Lewis. After decades of disdain, Furness' ideas, which influenced the likes of Louis Kahn, Louis Sullivan, and Frank Lloyd Wright, have regained respect.

the prominent gentlemen of West Philadelphia . . . their moral support was wanted as well as their pecuniary assistance." After all, the neighborhood "should want to support a West Philadelphia institution of such prestige and renown as our club." Two hundred flyers were printed and "duly addressed to gentlemen of wealth and standing in this section of the city." Few such gentlemen must have stepped forward because two years later, the club had raised only $2,100 of the $3,500 they sought. Furthermore, its hopes of building in less costly brick were dashed when the park insisted it build in stone, raising the estimated cost to $3,700.

"If we can't build, then all must bear shame," the chair of the club's building committee declared, throwing down the gauntlet. West Philadelphia finally pushed through with a builder who sliced the cost to $3,000 (about $71,400 today). Their boathouse, at #12, added a new feature to the Row: an off-center boat bay with a second-floor porch that extended beyond it. The porch offered members spectacular views of the other boathouses, without themselves being easily seen. It was a "social change as much as an architectural one," giving the club a "certain mysteriousness."

Money was less of a problem for Undine, which won permission to build at #13, between the West Philadelphia Boat Club and the Skating Club. Pleased with its Castle Ringstetten, Undine again turned to Frank Furness, now partnered with the socially connected Allen Evans, who would later found the Merion Cricket Club. This time, Furness seized the opportunity to give these fun-loving men, who valued strength and competition, a building that exuded both playfulness and muscular energy. In one of the few surviving examples of his writings, Furness explained his philosophy in 1878 in *Lippincott's Monthly Magazine*: "A design without action is merely a mechanical affair that might be produced by a mere machine."

He conjured up a building animated by an intriguing mix of geometric shapes, including windows in the shape of arches, squares, and rectangles; triangular roof peaks; and a witches' cap cupola. Adding vigor are protruding mini-balconies and a chimney, wider at the top and described by some as phallic-like or "priapal."

"The boathouse evoked the quality of its athletes," writes architectural historian Thomas Beischer, "a fundamental solidity binding the pent-up energy displayed in its combination of tension and compression, presenting an architecture unlike that of earlier boathouses."

Adding to both the strength and functionality of the building was Furness' modernistic use of iron and steel—the latest in construction technology. He creatively employed a steel tie-rod truss system with cast iron struts to support the roof of a generous boat bay the width of the building, uninhibited by interior columns. He kept the staircase out of the space by placing it in an adjacent tower, an element of industrial design at the

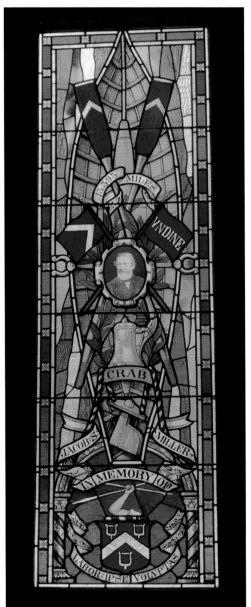

time, which kept workspace unencumbered. A boat bay ceiling higher than any other on the river allowed four levels of boats to be hung in slings and hoisted up and down by ropes.

Beyond reflecting Undine's competitive goals, Furness made sure his design met their social desires as well. He devoted the upstairs to balconies, parlors—including one for women—and for the men, the mother of all locker rooms: 140 wooden "closets," each numbered, assuredly taking care of the locker problem.

A large covered porch, facing the river, stretched the width of the building. But in a radical move for the Row, Furness also designed a castle-like, "Nuremburg"-style corner balcony, facing the park. From here, club members could look through railings, with cubes, spheres, and cylinders playfully perched atop one another, to view passersby while being seen by them as well.

With all that, Furness made sure that the "delight of the eye," as he called it, also was addressed. The details that fill the building include an elaborate staircase newel with a multiplicity of geometric shapes, and a carved mahogany fireplace with blue and white tiles depicting the story of Undine by A. B. Frost, a noted illustrator and Undine member. And as he did in many of his buildings, he brought in greens and reds—the colors of nature, which, he wrote, "never makes a mistake in taste."

Furness gave the ensemble on the Row "a place of festive pageantry . . . its most poetic and imaginative building, his colorful Nuremberg-style operatic fantasy," said architectural historian and Furness biographer Michael Lewis.

Undine's boathouse was instantly the most expensive on the Row—about $326,000 today, though that is a fraction of what it would take to replace it. Furness' firm received $560, equivalent to about $13,000 now.

———

Having left his mark on Boathouse Row, Furness was followed by other prominent architects who carried his eccentric ideas even further, as the ever-competitive boat clubs sought additions and modifications to give them more space, more prowess, and more prestige. They pushed out the back of their houses to make room for eight-oared crew shells, which became popular in the 1880s. They built upward for locker rooms and entertainment spaces. They added balconies facing the park. And with more and more boat bays, they began eating up the gracious green spaces that the Park Commission had so carefully laid out between them.

In 1891, the University Barge Club hired two architects who had left the Furness firm to form their own practice—Louis C. Baker and James E. Dallet. They revamped the serpentine stone boathouse with "elaborate woodwork, high chimneys, decorative terra cotta ornamentation, and a high-pitched roof that replaced the mansard roof." Besides doubling the number of boat bays to four and adding locker space, they also added the ever more critical social rooms.

In 1893, Bachelors Barge Club hired Samuel Huckel Jr. and Edward Hazelhurst, who had worked in the Furness studio in the mid-1870s, to replace its 30-year-old brownstone with a far grander Mediterranean-style boathouse made of brick, a material that Fairmount Park had not permitted for 25 years. The ground

Penn's Boathouse: Outward and Upward

At its completion in 1874, the College Boathouse of the University of Pennsylvania is the most luxurious facility yet on the Row. Today the original architecture is outflanked by modern additions that greatly expand its capacity to house crew shells. A 1980 addition to add women's locker rooms further obscures the original structure.

1904

The College Boat Club of the University of Pennsylvania, 1904.

From the University Archives and Records Center, University of Pennsylvania.

2015

The College Boat Club on a rare day of Schuylkill ice in 2015, with additions flanking the original stone structure.

floor makes a statement on the Row, with its elongated orange bricks—two inches high and a foot long—while the second floor, with its enormous balcony facing the park, is faced in pebble-dashed stucco. With Furnessian geometric liveliness, the house has an octagonal pavilion, arched windows, and a square porch—"a play of the symmetrical and the asymmetrical," Beischer writes of the building, which cost $10,500 (about $276,000 today).

In 1901, the brothers George and William Hewitt designed an expansion of the Malta Boat Club, which had originally started out as the only rowing club on the Delaware River. Both Hewitts had worked with Furness; George had been his partner. In a bold move of one-upmanship on the Row, they added a third story, using a variety of building materials.

In a final architectural foray, in 1904 the Fairmount Rowing Association demolished the 44-year-old Pacific Barge Club at #2, which it had acquired in 1887, and replaced it with the last house to be built on the Row. Unlike any other, it is in the Georgian Revival style, using sand-colored Flemish bonded brick.

"With three porches, four boat bays, and almost three stories in height, the structure commanded space, and in this way represented the dominance of the Fairmount Club, the most feared on the river prior to 1904," Beischer writes of the design by George Smedley. Not bad for a neighborhood club that in the 1870s stored its boat on Brown Street and had to carry it six blocks to the river.

Fairmount absorbed the adjacent, long-inactive boathouse of the Quaker City Barge Club during World War II, ironically positioning the newest building on the Row next to one of the oldest.

Within only a couple of decades, Furness and the 600 buildings he had designed had fallen out of favor. Clean lines, massive office towers, and glass were on their way in. Eclectic, quirky, and rough-cut stone were out. By the 1960s, when noted Philadelphia architects Robert Venturi and Denise Scott Brown (his wife-to-be) fought to save another Furness triumph, the University of Pennsylvania's Fisher Library, the wrecking ball had already wiped much of Furness' imprint from the city.

By then, many of the boathouses were literally falling apart. Besides the toll of time, some that rested on the soft, silty soil trapped by the Fairmount Dam were sinking and cracking. Others had holes in their floors and leaks in their roofs. The clubs that were still in existence had survived hard times of recession and war by renting space and equipment to the growing high school and collegiate rowing programs. Now new winds were buffeting them—and benefitting them as well. Title IX of the Education Amendments of 1972, while

Going Bigger on a Balcony

With its ten arches looking out towards Kelly Drive, the porch of the Bachelors Barge Club—part of the building's 1893 reconstruction—is a statement of the prominence of its members of the era, including names such as Lippincott and Burpee. The contrasting materials of the structure—the pebbled-dashed stucco wall and Pompeian brick—create interest in this Mediterranean-style building, so unlike the older Victorian Gothic boathouses. In 2008, Bachelors, which like all the boathouses faces serious maintenance costs, agreed to lease space to Drexel University's crew program for 50 years, with two 20-year extensions.

Circa 1865

2015

aimed at creating gender parity in schools, also put pressure on the boathouses to finally admit women, though that meant carving out locker space for them, not to mention the culture shock it entailed. But with the women came a wave of suburban high school and collegiate rowers, as well as an explosion of older, often well-heeled, dues-paying masters rowers.

Still, for anyone who did not row or jog, Boathouse Row remained a quaint, crumbling backwater of the city. That all changed in 1979 when its architectural outlines were dramatically illuminated with 8,000 incandescent lights.

"It was simple to do but difficult to get done," said Ray Grenald, an internationally known lighting architect who created lighting designs for Carlsbad Caverns, the West Wing of the White House, the Benjamin Franklin Bridge, and the University of Noura in Saudi Arabia. In his travels, Grenald, based in Narberth, Pennsylvania, would look for posters of Philadelphia but find only the "boring" Liberty Bell and Independence Hall. "If you mentioned Boathouse Row to people, they would say, 'What's that?' Philadelphians are terrible at selling their city. I wanted to see a poster that was more exciting."

Flooding in 2006

Torrential rains in June 2006, create turbulence as water pours over the Fairmount Dam, flooding boat bays and floating boathouse docks, even as the lights stay on. Regularly spaced LED lights replaced the original, more twinkling incandescent ones, to the chagrin of lighting architect Ray Grenald, who lit up the Row in 1979. "With the lights multiplied on the water, I wanted to give Philadelphia an awareness that theirs is a river town," Grenald said.

John Costello/*Philadelphia Inquirer*.

Upstaging the Liberty Bell for many tourists today is the vista of Boathouse Row, dramatically lit up at night.

April Saul.

When Grenald proposed lighting Boathouse Row, many argued it would be ugly, a waste of money, but the idea delighted then-mayor Frank Rizzo. After Grenald finally got the go-ahead, he discovered that, besides having rotten wood and failing supports—in part due to subsurface woodpilings that had been exposed to air—many of the buildings were firetraps, with underpowered and overheating electrical boxes. The first thing he did was order electrical work. "We saved Boathouse Row," Grenald said.

His vision for lighting was to trigger the imagination. He had been inspired, he said, by Picasso, "who, with three lines, could show an angry bovine male." So Grenald plotted the outlines of the houses, then kept removing potential lighting locations so that what was left was just enough for the eye to connect the dots. "I call it the negligee effect. A naked woman is not as appealing as one wearing a negligee. I wanted to do that with lights." The incandescent lights also gave a twinkly, magical quality to the Row. They were the *pièce de résistance* for the Row, which in 1987 was placed on the National Register of Historic Places.

Frank Furness likely would have appreciated Grenald's approach. In an essay on drawing from nature, he advised: "When your first outline has a certain degree of spirit and action, stop short: preserve that action." And like Grenald, he would also have been dismayed when, for reasons of practicality, the lights were replaced in 2005 by an unwavering march of LED lights, which entirely outlined the boathouses, diminishing the sense of energy and movement.

Despite the change, Grenald celebrates the ultimate impact. Now when he travels, he finds posters of a Boathouse Row ablaze, accentuating the arresting visual lines of Furness and his followers and reflecting the exciting town he knows.

CHAPTER FOUR

JOHN B. KELLY

*An Irish Bricklayer Builds
a Legend and Legacy*

The year was 1920 and America's star rower, John B. Kelly ("Jack"), was about to be dealt a snub that would forever change his life and that of a son, yet to be born.

Jack Kelly had crated up his brand-new single scull and booked passage on the SS *Philadelphia* to England. But that summer, Henley Royal Regatta officials would bar him from competing in the world's most prestigious singles rowing competition, the Diamond Challenge Sculls.

How could this slap from the British have happened to an American ally so soon after the end of World War I? What had this tall, determined athlete with the winsome dimple in his chin done to offend? Was the rejection personal, or something else entirely?

The questions would linger for years, even as Jack Kelly persevered to become one of the greatest scullers of all time.

The Kelly name is inextricable from the legend, the legacy and the landscape of Boathouse Row. Jack Kelly would go on to win three Olympic gold medals, including two in a single afternoon, an astonishing feat. The bronze statue of him in mid-stroke, *The Rower*, overlooks the Schuylkill River reviewing stand along Kelly Drive. The drive itself is named for his Olympian son, John B. Kelly Jr. ("Kell"), who was pushed unremittingly by his father to become a rowing powerhouse

John B. Kelly Sr.

John B. (Jack) Kelly Sr. looks into the camera with the steely determination of a man who, by 1920, is proving himself one of the most remarkable oarsmen the United States has ever seen, winning race after race and every national title. Only one contest eludes the 29-year-old: the most prestigious sculling race in the world, the Diamond Challenge Sculls at Henley, England.

Courtesy of John B. Kelly III.

Watching over His Course

On a steamy July 4, 1981, the statue of Jack Kelly by sculptor Harry Rosin dominates the Schuylkill River, as Jack Kelly dominated the sport of rowing. Longtime Coach George Hines recalls the day in 1965 when the statue was dedicated. "Early in the morning, guys from Vesper went up there, got under the shroud, and taped a T-shirt on the statue. The ceremony progressed. They yanked off the shroud. And there it was: 'Kelly for Brickwork.' Young Kell just laughed with everybody else."

Sal DiMarco, *John B. Kelly Sr., the Rower*, October 1984. *Philadelphia Evening Bulletin*, Special Collections Research Center, Temple University Libraries, Philadelphia.

**Adding Allure: Grace Kelly
with Her Brother**

Grace Kelly, here at age 14, congratulates her brother Kell, who has just turned 17, on his single scull victory at the Stotesbury Regatta. Six years later, at age 20, she would embark on her acting career, quickly winning an Academy Award for best actress. At 26, she married Prince Rainier III of Monaco, giving the Philadelphia Kelly clan a majestic aura.

Philadelphia Evening Bulletin, May 27, 1944, Special Collections Research Center, Temple University Libraries, Philadelphia.

in his own right. A grandson, John B. Kelly III ("J. B."), continues their legacy—unbroken for more than a century—of making Boathouse Row a crucible of competition.

The Kellys lured promising rowers and talented coaches from around the country and abroad to Boathouse Row, mentored high school students, and supported oarswomen when few others would. Their dedication enabled generations of athletes to pursue their own competitive dreams. Many of their protégées in turn coached others, assuring that Philadelphia remained a wellspring of the sport.

Though not a rower, another family member helped beam a national spotlight on the Philadelphia Kellys, for Jack Kelly's daughter and Kell's sister was Hollywood actress and Princess of Monaco Grace Kelly.

John Brendan Kelly was born in Philadelphia on October 4, 1889. Jack's parents, John H. Kelly and Mary Costello were among the tens of thousands of Irish who had fled the economic devastation of Ireland in the decades following the great potato famine of the 1840s.

The Kellys settled in "the Falls" in the 1870s, a time when immigrants, at least half of whom were Irish, made up 27 percent of the city's population. It was not an easy time for the Irish, many of whom labored under miserable, pre-union conditions in mining or laying track across the United States. Not far from Philadelphia, in Schuylkill County, violent protests by coal workers, allegations of murder, rumors of a secret and violent Molly Maguire society, and tough measures by railroad interests resulted in the conviction and hanging of 20 Irish immigrants in 1877.

The Kellys had migrated to Philadelphia from Vermont after Jack's father heard of work at Dobson's—a massive textile mill at 4601 Ridge Ave., which had been the Union Army's biggest supplier of blankets during the Civil War. He joined the thousands of Irishmen it employed in its struggling East Falls neighborhood.

Jack Kelly's mother, Mary, the daughter of an Irish tenant farmer, like her husband, had little formal education. But she had a passion for literature that she passed on to her ten children, eight of whom survived to adulthood. She also held them to unwavering standards of comportment. Punctuality was critical. So was

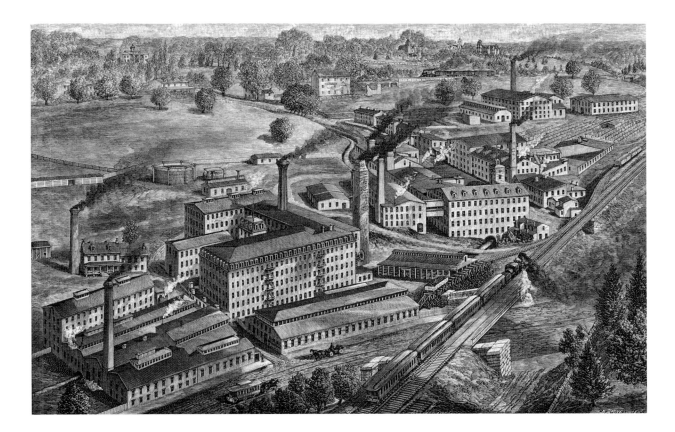

Dobson's Mammoth Mill

Before closing in the 1920s, Dobson Mill, a major producer of textiles, carpets, and blankets on Scott's Lane, employs more than 4,000 workers, many of them Irish immigrants living in East Falls. Dozens of children under the age of 16 work there, including Jack Kelly and his four older brothers, who all drop out of school to help support the family.

Dobson Mill, 1884. Courtesy of the Collection of Adam Levine.

keeping one's word. And when it came to money, she insisted they earn their own way. She demanded nothing less of them than success, though the doors to professional careers for them were largely still closed in the anti-immigrant, anti-Catholic America of the late 19th century.

Many of the couple's children would drop out of school at age nine or ten to work at Dobson's. They needed to supplement their father's meager income, even after he left Dobson's to become a conductor on the dangerous late-night run of the horse-drawn trolleys that ran on tracks inside the city.

To Irish youth, such as the Kelly brood, most avenues to the American Dream might have seemed out of reach at a time when help-wanted ads routinely used the phrase "No Irish need apply," and only one in four

Working with His Hands

———

Jack Kelly's early years in construction play a part in building the brawn that helps make him a champion on the water. On October 27, 1912, the 23-year-old sits front and center, hat in hand, posing with the construction crew of his brother's company, P. H. Kelly Co.

Courtesy of John B. Kelly III.

second-generation Irish could land a white-collar job. Those with ambition had little choice but to try to make their way by rising to leadership in heavily Irish labor unions, city politics, the arts, the church, sports, or as entrepreneurs.

The fortunes of the Kelly family soared after the eldest, Patrick Henry, known as "P. H.," found his ticket to success in a newspaper. The Philadelphia Press was offering a house worth $5,000 as a prize for "most popular employee of the year." With the skills of a well-oiled political machine, Mary Kelly sent her many children out to canvas the Falls for signatures. P. H. won, immediately sold the prize house, and used the money to launch a contracting business. Three years later, he was a millionaire. By 1923, the P. H. Construction Company would build the Free Library on the Benjamin Franklin Parkway.

The Kellys' second son, Walter, would grow up to play a marquee role in the vaudeville circuit, drawing crowds at the Garden State Pier in Atlantic City with his "Virginia Judge" routine and even performing to acclaim in Europe. His younger brother George wrote nine plays that made it to Broadway, including *Craig's Wife*, which in 1926 won the Pulitzer Prize for drama.

Jack, the family athlete, would find his way to success, as many from struggling families still do, through sports. But that would come later. Around 1899, at age nine or ten, like his brothers, Jack dropped out of school to work at Dobson's. At 12, he was dashing around the construction site for the new John Wanamaker's store, at 13th and Market Streets, as a "telephone boy," delivering messages. "I had to walk and climb the framework. . . . I often marvel now that I lived through it," he would later write.

Whenever he could, Jack would ride his bicycle along the Schuylkill River just blocks from the family home, then on Stanton Street. The scullers, with their grace and power, captivated his imagination as he would try to pace them on his bike.

Although he boxed and played some football, as well as the new game of basketball, he gravitated to rowing, the sport that had put Philadelphia on the world's stage. At the first modern Olympic Games of 1896, bad weather had washed out the rowing event, but in the next games of 1900 and 1904, the Vesper Boat Club's eight-man crew had triumphed.

Soon, the teenager was learning to row at the Chamounix Club, an early rowing group near East Falls with the virtue of affordable dues. "My hopes were high, but the bankroll low," he wrote. With extra money made by caddying for golfers on weekends, he switched to the nearby Montrose Boat Club, which had better equipment. By his late teens, he was making enough as a journeyman bricklayer to afford the top-ranked

Vesper Boat Club despite dues costing around $500 a year in today's dollars—approximately what membership in all the boat clubs still costs.

For the Olympics of 1900, the fiercely competitive Vesper had recruited the tallest, strongest men they could find, no matter their occupation or social standing. Among them were William Carr, a 24-year-old carpenter born in Donegal, Ireland, who lived with his widowed mother and four siblings; John O. Exley, 33, a teamster whose father had a farm on Hog Island, now part of Philadelphia International Airport; Harry DeBaecke, 21, a machinist; Roscoe Lockwood, a 24-year-old stenographer with two children; and the coxswain, 16-year-old Louis Abell, of Elizabeth, New Jersey, the son of a carpenter. Also on the boat was James Juvenal, 26, who worked in life insurance and would later become an Olympic coach.

It was into this new era of Boathouse Row that 19-year-old Jack Kelly, with his ideal physique for rowing, at nearly 6 feet 2 inches and 176 pounds, began to make his mark. His hands and arms were strong from his day job in construction, and he was relentless. He would be out on the river at 6:00 A.M., at work from 7:00 A.M. to 5:00 P.M., then back on the river again until dark. On Sundays, he rowed from morning till night.

His star quality was immediately evident. In his first year in junior competition, 1909, he stroked Vesper's four-oared boat, or "gig," to victory in the annual Schuylkill Navy Regatta. "Vesper proved a big surprise winning quite easily," Louis Heiland would write in his 1938 *The Schuylkill Navy of Philadelphia*. Within three years, Vesper members elected Jack, at age 22, club captain.

Rowing with others in a team boat requires an exquisite level of coordination—all oars dipping into the water in perfect harmony, all bodies pulling back in unison, all arms bringing in the end of the stroke together, everyone coming up the slide with seats rolling at the same speed so as not to check the forward momentum of the boat, all the while every muscle strains and the lungs scream for oxygen.

Jack preferred sculling in a single, where he could rely only on himself and his own conditioning. In his earliest races, he made classic and humiliating mistakes, sometimes flipping himself out of the boat. He caught "crabs"—placing an oar at a bad angle in the water such that it got sucked under, stalling the boat or even tossing him into the water. Even in those races, Jack would right himself and charge on, astonishingly coming near victory from behind.

He also developed an uncanny way to jump-start the competition by learning to recognize the particular facial motion or gesture made by the judge firing the starter pistol, in the split second before it went off. When a judge at a Boston race, catching on to his technique, warned, "There will be no beating the gun on me." Jack, so the story goes, waited until all the boats had left the mark before turning to him and asking, "Now?" Jack took off—and still won.

Jack Kelly, wearing his "luck of the Irish" green silk cap, was unbeatable. From 1909, when he joined Vesper, until 1920, when he was about to embark for the Diamond Sculls race in England, he had won almost every American sculling title—more than 100 consecutive victories.

World War I had brought a pause to his rowing, though not to his conditioning. He had made a name for himself in the ambulance corps, not so much for aiding the wounded in the trenches of France, but for the pounding he gave French opponents in local boxing matches. He was undefeated in 11 heavyweight bouts, even as he toned muscle and honed to an edge his drive to win.

He was 29 years old in 1920 and had just launched his own construction company, John B. Kelly, Inc.—soon widely known for its logo, "Kelly for Brickwork"—when he turned his focus to that summer's competition. At the top of his list was the Diamond Challenge Sculls at Henley, where he hoped to trounce the British champion, Jack Beresford. Victory would make Jack Kelly the world's singles champion. The Olympics, being held in Antwerp, Belgium, a site chosen to honor the valiant World War I nation, was almost an afterthought to him.

"I would rather row in the Diamond Sculls than in the Olympics," Jack told the *New York Times* that April, as he anxiously awaited British approval of his entry. "It is by no means certain that the English authorities will accept me," he said, citing a possible obstacle: the outrage in England following Vesper's ungentlemanly behavior at the Henley Royal Regatta 15 years earlier. In 1905, he explained, a Vesper crew had so violated the rules that Henley officials "resolved that they would never permit a Vesper oarsman to row there again. Of course it is foolish that any such reason should bar me but it is possible."

To assure that rowing was clean and fair—and remained a sport of "gentlemen"—Henley managers had promulgated a stringent amateur code, stricter even than that pronounced by Philadelphia's Schuylkill Navy, formed by nine local clubs in 1858 as the first amateur governing body for sports in the United States. The question of professional rowers preoccupied amateur groups in both the United States and England through much of the 19th century, as "the manly sport of rowing" threatened to be sullied by high-stakes races and the corruption that inevitably accompanied them.

Making It off and on the River

With construction booming and his finances looking up, Jack Kelly sits in his car, parked in front of the Vesper boathouse. Although he lost the nationals in 1916, he is still regarded as America's best sculler, having won 13 straight victories before that contest. Newspapers tout him as bringing "rowing fame to Philadelphia," but Jack's rowing stops when he, along with most of Boathouse Row, goes off to fight World War I.

Circa 1917. Courtesy of John B. Kelly III.

Schuylkill River Scene, 1920s

Rowers draw massive crowds along the Schuylkill, captured in this postcard from the 1920s.

Watching Races on the Schuylkill, Fairmount Park, Philadelphia, PA. Courtesy of James Hill.

99. WATCHING THE RACES ON SCHUYLKILL. FAIRMOUNT PARK. PHILADELPHIA. PA.

108533

The Schuylkill Navy's amateur standards, followed by those of the National Association of Amateur Oarsman formed in 1872, also reflected a broader national concern. Gambling was rampant in the mid-1800s, and stalwart citizens were battling back. Lotteries had cheated and impoverished so many that by 1840 most states, including Pennsylvania, had enacted laws against them.

Riverboat gambling was rife with professionals fleecing people on hundreds of paddleboats plying the Mississippi. Over the course of a three-day poker match in 1856, a plantation owner lost $100,000 to one of the more notorious gamblers, who also stung an Englishman. After losing his luggage and $8,000 to the professional, the distraught visitor shot himself in the head. The Gold Rush drew the gambling kind, so many that some outraged citizens in 1856 lynched professional gamblers in California. Closer to Philadelphia, gambling establishments were taking over Saratoga, New York, and spreading into New York City, where bettors would soon infiltrate the infamous Tammany Hall.

It was no wonder that the sportsmen of Philadelphia, intent on staying in the good graces of the city on whose parkland their boathouses stood, and wanting to preserve the integrity of the sport they loved, should create a clear definition of "amateur." Still, America remained enamored by the professionals, who continued to compete against one another to the end of the century. Men such as the Ward brothers, Ned Hanlan, Fred Plaisted, James Hamill, and the Biglin brothers were the sports heroes of their day, drawing adulation, crowds, money—and foul play.

The artist Thomas Eakins was among the admirers of the Biglin brothers who competed on the Schuylkill River in May 1872, in the country's first pair-oared race. The purse was $1,000 (nearly $20,000 today). Prizes for professional races would soon dwarf that amount, courting corruption. Charles Courtney, who went professional after winning at the amateur Centennial singles race on the Schuylkill in 1876, claimed that gamblers snuck arsenic into his food, sickening him before a race in 1877.

In England, where class divisions were more prominent, rowing organizations specified the kinds of people eligible to compete as amateurs. The London Rowing Club, returning from the Centennial races, where it felt the definition of "amateur" was far too loose, drew up new rules stating that an amateur must be "an officer of Her Majesty's Army, or Navy, or Civil Service, a member of the Liberal Professions, or of the Universities or Public Schools, or of any established boat or rowing club not containing mechanics or professionals."

In 1879, Henley stewards—reacting to several instances when foreign rowers whom they judged to be professionals had gained entry to their races—also tightened their amateur rules. Besides the prohibitions on rowers or coaches receiving money, no one could row as an amateur who had made money as a "mechanic, artisan or labourer."

The British had reason to be concerned. Americans competing in England occasionally roiled the waters of the Thames with unmannered behavior or worse. In 1881, the stroke of a Cornell crew cut a deal with a saloon in Ithaca to throw a race at Henley. The oarsman fainted in mid-course to assure payoffs to those back home who had wagered bets.

A few years later, Cornell raced on to the finish, fully aware that the British crew, experiencing some difficulty, had never left the starting line. Cornell's decision to race anyway was seen in England as "ungentlemanly."

Then came the incident that seemingly ensnared Jack Kelly. After a Vesper Boat Club crew rowed at Henley in 1905, its manager made the controversial decision to give the men spending money, a seemingly benign way to allow the athletes the means to enjoy the Continent. The decision to pay the men raised questions on both sides of the Atlantic. In the United States, both the National Association of Amateur Oarsman and the Schuylkill Navy investigated whether Vesper had violated amateur rules. Their findings, significant enough to make the newspapers, led to a yearlong suspension from competition of the Vesper Eight and its manager.

The reprisal by Henley officials went further: "No entry from the Vesper Boat Club of Philadelphia, or from any member of their 1905 crew [shall] be accepted in future."

Fifteen years and a World War later, a friend of Jack, who had talked to four of the six Henley stewards, assured him that the war had changed things "and that they'd be happy to accept my entry," Jack would tell the *New York Times*. But three days before Jack was supposed to board ship, a cablegram from the regatta's stewards landed: "The entry of J. B. Kelly in the Diamond Sculls not accepted. Letter follows." No letter ever did.

Angry, hurt, and resolute, Jack turned his focus to that summer's Olympic games, where he would get a second chance to race the same British world-class sculler he had so wanted to defeat in the Diamond Sculls— Jack Beresford.

But first, Jack Kelly burnished his image in the Independence Day race on the Schuylkill against the Canadian war hero Bob Dibble. He not only defeated him, but when the exhausted Dibble fell overboard at the finish, Jack dived into the water to save him from drowning. Some 20,000 people watched the race, according to the July 6, 1920, *New York Times*, and it was estimated that upwards of $10,000 were wagered on it (nearly $120,000 in today's dollars).

SCULLING AND SKULDUGGERY

Professional rowing in the 19th century was a bit like March Madness, and Ned Hanlan and Charles Courtney were two of its colorful heroes. The purses were huge, sometimes totaling as much as $80,000 in today's dollars and worth it for the entertainment. Gambling was rife. Races were thrown.

Hanlan, an unknown 21-year-old from Toronto, Canada, made a name for himself in Philadelphia at the 1876 Centennial's professional regatta. Mid-race, to the crowd's astonishment, Hanlan stopped rowing and watched his American contender from Boston, Fred Plaisted, creep up to his stern. Then Hanlan charged off to victory. Hanlan, among the first to use the sliding seat and swivel oarlocks, had the speed to afford such drama. He was called a "demi god" and champion of the world.

Courtney, who grew up on Cayuga Lake, New York, raced as an amateur at the Philadelphia Centennial, but undefeated in 88 amateur races, he quickly turned professional. An 1878 race against Hanlan generated several hundred thousand dollars in bets. At the finish, Hanlan was blocked by spectator boats that strayed, perhaps intentionally, into his path, but he somehow maneuvered around to win. A contest the following year between the two was thwarted when Courtney's shell overnight was cut in half with ice saws. Had Hanlan paid someone to do this? Had a fearful Courtney himself arranged to have it done? A biographer of Courtney wrote, "Never since the firing on Fort Sumter did an event so arouse the anger of the American people."

Ned Hanlan of Canada

Ned Hanlan's face appears on collectors' cards, called "premiums" and sold in packs of cigarettes, much like baseball cards are sold with chewing gum decades later.

Courtesy of the Bill Miller Collection.

Charles Courtney of New York

A photograph of Charles Courtney from the 1876 Centennial regatta in Philadelphia shows his use of a rowing advance that boosts leg power—the sliding seat.

The Library Company of Philadelphia.

That summer, Jack became a hero again when he miraculously dodged live electric wires to charge into a burning building near his Olympic quarters in Antwerp, to rescue its elderly occupant. Kelly believed in divine intervention; he also believed that adversity builds strength. Later, in an essay entitled "This I Believe," Jack wrote:

This I believe, that life has a peculiar way of balancing its books and you will find that we get out of life just about what we put into it. Many times the clouds are dark and everything seems to go against us, but that is the laboratory test we are put through to see how we react to disappointment and the same is applied to people who have a flare for success. Success and prosperity can hurt a person more than adversity. Beethoven said when he was near death that of all the experiences he had in his career, if he had to give up all the memories but one, he would keep his disappointments, as they taught him most. This I really believe."

Jack had prayed that God would assign him and Beresford to different brackets for the heats so that they could both progress to the finals, where they would face each other for the first time. Which is what happened. On the night before the race, Jack remembers going to bed with the stars "shining brightly through the open window. 'Thank you, God,' I said. You won't hear another word from me. You have done your part. It's up to me tomorrow."

Kelly and Beresford sculled all out for most of the 2,000-meter (1¼-mile) distance, each challenging the other for the lead with bursts of breathtaking power strokes. Thirteen years later, Jack described the battle which would set a world record:

Beresford tried to set the pace. I disputed for a time and then let him go to it. He led me all the way to the last quarter. I pulled up a high stroke, dug deeper and deeper, and put every ounce of strength I possessed into the fight. We were even for 200 yards with the crowds cheering frantically. Then Beresford cracked. I loafed the last 200 yards, content to win by a length. Even then I broke the world record, 7:38 . . . I did it in 7:35. I would have clipped five seconds more off the mark, if I had been pushed.

"Kelly was slightly exhausted after the hard race," the *Philadelphia Inquirer* reported, "but Beresford crumpled up in a heap." Jack had won by a full second.

The 1920 Olympic final in Antwerp, Belgium, between British rower Jack Beresford, 21, and Jack Kelly, 30, finally pits two of the greatest single scullers in the world against each other. Earlier that summer, Lord Beresford won the Diamond Sculls at Henley after officials barred Kelly from competing. Here, Beresford loses to Kelly by one second in what is regarded as one of the tightest margins in the event's history. After the race, Kelly, so the story goes, sent his green cap to King George V, with a brick and a note saying, "Compliments from a bricklayer."

Antwerp, 1920 Olympic Games. International Olympic Committee.

A half hour later, although Jack had not eaten and told his first cousin Paul Costello he was feeling ill, the two climbed into their double and won that race as well. For winning two gold medals in a single afternoon, John B. Kelly was hailed as the greatest sculler of all time. Nearly a century later, he remains the only rower in the U.S. Olympics Hall of Fame.

With an eight from the Naval Academy also winning gold, the surprise dominance of American oarsmen in the 1920 Olympics served notice "that American crews and rowers might hold their own with the best in the world." In Philadelphia, a crowd of 100,000, supported by the police and firemen's marching bands, cheered the return of their hometown Olympians. Many in the crowd wore green caps.

Vesper, the premier racing club on Boathouse Row, had once again brought the city international distinction. Still, Jack seethed. He had won every major sculling contest but the one from which he had been excluded. The question of why would haunt him. He vowed that if he ever had a son, he would do everything he could to make sure he won the Diamond Sculls.

In his first interviews after the rejection telegram, Jack told reporters he probably had been barred because of the 1905 Vesper incident. "I see no reason for the refusal of my entry," he told the *Philadelphia Bulletin* (June 4, 1920). "Possibly the Englishmen are considering the trouble which arose after the return of the Vesper Boat Club." Thirteen years later, still without official word from Henley, Jack repeated the same theory.

But when he entered politics, Jack took a populist route and began playing up Henley's bias against manual laborers as the reason for the snub. It was a log cabin sort of story for the popular Olympic hero whose Brickworks had expanded up and down the East Coast, and who in 1935 had nearly been elected mayor of Philadelphia, garnering 47 percent of the vote running as a Democrat in what was then a solidly Republican town.

"I was at that time in business for myself under my own name, John B. Kelly, Inc. and had not laid any bricks after 1910. And this was 1920," Jack told the *New York Times* (September 24, 1956) four years before his death.

John B. Kelly III ("J. B.") says it is plausible that his grandfather used the manual labor rejection to his advantage. "My grandfather was very serious about his image," J. B. explained. He was "very conscious of how he looked in public and carried himself in what he thought was in an appropriate and serious but also grand way."

Running for Mayor

John B. Kelly, Mayoral Candidate, November 4, 1935. Philadelphia Evening Bulletin, Special Collections Research Center, Temple University Libraries, Philadelphia.

With President Franklin D. Roosevelt

President Franklin D. Roosevelt, City Democratic Chairman John B. Kelly, and Senator Joseph F. Guffey Meet at the B&O Rail Station, 1936. Philadelphia Record, Historical Society of Pennsylvania.

Henley records, which came to light decades later, indicate that Jack was actually rejected for both reasons: the 1905 Vesper incident as well as the manual laborer rules. But the underlying issue may well have been something that neither Jack Kelly nor the British nor anyone else would publically voice: "the Irish problem."

In 1920, the Irish were fighting a bloody war of independence against the British. That spring, the Irish Republican Army had escalated its attacks, killing British policemen in Ireland and blowing up their barracks. "The thing I always heard growing up," said J. B., was that the British "were looking for a reason to excuse him because he was Irish Catholic."

Jack Kelly's 1920 Olympic gold in the single and his second gold with Paul Costello in the double elevated Vesper to the pinnacle of world rowing, a precarious spot for a club to be in when your star athlete decides to abandon ship. Which is what Jack did in 1923, abruptly moving two doors upriver to the Penn Athletic Club, which had just bought the West Philadelphia Boat Club at #12 Boathouse Row. He took with him Vesper's best rowers, including his Olympic partner Costello, who had won the 1922 national single sculls championship. Also joining them was former Vesper coach Frank Muller, whom Jack lured back from Harvard.

Did Jack leave because he believed his affiliation with Vesper had hurt him at Henley? Had the club dealt him some sort of insult? Joe Sweeney, who wrote an extensive history of the Pennsylvania Athletic Club Rowing Association (Penn AC), heard several theories. One was that Jack sided with the Pennsylvania Athletic Club, a wealthy sports club then based on Rittenhouse Square, which wanted its name on a rowing club—specifically, Vesper. But Vesper refused to bend. So it took over the West Philadelphia Boat Club instead. From an old rower of that era, J. B. says he heard a different story, though he has no idea if it is true: Costello was caught entertaining a woman in the boathouse, and in the fallout Jack split along with his cousin.

Whatever the reason, Jack's move proved a tsunami on Boathouse Row. Even as it devastated Vesper, it swept a trove of talent into the boathouse two doors away. For the next quarter century, Penn AC would reign as the dominant club on the Row and a major world contender.

Almost immediately, Jack Kelly and Paul Costello, now rowing under the Penn AC banner, won first place in their double in the 1924 Paris games. It was Jack's third Olympic gold rowing medal—a historic feat. Costello won his third Olympic gold medal in 1928, again for Penn AC, rowing the double with Charles V. McIlvaine Sr., another cousin and Vesper expat.

Overall in the 1928 games, Boathouse Row medaled in four of the seven rowing events. Ken Myers of the Bachelors Barge Club, in a single, won silver. Members of the Pennsylvania Barge Club won two medals—a bronze in the pair without coxswain and a silver in the four without coxswain. (One of its rowers, Ernest Bayer, fearing that a married man would not be selected to compete, had kept his elopement secret, but more about that in a later chapter.)

For Jack—now in his 30s, married, a father, and a national celebrity, having won 126 sculling races, including 11 national championships and three Olympic titles—competitive racing was over. Not so his commitment to Boathouse Row.

Little Kell's First Strokes toward Henley

In September 1935, when John B. Kelly Jr. is eight years old, his father, wearing his 1924 Olympic singlet, takes a break from his mayoral campaign to take Kell out for his first row. He had vowed that someday a son would win the Diamond Challenge Sculls at Henley.

Philadelphia Evening Bulletin, Special Collections Research Center, Temple University Libraries, Philadelphia.

A 12-year-old and His Coaches

At age 12, Kell stands outside Penn AC with the famous former professional rower, Coach Fred Plaisted, 90, after whom Plaisted Hall (now Lloyd Hall) was named. Also coaching him is Joe Burk, arguably the world's greatest single sculler of the late 1930s.

Philadelphia Evening Bulletin, September 14, 1939, Special Collections Research Center, Temple University Libraries, Philadelphia.

Even as he grew his business into one of the largest brickworks on the East Coast; even as he became a Democratic powerhouse in Philadelphia, Jack poured his new wealth and seemingly endless energy into the Row. Needed was a backfield of strong young men who would grow up to be future champions. To bring reinforcements into Penn AC, he turned to youths who were as hungry for success as he had been—the children of German and Irish immigrants, who filled the halls of the city's Catholic high schools, especially West Philadelphia Catholic High School for Boys.

Under Coach Muller, Penn AC 's "Big Eight," made up of many West Philadelphia graduates, won the world championship in 1930 in Liege, Belgium, and, with the help of a tailwind, smashed the world record for the 2,000 meters in one of the heats. That record, 5 minutes and 18.2 seconds still holds.

From 1929 through 1931, as the nation suffered through the Depression, this mostly Irish crew won 31 consecutive victories, including the U.S. and Canadian championships in 1931. The Associated Press named it the greatest crew of the first half of the 20th century.

For Jack, one more challenge remained: to see the name "John B. Kelly" on the Diamond Sculls, the one race he had not won only because the English had not allowed him to compete. In 1935, two weeks after his son, John B. Kelly Jr., turned eight years old, his father took him out for a row in a double. By age nine, Jack had Kell in training. At age ten, the 90-pound fourth grader at the private William Penn Charter School made his debut at Penn AC as cox of a junior four-oared gig. His father had bought boats for the elite Quaker school, which in the 1940s had a team for five years—essentially the time that Kell was there.

Then, in the midst of World War II, Jack once again turned the Row upside down. He abandoned Penn AC and returned to the Vesper Boat Club, taking his stable of champions with him. Why? Maybe it was the stab of club politics. Or perhaps Jack saw this cradle of his own career as the best place for Kell to succeed.

Every day after school, Kell's older sister Peggy would drive him down to Vesper to be coached by Muller and Costello. Using his influence, Jack had helped these men get City Hall jobs that allowed them to be at the boathouse by 3.30 P.M. every day to coach Kell.

"He wasn't out with the kids having fun and getting bubble gum and drinking Coke," a Kelly relative told Arthur Lewis for his book *Those Philadelphia Kellys*. "He was always in training, meeting his father every day after school, going out on the boat slip."

With a record of wins that was rivaling that of his father, Kell in 1946 was deemed ready for the Diamond Sculls at Henley, for the victory Jack had vowed a son would someday achieve. The 19-year-old lost the race by

Racking up a Record

By age 17, Kell, already piling up victories, rows past Sedgeley on the Schuylkill, practicing for the Stotesbury Regatta. He still wears a Penn AC shirt, but his father, in a disagreement with the club, is abandoning it to return to the Vesper Boat Club, where he will use his wealth and clout to rebuild both its boathouse and reputation.

Philadelphia Inquirer, May 5, 1944, Special Collections Research Center, Temple University Libraries, Philadelphia.

a humiliating three lengths and for a long time afterward sat in the boat, his hands frozen on the oars, unable to face his father.

But the next year, 1947, Kell captured the trophy, a gilt goblet in a pineapple design. And he did so by an impressive eight boat lengths. The American Amateur Athletic Union recognized John B. Kelly Jr. that year as the country's most outstanding amateur athlete, honoring him with its Sullivan Award, the Oscar of the sports world. In 85 years of the award, only Kell and Joe Burk, another protégé of Boathouse Row (and the subject of the next chapter,) have ever won a Sullivan for rowing.

Vindication, at Last

After disappointing himself and his father at his first attempt at winning the Diamond Sculls in 1946, Kell returns to Henley, England, a year later. Wearing a replica of his father's trademark green cap, and rowing before 20,000 spectators, he finishes an astounding eight boat lengths ahead of his nearest rival.

Philadelphia Evening Bulletin, July 8, 1947, Special Collections Research Center, Temple University Libraries, Philadelphia.

Kell continued on his journey to the pantheon of great American rowers. He won the Diamond Sculls a second time in 1949, the U.S. single sculls championship eight times, the Canadian single sculls six times, as well as nabbing two gold medals at the Pan American games and competing in four consecutive Olympics.

Kell's 1956 Olympic bronze, as of this writing, was the last time an American has won a medal—gold, silver, or bronze—in men's single sculling.

"Sports were my most important priority. *Everything* was sacrificed to that end," Kell would say after his marriage fell apart and he jumped into a whirlwind of women. He, too, would go into the family business and into politics, becoming a popular city councilman. But his first and last love remained Boathouse Row. Because he cared, because he recruited, a Vesper Boat Club crew would, under his watch, for the first time in six decades, again prove itself the fastest in the world.

Vesper would also become the first club on the Row to break ranks and go coed. "He was very proud of that," said J. B, a competitive racer who helped lead Vesper into the 21st century.

"He never told me why he wanted to do it. Maybe because he had three sisters and five daughters."

From Kell to J. B.: Sharing a Love

Kell and son J. B. Kelly III share a moment at the Vesper Boat Club during the Head of the Schuylkill Regatta, probably in 1980. Try as he would to find another sport, J. B. ends up rowing for Harvard, where his crew defeats Yale. Five years after this photo, the 56-year-old Kell, who had just been elected president of the U.S. Olympic Committee, dies of a heart attack while on his morning jog along Kelly Drive. Like his father and grandfather, J. B. Kelly has played a leadership role at Vesper and on the Row.

Courtesy of John B. Kelly III.

CHAPTER FIVE

TOM CURRAN AND JOE BURK

The Collegiate Calling
of Two American Champions

One frigid Philadelphia day, so bitterly cold your breath turned to steam, Joe Burk entered the University of Pennsylvania boathouse only to find his rowers hanging out upstairs. Spurning indoor training, Burk had his boys out on the Schuylkill River almost every day, no matter how miserable the weather.

"Why aren't you dressed to go on the water?" he demanded.

"It's so cold, we could die!" one student protested.

Coach Burk, so the story goes, left the boathouse, jumped into the freezing water, then came back in, dripping.

"I'm still alive," he announced. "Now get out there rowing!"

Around the same time in the 1950s, La Salle College coach Thomas Aloysius Curran, returning to his car parked near Boathouse Row one evening, confronted a man looting his glove compartment. The thief threatened Curran with an automatic pistol and took off running down 22nd Street. Curran gave chase, braving "a hail of gunfire."

It was in character for a man everyone called "The Bear."

World War II had largely put a halt to competitive rowing in the United States and around the globe. But by the early 1950s, two of Philadelphia's foremost rowers of the 1930s were back, infecting a new generation of young athletes

From Winning to Coaching

Tom Curran and Joe Burk are among the world's great rowers of the 1930s, setting records that endure for years; Joe Burk does it in a single; Tom Curran, in an eight. Two decades later, both are coaching on Boathouse Row, steering their charges to the pinnacle of their leagues. Joe Burk is at the University of Pennsylvania; Tom Curran, at La Salle College. Both demand dedication and discipline, but their other secrets to success diverge.

**Tom Curran,
La Salle College**

Philadelphia Daily News. Special Collections Research Center, Temple University Libraries, Philadelphia.

with their passion. Both were extraordinary athletes who had trained at the Penn Athletic Club power-house that Olympian John B. Kelly Sr. had nurtured. Both had become international champions. And both were determined to instill an extraordinary level of discipline and commitment in any youths willing to pull an oar, some of whom did not know a bow from a stern. Each brought his own style of coaching and technique, ideas that some of their most talented disciples would carry out into the rowing world for decades after.

They led the two best college crews in Philadelphia. Yet their oarsmen rarely competed against one another. Under Joe Burk, the University of Pennsylvania would go on to dominate the Intercollegiate Rowing Association (IRA), made up of Ivy League and big university schools. Under Tom Curran, La Salle College (now La Salle University) would star in a burgeoning national competition of smaller schools, the Dad Vail Regatta.

These two men, Joe Burk and Tom "The Bear" Curran, would bring their protégés to the heights of international competition. Through dint of their personalities and drive, they would inspire a dynasty of coaches who would help spread the gospel of rowing in the second half of the 20th century.

———

Varsity rowing did not have its start in Philadelphlia. Penn was actually a late bloomer when compared with New England colleges, especially the other Ivies. In 1852, Yale had squared off against Harvard on Lake Winnipesaukee, New Hampshire, in what is considered the first collegiate competition of any kind in the United States. Penn students soon started rowing, but the university would not compete in its first varsity race for another 27 years.

The infancy of Penn rowing dates to 1854, when a group of students who enjoyed exercising at Tom Barrett's Gymnasium and renting boats from Charlie's Boathouse raised $100 (about $2,800 today) and bought a used four-oared boat from the Bachelors Barge Club, which had organized the year before. They called themselves the University Barge Club (UBC). To store the *Hesperus*, they built a one-story brick boathouse, measuring 25 by 50 feet, together with the Philadelphia Barge Club for $550 (nearly $16,000). Those early years were what John B. Thayer, a founder of UBC, called the "dawn of organized athletics" at Penn, but the school itself offered no support, and rowing was not against other colleges. UBC, which also admitted Penn alumni, was just like the other well-heeled affinity groups that were forming social sport clubs along Boathouse Row and racing one another.

In 1870, after rowing's hiatus during the Civil War, four New England schools—Harvard, Amherst, Brown, and Bowdoin—organized the Rowing Association of American Colleges, widely recognized as the first collegiate athletic organization in the United States, and began an annual race. Still, the University of Pennsylvania stood on the sidelines as eight other schools—Columbia, Cornell, Dartmouth, Massachusetts Agricultural College (now U. Mass Amherst), Trinity, Wesleyan, Williams, and Yale—joined in, soon followed by Hamilton, Princeton, and Union College. Though not in the group, Rutgers had its first race—against Harvard—in 1870.

Yale, which prided itself on having the first American collegiate crew, dating from students' purchase of a shell, the *Whitehall*, in 1843, looked with disdain on the newcomers.

"New crews were being formed at colleges that, in Yale's estimation, hardly compared in prestige to their own college or to Harvard," wrote Peter Mallory in his four-volume *The Sport of Rowing*. "For Yale, this represented a crisis of epic proportion. Once they had been a power in an elite sport. Now they were becoming increasingly marginalized in an increasingly common, plebian sport."

Yale saw itself and its rivalry with Harvard as the American equivalent of the Cambridge–Oxford matchup in England, which had been held annually since 1856 (their first race was in 1829). To reestablish Yale's dominance, its undergraduate crew captain, Bob Cook, took a semester off in 1873 to study rowing technique in England. He brought back to Yale the "English stroke," and its oarsmen abandoned "the vicious short dig" and adopted "a longer and more logical sweep." Through the end of the century, even after Cook became financial manager of the *Philadelphia Press*, he spent his vacations coaching Yale.

Penn students, meanwhile, were still not competing much beyond the clubs on the Row. The college had no athletic organization of any kind. And UBC's appeal to undergraduates had dimmed as it admitted more and more older Penn alumni to help raise money for its elegant new double boathouse, shared with the Philadelphia Barge Club at #7 and #8 Boathouse Row.

But in 1872, Penn sophomore Effingham B. Morris, whose father, Israel, had started the Bachelors Barge Club 19 years before, organized the College Boat Club. At first, Effingham and his enthusiastic classmates raced only the other boat clubs on the Schuylkill River. They finally confronted their first Ivy peers on June 24, 1879, in a battle with Princeton and Columbia for an ornate silver cup donated by George Childs, publisher of the *Philadelphia Public Ledger*. The opposition was tough, particularly Columbia, which had just won the Visitors' Cup at the Henley Royal Regatta in England. Nonetheless, Penn's four-oared boat won the 1½-mile race by a second. This sweet victory—followed by Penn's winning streak in the Childs Cup of 1882, 1883, and 1884—catapulted the late arrival into the top rank of collegiate rowing.

Surely key to their success was Penn's first coach, former professional rower and boat maker Ellis Ward, who, like the revered coaches who followed him—including Rusty Callow, Joe Burk, Ted Nash, and Stan Bergman—brought his own technique, technology, personality, and whatever magic he could muster to get his boys to the finish line fastest.

Starting in 1878, Ward developed the "Pennsylvania stroke," which emphasized a strong leg drive, and coached Penn rowers in whispers through his megaphone so that rival crews would not learn its secrets.

**The Son Who Starts
College Boathouse**

*Effingham Morris, University of Pennsylvania
Class of 1875.* From the University Archives and
Records Center, University of Pennsylvania.

The Father Who Starts Bachelors

Israel Morris. Courtesy of the Bachelors Barge Club.

THE LITTLE-KNOWN MORRIS LEGACY:
TWO CLUBS ON THE ROW

It is not surprising that in 1872, Penn freshman Effingham Buckley Morris was eager for the university to have its own undergraduate varsity crew and boathouse to race against other Ivy League schools. A generation earlier, his father, Israel Wistar Morris, had been a founder of the Bachelors Barge Club, the oldest surviving club on the Row. Bachelors' minutes show that monthly meetings of the club, founded in 1853, were often held at the Morris mansion, which had been in the family since the American Revolution.

Curiously, today the Morris family connection to 2 of the 11 functioning boat clubs on Boathouse Row is lost to the fog of history. Neither members of Bachelors nor the College Boat Club of the University of Pennsylvania are aware of their ancestral ties. Census records prove that Effingham, born in 1856, grew up in the house at 225 S. 8th Street (now the Morris House Hotel) with his parents, Israel W. and Anne Buckley Morris; his grandmother; and two Irish maids in their 20s.

Israel Morris became one of the nation's leading mining experts and owner of an anthracite coal shipping company; his son would later become president of the Girard Trust Company and a director of the Pennsylvania Railroad. But first, at 17, Effingham launched the College Boat Club at a time when most other Ivy institutions were already competing with one another.

Students in 1873 elected Effingham president of the university's first athletic association, and in 1874, the club completed its own spacious and gracious boathouse, with Eastlake Victorian touches, leaving a prominent Philadelphia family's imprint on two landmarks on the Row.

More typically, families pass along their clubhouse allegiance, and each club has its dynasties: the Kellys, the Colgans, and the Horvats of Vesper; the Sonzognis of Fairmount; the Bargees of University Barge Club; the Joniks of Philadelphia Girls' Rowing Club, and so on.

The Family Mansion, Now Morris House Hotel

The Morris Mansion, at 225 S. 8th Street, was home to generations of Morrises, whose history dates back to the American Revolution. Israel Morris and his son Effingham each start a boat club on Boathouse Row—Bachelors Barge Club and College Boat Club, respectively. Today the mansion is the Morris House Hotel.

The University of Pennsylvania is still standing on the shorelines of competitive collegiate rowing in 1875 as Cornell, Harvard, Yale, Columbia, Dartmouth, Wesleyan, Amherst, Brown, Williams, Bowdoin, Hamilton, Union, and Princeton famously race one another in Saratoga. But four years later, under their first coach, Ellis Ward, Penn's four-oared crew triumphs over Princeton and Columbia to win the solid silver Childs Cup donated by George W. Childs, publisher of the *Philadelphia Public Ledger*. The Childs Cup race continues today, but as an eight-oared event. George Childs gave to many causes, saying, "I sometimes feel that the only money I have is that which I have given away." He helped his good friend Anthony J. Drexel start the Drexel Institute, now Drexel University. Together, the two also built the "model town" of Wayne, Pennsylvania.

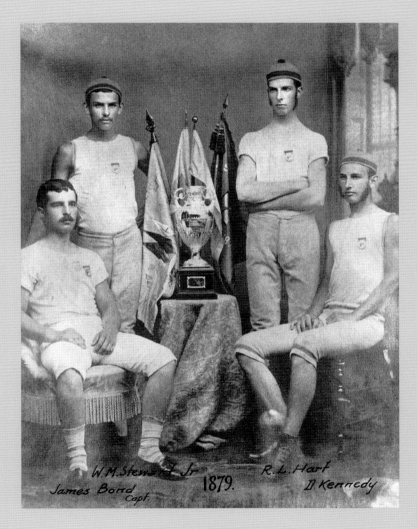

Penn's First Varsity Crew, 1879

The Professionals: The Ward Brothers

The Ward brothers, sons of a Hudson River waterman, were world-renowned professional rowers during the second half of the 19th century. In this photograph, the four Wards—Henry (Hank), Joshua, Gilbert, and Ellis—are portrayed with a list of their many competitions. Among them is the 1865 "Championship of America" where they defeated the Biglin brothers at Sing Sing, New York, pocketing a $2,000 purse (nearly $30,000 today). In 1871, they won the world title in Saratoga. Like other professional rowers, including Charles Courtney, Ned Hanlan, Fred Plaisted, and the Biglin brothers, some of the Ward brothers turned to collegiate coaching. Courtney, for instance, would coach at Cornell and Hanlan at Columbia. Ellis, the youngest Ward, settled in Philadelphia, where he worked as an oar maker, as a coach of the Fairmount Rowing Association, and at the University of Pennsylvania for most of the years between 1878 and 1913. The notion of colleges hiring crew coaches was controversial. Coaching "needed justification to those who scorned the idea of rivalry among gentlemen pursuing higher intellectual attainments," the University of Pennsylvania Record wrote in its 100th yearbook in 1952.

Besides its Childs Cup victories, Penn quickly began placing first or second in the annual Rowing Association of American Colleges regattas. When that organization stumbled, Penn, in 1895, helped found its successor group—the IRA, whose post-season regatta determines the nation's champion college crews.

Under Ward, Penn's crew thrived, winning the IRA in 1898, 1899, and 1900. In 1901, with ebullient media coverage, his crew traveled by ship to England to compete at Henley, the pinnacle of amateur rowing.

Although Penn won trial heats at Henley, it ultimately lost to the English club Leander. Still, "Penn left Henley with the distinction of being the only American eight-man crew to mount a serious challenge to Britain's retention of the Grand Challenge Cup, the most prized trophy in amateur rowing."

That, at least, was the American perspective.

The British, however, saw the Penn crew as uncouth upstarts. They frowned on Ellis Ward, whose history as a professional, they felt, tainted the team's amateur credentials. And they regarded Coach Ward's protests about foul play in the draw for lane assignments as ungentlemanly—no cultured person would stoop to such a single-minded pursuit of victory. In a prescient insight into the benefits that still accrue to U.S. colleges with winning sports teams, one British coach speculated on what a Penn victory in 1901 at Henley would have meant: winning the Grand Challenge Cup, Penn's crew "could not have been refused a contest with Harvard and Yale and the prestige of the whole university would have enhanced."

If rowing could enhance a university's prestige to that degree, one would not know it by the number of Philadelphia area colleges jumping into the sport. By the 1930s, the University of Pennsylvania, after more than a half century, was still the only area college with a varsity crew.

And Joe Burk and Tom Curran were still just kids with big dreams, racing their hearts out.

———

Tom Curran was a burly Irish kid who was willing to push himself beyond the possible, the kind of rower that Jack Kelly Sr., after his Olympic victories of the 1920s, began recruiting to his boat club from West Philadelphia Catholic High School and other Catholic high schools.

Under Ellis Ward, Penn's oarsmen quickly become among the best in the world, winning the Intercollegiate Rowing Association championship in 1898, 1899, and 1900. In 1901, to much fanfare—including news stories, a mobbed farewell, and a photographer on board—they travel to England. This is the university's first time at Henley and the British, with their restrictive amateur standards, frown on Penn sporting a former professional rower as their coach. Penn is the first "foreign" crew to reach the finals for the Grand Challenge Cup but loses to England's Leander Club. Fifty-four years pass before another Penn Crew wins this cup.

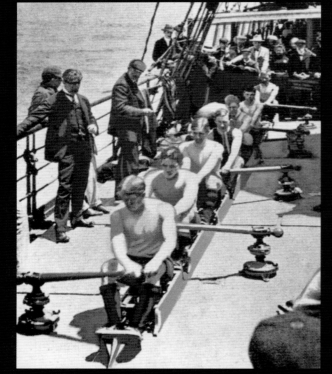

Aboard Ship: *Philadelphia Evening Bulletin*, Special Collections Research Center, Temple University Libraries, Philadelphia.

Poster Boys: *Penn's 1901 Crew Works Out at Henley*. From the University Archives and Records, University of Pennsylvania.

The Defeat: *Penn Loses to Leander by a Length, July 5, 1901*. From the University Archives and Records, University of Pennsylvania.

At 19, Curran was the youngest member of the Pennsylvania Athletic Club's high flying "Big Eight." In a heat at the 1930 FISA world rowing championships in Liege, Belgium, the crew broke the world record for 2,000 meters and went on to win the world championship by a resounding two boat lengths. Among those Penn AC men rowing with Curran were Charley McIlvaine, who had won an Olympic gold medal in 1928 in the double with Paul Costello; Joe Dougherty, who had rowed a pair with coxswain in the same Olympics but had lost; and Tom Mack who had been Dougherty's coxswain. Also in the Big Eight was Dan Barrow, who, like Curran, hoped to make it to the 1936 Olympics.

While Curran and his crew were racking up victories, Joe Burk, three years younger, was just starting at Penn, intent on playing football as he had at South Jersey's Moorestown High School. Penn's rowing coach, Rusty Callow, immediately recruited the towering lad with the spiky reddish-blond hair. At 6 feet 2 inches and about 195 pounds, Burk, who had grown up working with his family on an 80-acre peach and apple farm in Beverly, New Jersey, had the height and the strength of the ideal rower.

Through his four years at Penn, Burk majored in business while playing football every fall and rowing every spring. The university's crew was successful during those years, though not world-class like Penn AC's Big Eight, into which Olympian John B. Kelly

F MULLER · TURNER · BARROW · DOUGHERTY · JANES · McNICHOL · BRATTEN · CURRAN · McILVAINE

NATIONAL CHAMPIONS SPRINGFIELD MASS. 1929

WINNERS of STEWARTS CUP AMERICAN HENLEY 1930

TIME 6.22⅗ NEW RECORD

Early Days of the "Big Eight"

Penn AC's "Big Eight"—with Tom Curran (second from right)—are just beginning their stupendous run of victories in 1929, when they win the nationals in Springfield, Massachusetts, where this photo is taken. In 1930, they win the Stewarts Cup at the American Henley, then break the world record for 2,000 meters in the European championships. Several become crew coaches, fostering generations of champions. From left: Coach Frank Muller, Chester Turner, Dan Barrow, Joseph Dougherty (coach, Penn AC), Myrlin Janes, John McNichol (coach, West Catholic High and Penn AC), Jack Bratten (La Salle College's first coach), Tom Curran (coach, La Salle College and Temple University), and Charlie McIlvaine (La Salle College High School coach).

Courtesy of Kevin Curran.

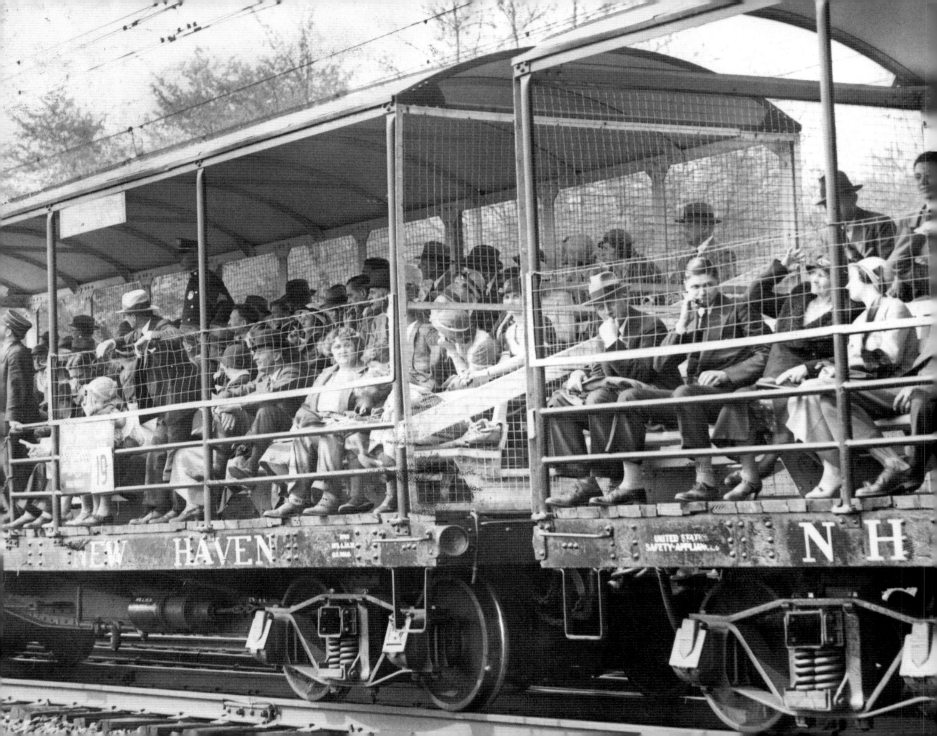

Kelly Sr. and Jack Dempsey, Observing

With railroads in the country often running along rivers, observation trains are the rage for big races, especially those by the Hudson River at Poughkeepsie. In 1932 in Philadelphia, 25,000 people watch Yale defeat Penn and Columbia on the upper Schuylkill for the Blackwell Cup. An observation train follows the racers between the Spring Mill and Shawmont stations. Among those aboard are John B. Kelly Sr. (first row, right side, hand on chin) and his friend professional boxer Jack Dempsey (with cigarette). The two met on a beach in Ocean City before they became world champions.

Philadelphia Evening Bulletin, May 1932, Special Collections Research Center, Temple University Libraries, Philadelphia.

Joe Burk, Not Yet Famous

University of Pennsylvania Coach Rusty Callow convinces Joe Burk, a football player, to also come out for crew. Burk plays both sports, and by 1934, the 20-year-old is considered the strongest and heaviest man on varsity crew, though he is only beginning to hit his stride.

Joseph William Burk with Oar on the Boat House Dock, 1934. From the University Archives and Records, University of Pennsylvania.

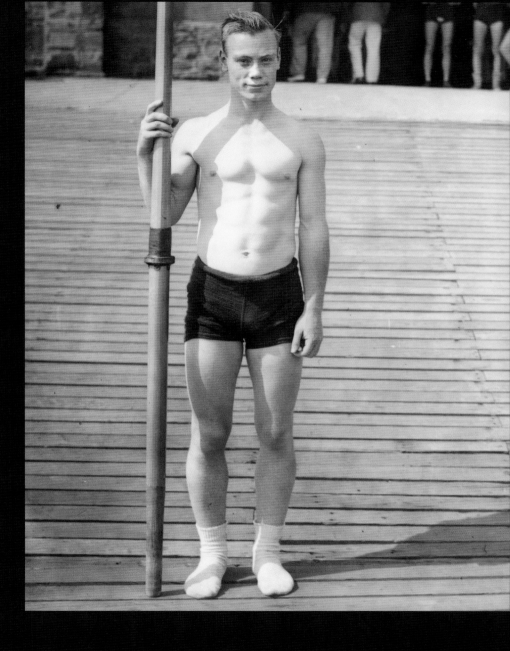

Sr. and coach Frank Muller had been pouring love and money. In 31 races between 1928 and 1932, Penn AC oarsmen were undefeated. And at the 1932 Los Angeles Olympics, where the entire U.S. team (except for the University of California eight) came from Boathouse Row, 10 of those 17 Philadelphia rowers and Coach Muller were from Penn AC. (The seven others belonged to Bachelors, the Undine Barge Club, and the Pennsylvania Barge Club.)

Meanwhile, Penn's eight, rowing with Burk, were winning some collegiate cup races but typically finished fourth or fifth in the national IRA meets and never went to Henley. Penn crew was also struggling financially in the aftermath of the Depression. The "athletic budget is not of sufficient strength to provide the necessary funds to send varsity to this national event [the IRA]," the U. of Penn 1934 class yearbook, *The Record*, reported. Callow hustled, picking up enough support from alumni and parents to get the crew to Poughkeepsie, where it placed fifth.

Graduating in 1934—the "strongest and heaviest" on Penn's Varsity 8—Burk, smitten by crew, focused relentlessly on making it to the 1936 Olympics in Penn's eight-oared boat. "To keep in shape," Burk said in his understated way, "I joined Penn AC."

Although in crew—sweep rowing—each oarsman rows with only one oar held with both hands, Coach Muller insisted that his men cross-train by sculling, rowing with two oars. Burk proved so good at it that he bought a single shell from master boat builder George Pocock in Seattle. The 22-year-old now believed he had two different shots at making the 1936 U.S. Olympic team: as a single sculler; or in the University of Pennsylvania's eight, open to alumni. But at the Olympic trials, Burk lost in his single by a humiliating 1½ lengths to his more experienced Penn AC club mate, 26-year-old Dan Barrow, a graduate of West Philadelphia Catholic High School who had rowed in the renowned Big Eight.

On the afternoon of July 4, 1936, at the Olympic trials on Lake Carnegie in Princeton, New Jersey, Burk and his Penn crew were hopeful of victory as they lined up against the three other finalists—the New York Athletic Club, the University of California, and the University of Washington. Determined to keep the lead, the Penn eight rowed at a punishing pace down the 2,000-meter course, in a heart-pounding race recounted by Daniel James Brown in his book *The Boys in the Boat*:

The New York Athletic Club went briefly to the head of the pack, but Penn, pounding the water at a high cadence of forty strokes per minute, quickly snatched the lead back. California, rowing at thirty-eight,

Boathouse Row sends eight rowers to the 1936 Olympics in Berlin—six oarsmen from Penn AC and two from the Undine Barge Club, making up nearly a third of the U.S. contingent. Only one, Dan Barrow, medals, winning a bronze in the single. The University of Washington eight, to the shock of the Germans, takes gold.

Sailing to Germany: Boathouse Row's 1936 Olympic hopefuls from Penn AC are: the pair with cox, coxswain George Loveless (lowest step), Tom "the Bear" Curran (behind Loveless on right), and Joe Dougherty (next to Curran); single sculler Dan Barrow (standing to the right, hands behind his back); and coxless pair George Dahm and Harry Sharkey. From Undine are double sculls contenders John Houser (top row left) and Bill Dugan (right).

Courtesy of Kevin Curran.

settled into third place, ten feet in front of Washington's bow. [Washington] took the rate up to thirty-nine to gain momentum, but once that was accomplished they immediately began to lower it again . . . to thirty-five. . . . Out front, Penn was still thrashing the lake white at thirty-nine. . . . As they approached the halfway mark, the New York Athletic Club suddenly began to fade. . . . Penn remained out in front by three-quarters of a length, and even continued to slowly draw farther ahead of California. . . . [Washington] continued to row at thirty-four. But what a thirty-four it was . . . long, slow, sweet, fluid strokes . . . eight white blades dipped in and out of the mirrorlike water at precisely the same instant.

Germany

Austria

**Dan Barrow
USA**

The "Hitler Olympics"

Single sculler Dan Barrow, who defeats Joe Burk in the 1936 Olympic trials to represent the United States in the single scull, receives his bronze medal as the German victor, Gustav Schafer, gives the Nazi salute. The oldest of 12 children, Barrow rowed stroke for West Catholic's eight-oared crew, which won the first Stotesbury Cup competition in 1927.

Dan Barrow at 1936 Olympics. Courtesy of Mary Ann Barrow.

With 500 meters left, Penn was in the lead, rowing at a "killing forty-one." Only then did Washington pick up its pace to forty. "For five or six strokes the bows of the two boats contested for the lead, back and forth like the heads of racehorses coming down the stretch. Finally Washington's bow swung decisively out front by a few feet. . . . With four hundred meters to go, Washington simply blew past the exhausted boys from Penn, like an express train passing the morning milk train."

At the "Hitler Olympics" in Berlin, Penn AC's Dan Barrow, rowing in the single spot that Burk had coveted, would win a bronze medal. Of the 26 U.S. rowers who competed in Berlin, eight would hail from Boathouse Row, as would their coach, John McNichol of Penn AC, a former coach at West Philadelphia Catholic High School. Among them was Tom "the Bear" Curran, who raced with Joe Dougherty in the pair with cox, though the Penn AC duo failed to medal.

As German filmmaker Leni Riefenstahl trained her cameras on her nation's crew, the underdog University of Washington's eight would famously outdo them to win gold.

———

After the crushing disappointment of the Olympic trials, Joe Burk vowed that he would never lose another race. He approached his performance with the clinical detachment of a scientist. He taped a stopwatch to his toes to time himself. He dissected his sculling stroke. Between his farm chores, pruning trees and carrying 50-pound baskets of apples, Burk worked out daily, rowing 3,000 miles on the nearby Rancocas Creek, even axing through ice in winter to get in his miles.

"Crew takes a lot of time," he would later say. "If you only put in three-fourths of the time, you are still putting in an awful lot, so you might as well put in the extra time and be successful."

Burk's Winter Workout

Determined not to miss a day of practice, Joe Burk breaks the ice with an axe on South Jersey's Rancocas Creek, near his family's farm. He purchased his scull from master craftsman George Pocock in Seattle and corresponds with him about technique for four decades. Having missed out on the 1936 Olympics, Burk set his sights on the Summer Games of 1940.

Joe Burk on Rancocas Creek, 1938. Courtesy of Kathryn McCaffrey.

He bounced ideas off Pocock. He found that rowing shorter strokes at a blistering pace of 40 per minute—assuming you were in the extraordinary form required to keep it up—was faster and more efficient than the slower, smoother stroke that coaches then favored. In a newspaper account written under his byline, Burk explained the rationale for his technique.

Imagine that the power of a stroke, he said, is like a triangle, with the greatest force at the peak. If the base of the triangle is wide—namely, if the stroke is long—it takes longer to get to the point of maximum power.

"Herein lies the essential difference in my style. I do not 'reach' so far, nor do I take such a pronounced 'layback.' . . . This enables me to strike a higher beat, utilizing the most powerful portion of the stroke."

Home from Henley

After winning the world's most prestigious single's race, the Diamond Challenge Sculls at Henley, Joe Burk is congratulated by Philadelphia Mayor S. Davis Wilson. On left are Olympians Paul Costello and John B. Kelly Sr. Second from the right is Olympian Charley McIlvaine.

Philadelphia Evening Bulletin, July 13, 1938, Special Collections Research Center, Temple University Libraries, Philadelphia.

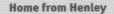

No Last Hurrah

Having won everything there is to win except the 1940 Olympics, which are cancelled, Joe Burk retires from rowing and goes off to war. His heroics on a PT boat off New Guinea make news in Philadelphia. "Give Joe Burk a boat and he'll set a record," the *Philadelphia Inquirer* writes in 1944, calling him "the champion bumper-off of Jap boats" after he destroys 13½ barges. He earns a Navy Cross for "extraordinary heroism . . . in aggressively pursuing Japanese barges." His younger brother, Jim, also a rower and also serving in the South Pacific, does not return from war.

Courtesy of University of Pennsylvania Athletics.

Some called his unconventional style jerky and robot-like, but if less elegant, it did the job. In his single, Burk won the U.S. and Canadian Championships in 1937, 1938, 1939, and 1940. He won the Diamond Challenge Sculls at Henley in 1938, the race from which John B. Kelly Sr. had been so bitterly barred in 1920. And he stunned onlookers by rowing its entire length of $1^{15}\!/_{16}$ miles at nearly 40 strokes per minute—an unprecedented, exhausting pace that slashed the course record by eight seconds. Arriving home in South Jersey, more than 40,000 people turned out to cheer him. The next year, he won the Diamond Sculls yet again—a back-to-back feat that no other American to this day has ever accomplished.

Burk credited his wins to his rigorous stopwatch training, which, unlike racers themselves, never speeds up or slows down. In all, Burk amassed 37 consecutive victories between 1936 and 1939. He was called "the world's greatest sculler."

Capping his triumphs was national recognition of his sportsmanship and athleticism by the Amateur Athletic Union. On March 9, 1940, Burk received its prestigious James E. Sullivan Award, given each year to the "outstanding amateur athlete in the United States." Between the award's founding in 1930 and this writing, only two people would be honored with a Sullivan for rowing. Both of them trained on Boathouse Row: Joe Burk in 1939 and John B. Kelly Jr. in 1947.

Burk, 26, again set his sights on the Olympics, the one world match he had yet to race after missing out in 1936. But war crossed his trophy-strewn path. Japan, which was to have hosted the 1940 summer games, cancelled after international rebukes for invading China and the death of 300,000 in the "rape of Nanking." Next up was Finland, which pulled out of hosting the Olympics after it was invaded by the Soviet Union in April.

Joe Burk after Practice on Rancocas Creek, Days before Leaving for Henley, June 15, 1939. Philadelphia Evening Bulletin, Special Collections Research Center, Temple University Libraries, Philadelphia.

At the peak of his career that summer, Burk, indisputably the world's top singles contender, suddenly announced his retirement from rowing. In August 1940, he told *Philadelphia Inquirer* columnist Cy Peterman, "Yes, Cy. I'm through. . . . There's no sense going on with what you've already done; no percentage in waiting for the inevitable decline." Besides, he added, he might be keeping others from winning.

Instead, Burk went off to war, as did Tom Curran, as did Penn coach Rusty Callow, as did so many men from Boathouse Row. Returning, they found the private clubhouses withered by war's toll on a generation of young men, but college crew was bursting into bloom.

———

Rusty Callow had sown the seeds of collegiate crew's flowering: Gazing out at the uneven landscape of rowing from his perch at Penn in 1934, he had felt empathy for smaller colleges with struggling crew programs. In particular, he admired Harry Emerson Vail, who was valiantly building a rowing team under the freezing, short-season conditions at the University of Wisconsin–Madison. When the school made money available, which was rarely, the much beloved Vail, whom everyone called "Dad," would take his tiny crew to the IRA in Poughkeepsie and compete like a David against the Goliaths. It was tough for small schools with hand-me-down equipment, inexperienced oarsmen, and little support to find the competition they craved.

So Callow invited small college rowing programs to compete with one another in a regatta he named the "Dad Vail." The first few years, only a handful of schools showed up—Marietta College, Manhattan College, the University of Wisconsin, Rutgers, and Rollins. Despite its origins on the Schuylkill River, there was no representation from Philadelphia, which, aside from Penn, was still bereft of crew. But by war's end, La Salle College—a destination school for West Philadelphia Catholic, North Philadelphia Catholic, and La Salle College High School—was bustling with young rowers. They were the hatchlings of John B. Kelly Sr.'s rowing incubator, which had moved from Penn AC to the Vesper Boat Club, and were eager to compete.

With volunteer coach Jack Bratten, who had raced with Penn AC's legendary Big Eight, La Salle in 1947 launched a rowing program—the first varsity crew on the Schuylkill River in the seven decades since Penn's first Ivy League race. In another milestone, in 1951, La Salle won a surprise victory in the Dad Vail, held that year in Boston, thus becoming the first Philadelphia school to win the nation's new small-college regatta. That fall, Bratten moved on to become commodore of the Schuylkill Navy, and from his leadership position successfully argued that Philadelphia become the Dad Vail's permanent home.

Tom Curran, Coach

Tom Curran stands to the side, watching his La Salle College crew carry its eight at the start of spring practice in 1952, his first year of coaching. No one knows why he's called "the Bear," says George Hines (third from left), then a senior. "It was always, 'The Bear said this or the Bear said that.'" La Salle in 1947 became only the second college in Philadelphia, after Penn, with a varsity crew. It took over the Crescent boathouse in 1950, when that club stumbled after the war.

Philadelphia Evening Bulletin, March 2, 1952, Special Collections Research Center, Temple University Libraries, Philadelphia.

He handed La Salle off to his crewmate from that world champion Big Eight—Tom "the Bear" Curran.

George Hines has a vivid memory of his first encounter with "The Bear" in 1952, his senior year. Despite La Salle's Dad Vail coup the previous spring, only nine men showed up at the first practice, just enough for a single crew—eight rowers and a coxswain. Whether the pitiful turnout was the result of Curran's nickname or his reputation for toughness, Hines does not know. But Curran made the situation abundantly clear: "We were it. Just him and us. It was us against the world. We have no subs. His approach was, 'We have no choice.'"

Hines soon came to appreciate Curran's coaching, even if it was delivered with an iron fist and a sarcastic wit. Almost every afternoon, Curran, by day a New Jersey beer distributor, would drive his Karmann Ghia to

the Row from his home near Atlantic City. "When he got in his little two-bucket, it started to lean on one side," Hines said, laughing at the memory of the big man in the tiny sports car.

"The strong, silent type," Hines called him, but when Curran spoke, it was to make a point. "He'd make cracks while you were rowing, to rattle you," like calling you a "chicken looking for the hen house" if you were turning your head back and forth. "His favorite expression was 'I don't have to look at your oar in the water. I just hear the flushing of a toilet.'"

Unlike Burk, with his short, powerful, high-rate strokes, Curran insisted on strong, slower ones that maximized momentum—the glide between strokes. "The idea was to keep with another crew that's rowing at 38 strokes per minute but do it rowing at 36 or less by being smooth, efficient, and together. . . . It was our incentive to make every stroke count. We wanted to put the Rockettes to shame every day," Hines remembers.

They practiced their racing starts over and over again, and learned how to anticipate the official's starting command. "The Bear's method was first of all to scout who's starting. Or watch him start earlier races. He would show us the method, by [having us use] our ears, the phrasing of the starter's delivery. That's where you got the handle on it. It works. I used it myself," said Hines, who would later coach at La Salle College High School while working in law and real estate.

Hines is not sure what precisely spun the magic of Curran's crew—the relentless practice, the smooth technique, the crew's absolute synchronicity, or simply their collective will to win against all odds. But that spring, the nine determined men of La Salle's crew were once again victors at the Dad Vail. Under Curran, they became a legend. La Salle College crew, which had taken over the boathouse of the war-decimated Crescent Boat Club, dominated the Dad Vail in the 1950s. Its crew won six years out of eight, even as the number of competing colleges doubled from 10 in 1954 to 20 by 1961.

By then, both St. Joseph's University and Drexel Institute (now Drexel University) were rowing (both had varsities by 1959). And Temple University would weigh in with crew in 1966 after lobbying by about ten students—admitted from St. Joseph's Prep, Monsignor Bonner, and La Salle College High School, which all had rowing programs far older than the colleges.

Who did Temple hire as its first coach? The Bear. Moving on from La Salle College, Curran left his vaunted crew in the hands of another of the Big Eight fraternity, Joe Dougherty, while Curran created an overnight powerhouse at Temple.

A "Bear" for Details

In 1956, Curran's La Salle College Explorers win the Dad Vail for the fourth time in six years, competing against about nine other schools ranging north to Amherst and Brown and south to Rollins, Tampa and Florida Southern. His men win again in 1957 and 1958.

"He was very precise," remembers crew member George Hines, who went on to coach La Salle College High School crew. Curran would put a thumbtack on the gunwale, beyond which the oarsmen were not supposed to reach. "Thou shalt not go beyond that tack!" Hines recalls him saying. "His crew was 99 percent straight in line, and the boat ran smooth."

Philadelphia Evening Bulletin, Special Collections Research Center, Temple University Libraries, Philadelphia.

Gavin White was an undergraduate rower at Temple in 1971 when Curran arrived. White was immediately struck by his hands. "He had the biggest paws. He was husky. You could almost see his posture was like a giant bear."

White, who succeeded Curran as Temple's head coach, remembers how gruff he could be, especially if you disagreed with him. But he was also funny. One time, at a national meeting of Dad Vail coaches in Philadelphia, Curran whispered to White, by then his assistant coach, to cover for him while he stepped out to buy sandwiches. It was Curran's responsibility to provide lunch, and he had forgotten. "While you're gone, how should I vote?" White whispered back. "The opposite of St. Joe's," Curran instructed.

By the time Curran returned, White had voted three times the opposite of St. Joe's. Then Curran made a proposal of his own and asked for a vote. Everyone, including St. Joe's, voted for it. What did Curran do? "He voted against his own motion! Just to be contrary."

At the same time in the 1950s, that Curran, at La Salle, was building one of the best small college teams in the country, Joe Burk arrived at Penn, just a few boathouses away, equally committed to excellence. Burk had returned from the South Pacific with the Silver Star, the Bronze Star, and the Naval Cross for "extraordinary heroism and intrepidity in action against the enemy," his citation said. His PT boat had sunk dozens of Japanese supply barges. Once celebrated by the local press as a sports hero, he was now hailed as a war hero.

Penn coach Rusty Callow, returning from his own service at a Seattle munitions plant, had helped Burk get a coaching job at Yale. In 1950, when Callow left a two-decade career at Penn to coach Navy, he made sure his protégé replaced him. Burk would bring to Penn crew the same intensity and concentration that he had brought to Henley—and to battle. Believing that what moved boats came down to power and endurance, he instituted weight training, one of the first rowing coaches in the world to do so, and affixed heavy weights to "pull machines."

Discipline was also critical. His rowers had to stick to his rules. There were curfews. Drinking was forbidden. Concerned about the carbonation, he even banned Coke. The men were weighed weekly and ordered to run for miles if they came in too heavy. In the 1960s, Burk checked hair length. And when on tour, his charges wore ties and jackets.

Having his boys toe the line was not just about crew. "A boy needs to have some physical strain, to know what it is to work hard and sacrifice," Burk would say. "Life is getting easy now, and they need something that tests them and teaches discipline. If crew were only victories, I wouldn't do it."

In winter, he did not view indoor rowing tanks as an acceptable alternative to outdoor practice. Still water, he thought, threw off the crew's timing. So his students were out on the Schuylkill six days a week, no matter the season. "In my four years at Penn, we only missed one day of rowing on the river, and that was because the buses could not get through the snow," said an oarsman from the Class of 1968.

"He did not seek 'perfection,' because that always led to disappointment," Burk's daughter, Kathryn Mc-Caffrey, explained. "His goal was to strive for 'excellence,' a reach which you could always take one notch higher."

With his scientific bent, Burk went beyond his stopwatch to find technology to improve his men's speed. He asked a former Penn coxswain turned engineer to devise a system to measure how hard each man was pulling, then installed spring-triggered lights on the rowlocks. Each oarsman had four lights, with all four lighting up at a stroke's maximum performance. Although the paraphernalia added 50 pounds to the weight of the boats, the men appreciated how the lights revealed precisely when to apply the most pressure.

While Curran looked to the power of omens—rain on the first day of practice signaled a good season; a late night "good luck" call from a friend meant a win the next day—Burk was all about statistics. He even had a system that avoided entirely the possibility of coach favoritism, especially his own, in picking the right men for a boat.

Using a deck of cards, he would put one oarsman's name on each card, shuffle, then deal out that day's lineup for each boat. The shells would race, with those in the winning boat each getting three points and the losers, two. He would then select the starters for big races according to the sum of the previous 50 races.

Said Ted Nash, an Olympian who became Burk's freshman coach: "Using his system, there's no way a coach will judge against a boy purely because he doesn't like his personality or his attitude or the length of his hair."

For 19 years, Joe Burk would lead the University of Pennsylvania in one of its most glorious eras in rowing. In 1951 and 1952, the Quaker lightweight varsity won at Henley. In 1952, his heavyweight crew won the Childs and Blackwell cups, defeating Columbia, Princeton, and Yale.

Pushing to the Limit

Joe Burk demands no less of his Penn oarsmen than he does of himself. His crew rows no matter the weather. Going beyond such discipline, he turns to science, commissioning a light system so each rower can recognize his maximum power by the number of lights that turn on. "His knack for building good crews from inexperienced material has won him the respect of coaches throughout the country," the Penn Class of 1963 writes.

Philadelphia Evening Bulletin, February 4, 1958, Special Collections Research Center, Temple University Libraries, Philadelphia.

Burk's Light Boat

Burk's special lights, that measure each rower's effort, are attached to the gunwales of a crew shell (facing page).

The Record, Class of 1965, 348. From the University Archives and Records Center, University of Pennsylvania.

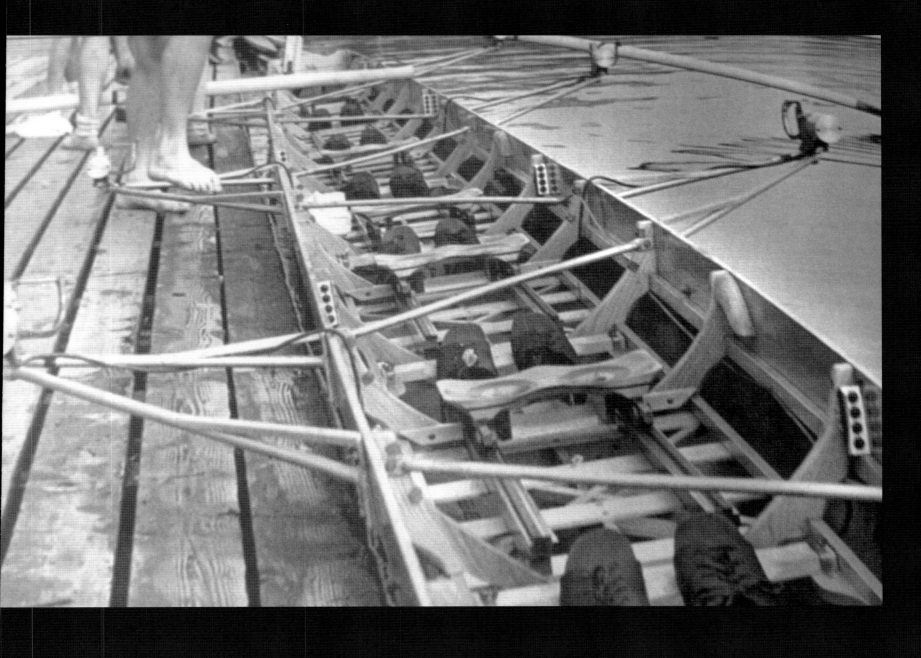

The year 1955 was particularly stupendous. The heavyweight crew, with future Harvard coach Harry Parker in the two seat, won every major race and broke Navy's four-year winning streak, defeating them in the Adams Cup. "They shattered the longest crew winning streak since Cleopatra's barges swept the Nile," the *Daily Pennsylvanian* gushed in a May 10 editorial. "The crew has brought more silverware to our trophy cases this season than in any year except 1935." Penn's crew that year went on to win the Canadian Henley as well as the Grand Challenge Cup at Henley, England, where they trounced the British, Soviets, and Canadians. It was the first time a Penn crew had competed for the Grand Challenge since Ellis Ward's crew had done so in 1901.

"To European observers, Penn seemed to defy the laws of physics that applied to all other crews," Mallory wrote. "The strength and speed of the Penn pullthrough, the endless run on the impossibly long recovery, seemed as unattainable in its own way as Joe Burk's high-rating sculling technique had seemed to them 17 years earlier."

In 1962, Penn went to Henley again. But 1964 proved a disappointment as Penn lost in the Olympic trials to a motley, miraculous Vesper Boat Club crew. So, too, despite a stellar year, his eight-oared crew failed again in the 1968 Olympic trials, losing to Harvard by a painfully tiny $\frac{5}{100}$ of a second. However, Penn's coxed four made it to the 1968 Mexico City Olympics, where it placed fifth. With a national camp selection process taking hold, that Harvard eight and Penn four would be the last single-college crews ever chosen to represent the United States in an Olympics.

A generation of great rowers who became great coaches was moving on.

In 1969, having infected his rowing progeny with a lifelong obsession, Joe Burk, at age 55, left coaching much as he had left competition, modestly passing on to others the opportunity to lead.

A decade after that, Curran, at age 68, handed the baton to his assistant coach, Gavin White, who would coach Temple crew for the next 37 years.

The era of Joe Burk and Tom Curran left a large and continuing legacy. Many of their prodigies would move away from rowing but carry with them into careers the confidence and self-discipline that comes with early rising and rigorous training. Some of their most successful rowers became some of the nation's most stellar coaches, men who would in turn inspire the next generation, which finally included women.

Some examples of their influence:

- After witnessing the success of Burk's strength training at Penn's 1955 Henley triumph, Karl Adam, coach of Germany's Ratzeburg Rowing Club, developed the technique of "interval training"— involving running, swimming, boxing, weight lifting, and other endurance sports.
- Dietrich Rose, who trained at Ratzeburg, brought interval training to the United States, where he helped coach the Vesper crew to victory in the 1964 Olympics.
- Star rower Harry Parker, who trained at Penn under Burk, became one of the nation's most revered rowing coaches, with a 50-year career at Harvard. Starting in 1963, under Parker the Crimson racked up an extraordinary 285–43–1 record, with 17 national championships, more than any school

in the country. In 1968, the student outdid his master when Parker's Harvard crew beat Burk's by ⁵⁄₁₀₀ of a second—four inches—winning the right to represent the United States at the 1968 Olympics in Mexico City. Parker also broke rank with many male coaches by agreeing to coach the first women's national contenders. His "Red Rose" crew won silver in 1975 at the world championship and bronze at the 1976 Olympics.

- Ted Nash, freshman crew coach under Burk, succeeded him in 1969 and led Penn to a wave of victories, including two undefeated seasons over 14 years. He also served several times as national Olympic coach and advocated for women rowers as a founder of the National Women's Rowing Association.

- George Hines, who rowed under "The Bear" at La Salle College, spent his career supporting youth rowing. He trained hundreds of teenagers at Philadelphia's La Salle College High School from 1955 to 1968, among them John Lehman Jr., who became U.S. Secretary of the Navy. Hines and his wife, women's rowing pioneer Lois Trench-Hines, also built the Hines Rowing Center in Conshohocken, opening the upper Schuylkill River to suburban universities and high schools unable to find space on crowded Boathouse Row.

- Stan Bergman, who started out rowing in a lifeguard boat at the Jersey shore, was mentored by Curran at the Viking Rowing Club in Ventnor. Bergman first coached crew at Holy Spirit High School in Absecon, and then at Penn for 22 years (1984–2006), before retiring in 2006.

- Gavin White, an undergraduate rower at Temple University under Curran and his successor as coach, took his rowing Owls to Henley at least seven times and won 20 Dad Vail varsity eight titles, including 13 consecutively, from 1989–2001. "The Bear taught me everything I know about rowing," White said. "He was an amazing character, almost bigger than life." Under White, the stature of Temple's crew was such that in 2013, an outcry went up around the country after the university announced that it was eliminating its men's and women's crew in an economy move. The rowing program and its dilapidated boathouse were rescued with funds from the city and a $3 million gift from philanthropist H. F. "Gerry" Lenfest, who had just been named by Pennsylvania's governor to the Temple University board of trustees. "I couldn't believe that Temple, the city's principal university, with the most graduates, couldn't have a place on the Schuylkill," explained Lenfest, who is neither a rower nor a Temple graduate. "The sport is so germane to the city."

CHAPTER SIX

ERNESTINE BAYER

Women and Their Fight for the Right to Row

Before Ernestine Bayer got it into her head that she had a perfect right to row; before she arm-twisted her competitive-rower husband in the 1930s to find a way to get on the river; before she and other strong-willed Philadelphia women passed the baton, one to the next, in a decades-long campaign to upend the no-women-here culture of Boathouse Row and American rowing; before all of that, a few—*very* few—women rowed for sport, and when they did, they were mostly regarded as spectacles.

In 1870, Lottie McAlice and Maggie Lew, two Pittsburgh 16-year-olds, raced each other for 1⅜ miles on the Monongahela River in what was touted as the "first female regatta." An estimated 8,000 to 12,000 onlookers crowded the shores to watch the oddity, including press from Chicago, Cincinnati, and New York. McAlice, the victor in just under 18 minutes 10 seconds, won a prize of a gold watch.

On New York City's East River that same year, five teenage girls wearing dresses competed in a three-mile race in heavy 17-foot workboats as spectators lined the banks "for a considerable distance," with the water "fairly covered" with pleasure boats, barges, and steamships.

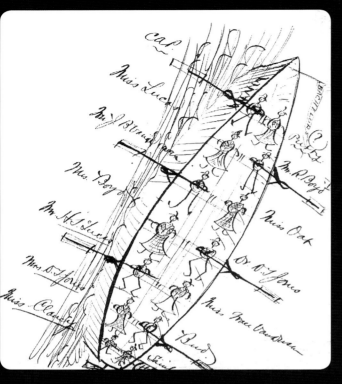

"Ladies Boat" I

A guest at the Bachelors Barge Club draws a sketch of the "ladies boat," showing the seating of a boatload of club members and their dates, presumably as they rowed upriver to the Button. Ladies boats, common among all the clubs of Boathouse Row in the 19th century, were wide enough for the ladies to sit next to their beaux, who did all the rowing. The arduous sport could hurt a woman's fragile body, the Victorians believed.

Logbook, the Button, July 18, 1890. Courtesy of the Bachelors Barge Club.

"Ladies Boat" II

Another sketch recorded in the Button's social logbook shows a T-shirted Bachelors' rower ferrying his elegantly dressed date. It is titled "Sans souci," or "No worries."

Logbook, the Button, May 1884. Courtesy of the Bachelors Barge Club.

In 1888, Newport, Kentucky, oarswoman Mollie King publicly challenged any "female" for a "two mile race for stakes." It's unlikely that anyone took her up on it because the many newspapers that announced the contest never published a story on the results.

Sure, women figured in the muscular, masculine, high-energy culture of crew, but mostly as dates, not athletes. On Boathouse Row, they sat next to their beaux in "ladies boats" for outings upriver or were entertained in the boat clubs' "ladies lounges." The notion that women's rowing would be taken seriously—even becoming an Olympic sport—was so far-fetched as to be laughable.

Epitomizing the opposition to women's participation in sculling—and other endurance sports, for that matter—was Pierre de Coubertin, the Frenchman who launched the modern Olympics. He was outspoken about his views, famously saying in 1889, "Women have but one task, that of crowning the winner with garlands. . . . It is indecent that the spectators should be exposed to the risk of seeing the body of a woman being smashed before their very eyes. Besides, no matter how toughened a sportswoman may be, her organism is not cut out to sustain certain shocks."

Even before de Coubertin made his declaration, women's push into athletics and competitive sports was moving apace. Still barred from walking into the voting booth, women were determined to prove themselves equal to men in every arena. In the last quarter of the 19th century, they conquered the highest U.S. peaks, crossed Niagara Falls on a tightrope (with 38 pounds on each ankle), swam across the Hudson River, defeated men in a walking race, ballooned solo, launched women's baseball teams (the Blondes vs. the Brunettes), brought tennis to America, and went at one another with boxing gloves.

A few American women even banded together to start rowing groups, though their main interest was health, fitness, and camaraderie, not competition. In 1875, Wellesley College, near Boston, became the first women's college to offer rowing, but it would be nearly a century before Wellesley women raced another school.

In 1882, four young women in San Diego formed the country's oldest surviving women's rowing club, ZLAC, an acronym of their initials. While the women did row, in whaling barges, ZLAC was largely a social club until 1962, when it bought its first racing shells.

It was not rowing, but rather the popularity of bicycling that was a game changer for women and sports. After all, how do you ride a bike in a long skirt? In 1895, the *New York Times* hailed the new "duplex riding skirt," with an inner layer that could be raised with a drawstring, as "an ideal suit for cycling, to which even

the most prudish could not object." Suffragist Susan B. Anthony remarked, "The bicycle has done more for the emancipation of women than anything else."

Some Philadelphia women who enjoyed bicycling, riding horseback, and canoeing in Fairmount Park broke into the all-male Boathouse Row in 1897 when they rented the Skating Club, not for rowing, but as a place to relax after their park outings and to socialize over luncheons and teas. But when they sought to build their own house in 1902, the park turned down the idea of a women's club on the Row as "a trifle advanced." The well-connected women, who now numbered 300, brought pressure to bear and won permission to build "Sedgeley" adjacent to the Lighthouse. In 1929, with its slip needing major repairs, the Sedgeley Club dispensed with its one canoe and conceded that it was "purely social."

Into this time of women's restraint and modesty, the feisty, do-not-tell-me-I-cannot-do-it Ernestine Steppacher (Bayer) was born on March 25, 1909. It was her mother's world and Ernestine—the first in a wave of Philadelphia women to break men's lock on competitive rowing—would have none of it. Her earliest memory, at age four, was of her brother mounting a horse for a photo shoot, while she was not allowed to do so. Her mother said the pose was not "ladylike." When Ernestine wanted a bike, her mother denied her for the same reason. Ernie should learn to knit and sew and cook so she could be a good wife, her mother told her.

She was 11 years old in 1920, when women finally won the right to vote. They had yet to win the right to row.

Despite her mother, Ernie played "captain ball," a game akin to basketball, on a team that won the city championship. She swam competitively and excelled at running cross-country. "The coach said she could make the national team, but she would have to quit dancing because it worked the wrong muscles," said her daughter, Tina Bayer. "So she stopped running."

Ernestine Steppacher met Ernest Bayer on a blind date. Ernie and Ernie fell in love. But how could they marry? Ernest was training for the Olympics and "newlyweds wore themselves out having sex. That was the thinking at the time. You wouldn't be strong," Tina explained. "My dad was afraid that if it was known he'd gotten married, they wouldn't let him compete."

On January 28, 1928, six months before the Summer Olympics, Ernie and Ernie quietly traveled from Philadelphia to New York City, where they secretly wed. She was 18; he was 24. That summer, with his Pennsylvania Barge Club crewmates unaware of his transgression, Ernest Bayer's four without coxswain raced to a

In 1875, Wellesley College in Massachusetts starts the oldest surviving collegiate rowing program for women. The idea isn't to compete, but to promote grace and posture. It takes nearly a century, until 1966, before a crew from the all-women's college races another school, the Massachusetts Institute of Technology.

Crew of the Argo, 1879. Courtesy of Wellesley College Archives. Photograph by Seaver.

Ernestine Bayer: "Mother of Women's Rowing"

Ernestine Bayer rows a single scull on the Schuylkill River, a year after a group of women quietly snag a lease for the Philadelphia Skating Club boathouse. The move gives women full access to rowing, which the men had only grudgingly and occasionally given their sisters or girlfriends. Even so, support for women's rowing was "minimal," said Ernie's daughter, Tina. The men, she said, saw them as "taking up space on the water. That attitude persisted for decades." For her vision and determination, Ernestine Bayer is known as the "mother of women's rowing."

Ernie Bayer, Summer 1939. Courtesy of the National Rowing Foundation Collection.

silver medal in Amsterdam. On September 18, the news that he had married broke in the *Evening Bulletin* under the headline "Cupid Hits Boat Clubs,"

"Marriage does not always mean the end of an oarsman's career," the article concluded, citing two married men who had gone on to win world single sculls, "but these scullers have been exceptions."

Now began the summers of Ernestine Bayer's discontent. In a story she would often repeat over the years, she recounted how, after work, she and Ernest would go down to the river, where she would sit on the porch of the Pennsylvania Barge Club and wait for her husband to finish his row.

One day, after years of this, she asked him, "Why don't girls row?" His response: "Oh, girls don't row."

"I accepted that for a while," she said. Until she saw a woman sculling alone in a single; her boyfriend had lent her his boat. "I decided then that if she could row, so could I." To which her husband, captain of the Pennsylvania Barge Club, replied: "Not out of my club you can't."

Ernestine stood her ground and Ernest changed course. With his medals and club standing, he had sufficient clout to grant her radical request. But not without blowback. A friend told him that by rowing, Ernestine could get tuberculosis and die, Tina Bayer said. "You should not permit your wife to row," he warned.

"The problem was that men on Boathouse Row did not want women rowing," said Tina. "They were taking up space on the water. That attitude persisted for decades."

Other women, mostly the girlfriends, wives, and sisters of oarsmen, were also yearning to row. Enter serendipity and fast reflexes. Ernestine, who worked at Fidelity Trust Company, heard from a coworker—a member of the Philadelphia Skating Club—that it was vacating its 1860 building on the Row and moving to an indoor rink on the Main Line, in Ardmore. In early 1938, before any oarsmen learned of the opening, Ernestine and club cofounder Ruth Adams (Robinhold) had pulled together 17 women and signed a lease.

Ernestine was named president. Ruth was treasurer. Lovey Kohut (Farrell), whose daring in a scull had sparked Ernestine's jealousy, was captain. The women, described as "secretaries, saleswomen, nurses, models, typists, and just plain ladies of leisure," voted to call themselves the Philadelphia Girls' Rowing Club (PGRC).

The press regularly chided the group as a "matrimonial club," pointing to the many young women who were dating and marrying men on Boathouse Row. But unlike ZLAC in San Diego, PGRC was intent on competing. Almost immediately, it hired a serious coach—Fred Plaisted. By then 89, he had been an internationally acclaimed professional sculler and respected college coach, with a public boathouse named in his honor, standing at the foot of the Row (replaced by Lloyd Hall). Ernest Bayer also helped coach, as did Tom Curran, who had rowed in Penn AC's championship "Big Eight" earlier in the decade.

On June 29, 1938, the women made a dramatic appearance, rowing in a crew shell wearing "lighted electric headsets," as part of a Schuylkill Navy pageant held that evening. In an era before television, a crowd estimated at 250,000 lined the river lit by anti-aircraft searchlights to see antics and races involving clowns, acrobats, surfboard riders, motorboats, and scullers.

Posing for the Press

The women are photographed in a Rockette-like pose on the wall outside their newly acquired boathouse. Philadelphia greets the "girls" of PGRC with amusement and condescension. Headlines call them a "matrimonial club" because some of the women are dating male rowers.

Philadelphia Girls' Rowing Club, 1938. The Library Company of Philadelphia.

A Historic First Row, 1938

On June 27, 1938, a month after the first women's competitive rowing club in the country is organized, the Philadelphia Girls' Rowing Club practices before its debut two days later in an exhibition row at the Schuylkill Navy Rowing Pageant. The *Philadelphia Inquirer* reports that 250,000 people crowd both sides of the river to watch the carnival, which includes an aerial show, surfboard acrobatics, canoe jousters, and sculling races. Prince Bertil of Sweden also attends the event, which marks 300 years since the Swedes landed in America.

Philadelphia Girls' Rowing Club Water Pageant, June 29, 1938. Philadelphia Record. Historical Society of Pennsylvania.

The next year, PGRC convinced the Schuylkill Navy to include an "exhibition race" for women in its July regatta. Three doubles, all from PGRC, competed in the first recorded women's race on the Schuylkill River. Ernestine and Jeanette Waetjen (Hoover) won.

The women of PGRC raced against one another, but finding others to challenge was proving futile. "The girls are endeavoring to find competition and have scoured the entire nation for rivals among their own sex. But there has been no response to their urgent appeal," the *Philadelphia Inquirer* reported on May 10, 1942, the club's fifth season. The women's colleges that had taken up crew, including Radcliffe, Mt. Holyoke, and Wellesley, had still not gotten beyond intramural rowing. Even the University of Pennsylvania, which had offered women's rowing as a class in 1934, would not field a varsity women's crew until 1975.

So the PGRC women continued to compete among themselves, even traveling out of town to do so. In 1953, at two major meets—the President's Cup Regatta in Washington, DC, and the Middle States Regatta in Travers Island, New York—PGRC oarswomen squared off against one another. No other women's crews had entered.

It would be 1955 before they finally met another club, a sorority team from Florida Southern University. A Lakeland, Florida, newspaper called the match-up historic: the day "women took over man's traditional eight-oared shell and launched intersectional competition." By then the intrepid Ernestine Bayer was almost

A PGRC quad carries their boat out of the boathouse in 1941. With no other women's crews to compete against nationally, PGRC rowers race one another. Sometimes, they are invited to do an "exhibition row" during one of the annual regattas on the Schuylkill, including the Stotesbury, the Dad Vail, and the Schuylkill Navy races, all still open only to men. "They would let us row in their regattas as exhibition races. They never looked at us as really racing," said Joanne Iverson, who began rowing a generation after PGRC's founding. "It was like patting us on the butt. Oh, aren't you cute. We provide entertainment."

Philadelphia Girls' Rowing Club Carrying Boats, 1941. Philadelphia Record. Historical Society of Pennsylvania.

At Penn, Intramural Only

Rusty Callow, who coached crew at the University of Pennsylvania from 1927 to 1950, helps undergraduate women get their eight on the water in 1935, albeit for intramural sport. An innovative coach, he also comes up with the idea for a smaller college competition at a time when the University of Pennsylvania is still the only college in the Philadelphia region with crew. The Dad Vail, which takes place in Philadelphia every May, starts in 1934 with six collegiate crews. It officially admits women only in 1976. Today the Dad Vail is the largest collegiate regatta in the country More than 120 schools compete, with the number of women edging out that of men.

46 and would not be dissuaded from racing, despite criticism that she was too old. Rowing in the eight-oared boat, she and her PGRC crew lost by only a foot.

As PGRC approached its 20th anniversary, the *New York Times* took the occasion to write a feature story about the club. "What the Lorelei is to the Rhine, the PGRC is to the placid Schuylkill River," wrote William Conklin on May 6, 1956. But unlike the Lorelei, which enchanted the Rhine, PGRC women were still battling old resentments.

"Some of the old-timers here are dead set against girls rowing," said PGRC Captain Nancy Wiegand. "But Grace Kelly's father and her brother are all for us. They have given us a lot of help and encouragement."

As Joanne Wright (Iverson), was growing up in the 1940s and 50s in Miquon, a dozen miles upriver from Boathouse Row, she knew nothing about Ernestine Bayer or PGRC or their difficulties developing women's rowing. She was just having fun on the Schuylkill, racing her brothers in the rowboats her father liked to build.

"I was 18 or 19," she recalled, when a friend in 1959 invited her to PGRC to try sculling in a "quad"—a four-person boat in which each person sculls with a pair of oars. Joanne found it nothing like her rowboat. The sliding seat meant she had to use her legs in a forceful rearward drive. The narrow hull and long oars demanded exquisite balance. There was so much technique to think about, and the boat moved so fast. "I had a blister on the ring finger of both hands, and the insides of my thumbs were raw . . . but I didn't care," she would later write. "I was absolutely hooked."

After that, Joanne was out sculling every morning and sometimes again that night, getting stronger, getting faster. She did not care what anyone thought. The stereotype was "we were either guy crazy and looking for marriage, or we were lesbians. . . . It wasn't feminine to be proud of being strong." She quickly began winning races against PGRC's top rowers, impressing even Ernestine Bayer. Within months, Joanne was elected club captain. With her string of victories, albeit against club members, she saw herself as the unofficial singles champion of the country and dreamed of rowing in the Olympics.

Pocock Boat Ad

A 1948 ad makes a macho appeal for the highly sought-after rowing shells handcrafted by George Pocock of Seattle.

National Association of Amateur Oarsmen, Rowing Guide, 1963.

On a Mission:
Joanne Wright Iverson

In her late teens, having fallen in love with sculling, Joanne Wright (Iverson) is shocked to learn that women's rowing is not an Olympic sport, so she pours her boundless energy into making that happen, if not for herself, then for others. She coaches young women at PGRC and in 1964 becomes the first women's crew coach at the University of Pennsylvania. No one back then understands how hard women's bodies can be pushed to train. "We didn't know what kind of weights they could lift. We didn't know if they could run Lemon Hill and stay alive and be able to not have a heart attack. We didn't know any of these things, and a lot of this had to be found out by trial and error," Iverson said.

Rowing

Joanne Wright Iverson in undated photograph. *Philadelphia Evening Bulletin*, Special Collections Research Center, Temple University Libraries, Philadelphia.

Coaching

FACING PAGE: Joanne Wright Iverson Coaching at Philadelphia Girls' Rowing Club with Bernadette Dubeck and Kathy McGovern, both 16, April 30, 1961. *Philadelphia Evening Bulletin*, Special Collections Research Center, Temple University Libraries, Philadelphia.

She was shocked to learn that it was impossible. Women's rowing was not an Olympic event. Men's crew had been an Olympic sport from the start of the modern games in 1896. Women had entered the games in 1900 with tennis and golf. Gradually, women's archery, figure-skating, swimming, fencing, gymnastics, alpine skiing, canoeing, and equestrian sports had been added. But in 1960, women's Olympic crew was still not a consideration. For that matter, in 1960 the National Association of Amateur Oarsmen (NAAO)—the national organization that set standards for amateur racing—had no women members. The college regattas—the IRA and the Dad Vail—had no women members. And no high school women had ever competed in the Stotesbury Regatta, formed in Philadelphia in 1927.

"All I wanted to do was get women racing," Joanne said in an interview. Like Ernestine Bayer, she single-mindedly tackled the challenge and found allies in two men from the West Coast, where tradition is less deeply etched than in the East.

Edwin Lickiss, founder of the Lake Merritt Rowing Club in Oakland, California, was recruiting women to race. So was Ted Nash, who was training for the 1960 Olympics with Seattle's Lake Washington Rowing Club; his wife, Aldina, also rowed. California and Washington women had started racing one another.

Resistance to women on the water came from the very top. As Nash was flying to Rome to compete in the 1960 summer Olympics, a member of the United States Olympic Committee asked Nash's seatmate to move "so he could talk to me," Nash said, recounting the incident. The official sat down next to the 6-foot 3½-inch Nash, who within days would win a gold medal in the four without coxswain, and warned: "You just stop this shit with the women; you're screwing everything up." After Nash's victory, a delegation from the NAAO

Russians on the Schuylkill

In the depths of the Cold War, over 50,000 people turn out in 1962 to watch Soviet rowers, especially world champion Vyacheslav Ivanov, race the Boathouse Row clubs in the Independence Day Regatta. John B. Kelly Jr., who rowed in the 1956 and 1960 Olympics where Ivanov won gold medals in the single scull, helped arrange the visit, and here gives Ivanov advice about the Schuylkill course. (Ivanov would win a third gold in 1964, tying the records of John B. Kelly Sr. and Paul Costello for three gold rowing medals.) During Ivanov's Philadelphia visit, Kelly introduces him to Joanne Wright as the country's " best female sculler," and they develop "a crush" on each other, she said.

Philadelphia Daily News, July 1962, Special Collections Research Center, Temple University Libraries, Philadelphia.

visited him in person to say that he was "making too many waves," that women now wanted to be in the men's national championships. "They reminded me that the governing body is the National Association of Amateur Oars*men* not Oars*women*."

Nonetheless, in 1961, the same year that President John F. Kennedy established a Commission on the Status of Women, the NAAO agreed to allow one Women's National Single Championship race during its 87th annual regatta in Philadelphia. Joanne was to race Nash's wife, Aldina. With her two-year record of eight wins and one loss, Joanne was training hard to finally claim the national title in an official race. But at the last moment, Aldina Nash took ill, and no women rowed.

In Canada that summer, the St. Catharines Rowing Club, which touted itself as "Building Character and Manhood for 53 Years," invited Joanne to do an exhibition row. She accepted. The more that men saw women on the water, the quicker their perception would change, she believed. Still, she felt that spectators viewed her as amusing—"a cute little girl trying to row."

On the other hand, that same summer the Schuylkill Navy asked the 22-year-old to be a regatta judge—a first for a woman on the Schuylkill. And the annual *NAAO Rowing Guide* asked her to write an article. In it, Joanne argued to the American rowing community that European women were racing (they had started to do so in 1954) and that the United States should step up its support of women rowers because, she wrote, in a leap of faith, "the day is coming when women's rowing events will be on the Olympics program."

To seriously compete, though, American women needed more support and more racing opportunities. Unlike the men who had national rowing organizations to finance their equipment and travel, the women were begging and borrowing. Without funds to pay for boats designed to their size and physique, they were still using oversized men's boats.

Joanne, who was racing out West in the meets that Nash and Lickiss were organizing, discovered that they shared an idea: a national rowing group for women. On July 3, 1963, the three met at an Oakland, California, restaurant and created the National Women's Rowing Association (NWRA). It had three members—Nash's Lake Washington Rowing Club, Lickiss' Lake Merritt Rowing Club, and Iverson's PGRC. That January, the all-male NAAO accepted the group's application for membership, "although most of the delegates said they did not favor the adding of women's events to a man's regatta," the *New York Times* reported on January 19, 1964.

Joanne Wright Iverson, 25, and Ernestine Steppacher Bayer, 55, the two most prominent and visionary women in American rowing, now saw their priorities differently. Joanne, still captain of PGRC, was obsessed with her national agenda of building the NWRA. She was reaching out all over the country for colleges and clubs to join in. Back home, though, club members saw her as high-handed. She was ignoring their equipment and training needs and committing the club to national events without consulting them.

Ernestine, concerned about the future of PGRC and fearing that the city could revoke its charter if the club languished, stepped in to wrest control from Joanne, who resigned from the club. To help with training, Ernestine brought in Ted Nash, who had arrived in Philadelphia in 1964 to coach freshmen crew at Penn. Despite the tension, the two women valued one another's work. Ernestine "was really good for

A legendary rowing family of Boathouse Row, "the three Bayers" take to the river. Ernest Bayer was a 1928 Olympic silver medalist, captain of the Pennsylvania Barge Club, and commodore of the Schuylkill Navy. His wife, Ernestine, started the Philadelphia Girls' Rowing Club in 1928. Their daughter, Ernestine (Tina), also made history by rowing in the first American women's crew to compete in Europe—in Vichy, France, in 1967.

Philadelphia Evening Bulletin, 1968, Special Collections Research Center, Temple University Libraries, Philadelphia.

publicizing the sport for women," Joanne conceded. "Much better than I was, because I didn't realize the value of it."

In 1966, the NWRA hosted its first regatta in Seattle. By then, Joanne's efforts had raised membership to nine groups. And Ernestine had built a strong eight-oared crew, which included her daughter, Tina. PGRC was victorious in the premier event, defeating the able West Coast teams. It would repeat the win again the next year.

But the real prize, what Joanne and Ernestine both had their eyes on, was international competition. They wanted American women—PGRC women—to participate in the European championships being held in Vichy, France, in September 1967. Getting to compete on the world stage was a critical step to finally opening the Olympics to women.

But to get to Vichy, the International Rowing Federation, known as FISA, would have to first approve the women's entry. Both Ernestine and her husband, Ernest, who was then treasurer of the NAAO, laid out their case to John Carlin, who headed the FISA governing body in the United States. Both groups operated out of #4 Boathouse Row, which the Pennsylvania Barge Club, on hard times after the war, rented to them.

Carlin denied the request. "He said, 'No. You're not in the same class as the Europeans. If the Communists win, they'll rub our noses in it,'" recalled Tina Bayer, then 22 and herself seeking to race in Vichy.

But Tina's mother, Ernestine, had a subterfuge. Through a connection with a Canadian sports writer, PGRC wrangled an invitation to row an exhibition race at St. Catharines in Ontario in early August. The event was a huge moment in rowing—the First North American Rowing Championships, which coincided with Canada's centennial.

The young PGRC women, yearning for competition, were slated to race a crew of distinguished older men, most of whom had rowed in the Olympics or European championships. Among the athletes was Thomi Keller, international president of FISA.

"They had never rowed together. We had," Tina said. "We beat them at the start and kept pace with them—and won! At the finish line, they did the sexist thing and kissed the woman in the corresponding [boat] seat. We were all invited that night to a cocktail party."

As mother and daughter were surveying the crowd that evening, Tina recalled, Keller walked over to them. "With his Swiss-German accent, he said, 'Ernestine, I vant your girls to come to Vichy.'

"'We'd love to but John Carlin won't let us,' Mom replied.

**Karin Constant:
"Good" Legs**

Karin Constant becomes one
of the first women to row at
the Vesper Boat Club in 1969
after Gus Constant spots the
26-year-old running a foot
race along Kelly Drive and is
impressed by her strong legs.
They quickly marry but
eventually divorce. A pioneer
of women's competitive
rowing, Karin later forms
Masters International, which
facilitates women's
international competition at
the masters level.

Karin Constant. Courtesy
of Karin Constant.

"'I'll take care of John Carlin if you take care of the entry and the money.'

"'The entry's due at midnight and we don't have the money,' Mom said. Keller pointed to a table and said, 'There's the entry.' Minutes later, Carlin signed off on it."

The money problem remained. PGRC needed $6,000 to get its crew and equipment to Vichy. The women, most in their early 20s and working as secretaries, students, teachers, and receptionists, did not have it. That same evening, Ernestine approached Horace Davenport, a former champion rower at Columbia University and head of the National Rowing Foundation. Would the foundation fund PGRC's expenses? she asked.

Davenport candidly confessed to Ernestine, "If the foundation funded a woman's boat, we'd probably lose all our contributors."

"Instead, he secretly loaned us the $6,000," Tina said. "We took 18 people to Vichy, and within a year every girl paid back the money. We could not reveal where we got the money, and the story was never told until after his death" in 1991.

Why was there still so much opposition to women's competition, so late in the game?

Tina believes that American women were held back by the traditionalism of Philadelphia, home to both the NAAO (now USRowing) and FISA until 1985.

"Boathouse Row had a stranglehold on the country," said Tina. Others, though, believed the reason was more than provincialism and that Carlin truly felt that women were not yet ready for international competition.

They got ready fast. With only three weeks before Vichy, the PGRC women moved from their homes into their boathouse. "We woke up, rowed, ate, went to our jobs, rowed, ate, went to sleep. In between we did fundraising. Our total focus was Vichy," Tina said.

On their last row past the boathouses before leaving for France, they were stupefied to see the men of the Row wave banners saying, "Good luck, PGRC."

In Vichy, Tina and the other PGRC women struggled with logistics and equipment and had to sew their own uniforms. They were awed by the towering heights of their European opponents. In a preliminary quad race, a rigger—the metal bracket that extends from the racing shell and holds the oarlock—broke, and they had to drop out. In the eight, PGRC came in last. Still, they were the first American women's rowing club to compete in Europe, and the European women treated them as equals, hopeful that their presence might open the door to the Olympics. PGRC's 1967 appearance in Vichy was a milestone for women rowers, and back home on Boathouse Row, where all the other clubs were still all male, the Vesper Boat Club took notice.

In Hollywood, future stars could be found working in soda fountains. In Philadelphia, they were spotted running along Kelly Drive. Which is how a 26-year-old with strong-looking legs in 1969 caught the attention of Gus Constant, a coach who was trying to assemble the first women's crew for the Vesper Boat Club.

The premier rowing club had never had a woman member in its 104-year history, but after PGRC's historic appearance at Vichy, it was clearly time for Vesper, if not all of Boathouse Row, to break with tradition.

"Here comes this little guy saying, 'Would you like to row?'" Karin Constant remembers. A native of Germany, Karin had always been intrigued by rowing but had never had the chance to try it, even in Europe, where women had been competing for 15 years.

"So when he asked me if I wanted to row, I said, 'Sure.' And he said, 'When would you like to start?' And I said, 'Well, I can start tomorrow.'"

Gus and Karin, who within six months would marry, began scouring the city for women with "good legs." They checked out basketball players and swimmers at recreation centers. They eyed passersby in front of Vesper. "There's a woman with good legs—let's ask her," they'd say to each other. By good legs, they meant muscular legs that could help drive the boat. They did not even have to be long legs.

The First Vesper Women

Preparing to compete in the Schuylkill Navy Regatta in 1970 are (from left) Jinx Becker, stroke (an early recruit of Vesper Coach Gus Constant); Sharon Pierce and Valerie Helenski (protégées of Coach Joanne Wright Iverson); and Karin Constant in bow. They did not realize that Gus paid their club dues.

Philadelphia Evening Bulletin, June 13, 1970, Special Collections Research Center, Temple University Libraries, Philadelphia.

"In those days it didn't matter. Rowing is legs. That's what we looked at," said Karin, herself only 5 feet 4 inches.

Among Gus' first rowers were Jinx Becker, who was training with Gus before Karin turned up, and Marie and Ann Jonik—18-year-old twins whose mother, Mary Prior (Jonik), was a founding member of PGRC. Joining them in 1970 was Diane Braceland (Vreugdenhil), who was home from Penn State that summer, looking for something fun to do. Her father, a member of the Malta Boat Club next door, suggested she try rowing.

"I really didn't know anything about the sport. I didn't know anything about Gus. He only had a handful of girls there, and so I said, 'Well, I'll give it a try and see how I like it.' And that's how I began rowing."

John B. Kelly Jr. ("Kell"), who, like his father, had focused so much energy on building Vesper into one of the world's most successful rowing organizations, wanted a competitive women's crew, and the club had carved out a cubicle with a single toilet for them to use as a locker room.

It was not a popular idea.

"One day we show up, and the guys had taken two-by-fours and nailed [the locker room] shut," Karin said. "Another time, we got into our eight at the dock, and one of the guys is up there with a shot gun and says, "We're gonna shoot you now. Then I showed up one day and they had taken the foot pieces from my single and hid them, and I didn't find them for about five or six years, and that's the kind of stuff that went on."

Gus Constant confirmed the story to the *Philadelphia Inquirer*. Although four members of Vesper's governing board backed women's crew, he said, "the rowers, especially the guys on the elite sweep team, they flipped. Now, these are bright guys. They had gone to all the best schools. At least 12 of them made the U.S. national team. And they'd do things like nail the girls' lockers shut. One guy pulled a rifle on me and pulled the trigger. Obviously, since I'm talking here, it wasn't loaded. But I was scared."

Diane, who started rowing with Gus in 1970, remembers how "it was strange to have people that you saw every day on the dock just ignore you and pretend you weren't there. . . . It was very evident and obvious that the women weren't accepted at Vesper. The guys didn't want us there. . . . They wanted us to leave. And that was for a number of years—it really was."

Even men next door at the Malta Boat Club, the only club on the Row that has remained all male, noticed. "We'd see seats out of boats and oars missing," said Chuck Patterson, who rowed with Gus at Vesper before

Diane Braceland: Committing

Diane Braceland (Vreugdenhil) joins the Vesper women's contingent after Gus Constant spots her rowing with her father, George Braceland, of the Malta Boat Club. Diane says she was looking for something active to do in the summer of 1970 and became hooked. "There were a lot of times when I wanted to quit rowing. . . . If you're going to row nationally, internationally, it takes a lot of your time, effort and energy. You have to really love it and have the desire to do it."

Don Camp/*Philadelphia Evening Bulletin*, Special Collections Research Center, Temple University Libraries, Philadelphia.

Racing on Lake Merritt in Oakland, California, a crew of women from the Vesper Boat Club pop champagne after defeating Radcliffe at the National Women's Rowing Association competition in 1974. The victory takes them to Lucerne, Switzerland, where they compete in the first FISA-sponsored World Rowing Championship to admit women. The Vesper crew places a respectable sixth. Among them is Ernestine Bayer's daughter, Tina, who also serves as team manager.

Associated Press, June 16, 1974, Special Collections Research Center, Temple University Libraries, Philadelphia.

moving to Malta. "It was just like the resistance to women in lots of other areas at that time. Gloria Steinem was writing. Women's Lib was growing. There was a male backlash to that, and these were bastions of male superiority. They didn't like girls coming in."

"Eventually," Karin said, Kell "put his foot down; then the guys shut up."

The Vesper women found that after Vichy, more and more racing opportunities opened up to them nationally. In 1971, they got the chance to compete at the World Championships in Denmark. They did not do particularly well, but they were there. No longer could the International Olympic Committee (IOC) justify the absence of oarswomen. In 1972, the IOC announced that women's rowing would be an event in the 1976 Montreal Olympics. Eight decades after men's rowing was declared an Olympic sport, the world's women would compete.

Anita DeFrantz arrived on Boathouse Row primed to break through any last remaining barriers to women's rowing. There still were some. She had learned determination from her parents and grandparents and from "growing up as an African American in the United States. We knew we had rights, and I had to stand up for them or they would be taken away from me."

Anita DeFrantz and Anne Warner

Arriving in Philadelphia in 1974 to attend law school at the University of Pennsylvania and train at Vesper, Anita DeFrantz (left) finds herself breaking ground not only as a woman. "In the early days, I did not see anybody who was African American which was odd because the boat doesn't care. And anybody could join the clubs," she said. Anita continues to make history by competing in the 1976 Olympics, the first year for a women's Olympic rowing event. One of her crewmates in the eight that summer is Anne Warner of Yale. Here, the two compete in the pair in the 1977 World Championships in Amsterdam; they finish sixth.

Courtesy of Anita DeFrantz.

Especially precious to her was sports—something unavailable to her at her public school in Indianapolis in the 1950s and 1960s, she said. "Public school had nothing for girls, little for African Americans. I was in orchestra and madrigals and the marching band. There were zero sports for girls."

At Connecticut College, Anita discovered that women were participating in varsity rowing and decided to try it after a coach, noting her height of 5 feet 11 inches, thought she might like it. That proved an understatement. Although she was only on junior varsity crew when she graduated, she chose to attend law school at the University of Pennsylvania—so she could row at Vesper.

Anita arrived in Philadelphia, the city of her birth, in 1974, a year after Title IX went into effect. The full force of this landmark legislation, which mandated gender parity in schools that received federal funding, was yet to reveal itself. At Vesper, Anita said, "I was shocked at how small the size of the locker room was." And she was disappointed that the women in training did not have the extra resources available to the men.

The men training at Vesper "had a place to live—in the boathouse; the women had to pay rent. Work was available to the men; it was much harder for the women to get support. Also, it was harder for women to get time off from work."

But at least the men were beginning to accept their presence on the dock.

Anita trained three times a day while attending law school and working nights at the Philadelphia police headquarters, interviewing defendants before bail hearings. It was a grueling routine, requiring an extraordinary level of desire and commitment. But it began to pay off.

In 1975, Anita made the national team that went to the world championships in England, coming in fifth in a four-oared shell. But it was the American women's crew, with women from Yale, MIT, Princeton, and elsewhere, coached by Harvard's Harry Parker, that stunned the rowing world. The Red Rose Crew, named for the roses tied into the laces of the women's rowing shoes, won silver, dispelling any doubts that American women could be contenders in their first Olympics.

Looking toward 1976, Diane Braceland immersed herself in Olympic training. Making the U.S. team "was a goal that I had to hunger after every day," she said. "Every time I got in a boat to practice, I had to remind myself why I was here, what I was doing, what my goals were, because you had to work extremely, extremely hard."

At Yale, Chris Ernst, a member of the Red Rose Crew, was also trying to train but was doing so under conditions that Title IX was supposed to remedy. The Yale women suffered with inferior boats and equipment to the men's, no locker room at the boathouse, and makeshift showers that had no hot water. Their worst indignity was having to sit on the bus, shivering in their sweaty clothes, waiting for the men to shower and change before riding back to campus.

On March 3, 1976, 19 women bared their torsos, on which they had penned "Title IX" with blue markers, and marched into the women's athletics office at Yale. They read this statement:

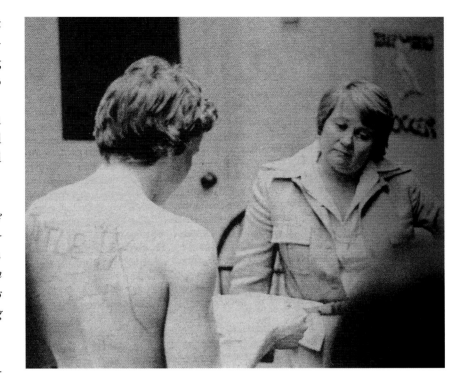

> *These are the bodies Yale is exploiting. We have come here today to make clear how unprotected we are, to show graphically what we are being exposed to. . . . On a day like today, the rain freezes on our skin. Then we sit on a bus for half an hour as the ice melts into our sweats to meet the sweat that has soaked our clothes underneath. . . . We're human and being treated as less than such.*

Yale's administration immediately got the women portable showers and quickly added a women's wing to the riverfront locker room as colleges around the country took note.

At the Olympic trials that summer, 27 women rowers were selected to represent the United States in six events. Seven of the women, including Diane and Anita, were from Boathouse Row, either Vesper or Penn's College Boat Club. Seven others were from the Long Beach powerhouse. The rest represented various colleges that had recently started women's varsity programs, including Cornell, Yale, and Wisconsin.

Diane would race in a double scull with Jan Palchikoff of Long Beach. Anita, team captain, was in the eight-oared crew along with Yale's Chris Ernst. Their biggest challengers, they knew, would be the communist teams—East Germany, Bulgaria, Romania, and the Soviet Union, which were backed by large state investments in support and training.

Women's First Olympics, 1976

Anita DeFrantz, (second rower from bottom), captains the historic American women's eight-oared crew which competes in the 1976 Montreal Olympics. Taking the risk to coach them is Harvard men crew's coach Harry Parker, who rowed varsity crew at Penn under Joe Burk. The women astound the world by winning bronze, but they are exhausted and miss seeing the American flag raised, as one of them turns green on the winner's podium. "I wanted to go all out. And see where all out was," Anita says afterwards. "I've seen crews lose races because they don't believe they can go through the pain barrier. . . ." Assured of a second try in the 1980 Moscow Olympics, Anita and other Olympic aspirants are infuriated when President Jimmy Carter cancels America's participation after the Soviet Union invades Afghanistan. A lawyer, she files a federal suit, arguing that athletes should have the freedom to compete where they want, but loses.

In this photo, the stern half of the crew shows Lynn Silliman (cox, back to camera), Jackie Zoch (stroke), Anita DeFrantz, Carrie Graves, and Marion Grieg. In 2016, the crew was inducted into the National Rowing Hall of Fame.

1976 United States Olympic Book.

Death on the Dock

Almost every year, the body of a victim of homicide, suicide, or accident is found in the Schuylkill River, often by rowers. Here a crew returns to its dock on Boathouse Row to find a body, recently pulled from the water, awaiting identification.

Jessica Griffin/*Philadelphia Daily News*, March 13, 2006.

In contrast, the American women "had no support at all," Anita remembers. "We had to work to support ourselves. We had to pay our own way to Europe for the world championship at Nottingham in 1975, to the 1976 Olympic games, the '78 games in New Zealand, the '79 games in Slovenia."

Even at the 1976 Montreal Olympics, she said, the women rowers were the last in line to go through uniform processing. By then, the U.S. Olympic Committee "had run out of the sweatshirts, rain gear and sneakers and the things that said 'U.S. Olympics' on them." At least they got their racing uniforms, which came from USRowing.

As expected, the communist countries dominated in Montreal, picking up 15 of the 18 possible women's rowing medals. Diane, in a double scull, again with Jan Palchikoff, came in fifth, after Bulgaria, East Germany, Russia, and Norway.

But in a surprise performance, Anita's eight-oared crew sped to a finish that was just five seconds out of first place—a bronze medal behind East Germany and the USSR. Joan Lind, a California single sculler, won silver, capping a triumphant first Olympics for the American women.

———

With women rowers busting through the long-standing dam of resistance, women of all ages poured in— from clubs, high schools, colleges, and even those in their retirement years. Encouraged by Lois Trench-Hines, a competitive rower who joined PGRC in the mid-1960s, the collegiate Dad Vail Regatta allowed several women's boats to race in 1973, though they were not officially admitted until 1976.

In 2016, 104 colleges floated varsity crews in the Dad Vail, with 2,779 participants, 51 percent of whom were women. At the high school level, girls slightly outnumbered boys as well. Such bench strength may account for America's ability to assemble the best women's eight on earth. From 2006 through 2016, year after year, U.S. women won the world championship, including gold medals at the 2008, 2012, and 2016 Olympics.

More gradually, the clubs of Boathouse Row began accepting women, though some resisted saying, "'Well, we don't have a toilet for you,'" Trench-Hines recalled. "By this time there were a lot of professional women, and they'd whip out their checkbook and say, 'How much do you want?'"

And what of the pioneering Philadelphia oarswomen who led the way for so many others? After the Bayer family left Philadelphia for New Hampshire in 1971, Ernestine continued to coach and row in Masters races almost until her death at age 97 in 2006. She came to be known as the "mother of U.S. women's rowing."

If victory was sweet back then, it still is in 2015 for sisters Ann Jonik (left) and Marie Jonik in a crew that wins the Masters Women's Eight event at the Head of the Schuylkill Regatta. Their mother, Mary Prior Jonik, was a founding member of the Philadelphia Girls' Rowing Club, and both daughters rowed in the 1976 Montreal Olympics. "I love winning," said Marie, "but at this point I go for the atmosphere, for the camaraderie of being there with my rowing pals."

Head of the Schuylkill, October 2015. April Saul.

Joanne Iverson began coaching women's crew at the University of Pennsylvania in 1968 and served as a manager of the U.S rowing team at the 1976 Olympics. In 1986, the group she founded, the NWRA, merged with USRowing (formerly the National Association of Amateur Oarsmen). She was elected president of the Vesper Boat Club in 2010, serving for six years—proof of an upended landscape.

Karin Constant became a major figure in the Masters women's rowing movement. Lois Trench-Hines, who rowed in a quad with Karin and Diane Braceland in the 1973 European Championships in Moscow, opened the upper Schuylkill River to numerous schools with her husband, former La Salle College High School rowing coach George Hines, by building the Hines Rowing Center as well as a boathouse for high school girls at Mount St. Joseph Academy.

Diane Braceland married Darrell Vreugdenhil after they met while competing at the 1973 World Championships in Moscow. A Montessori teacher, Diane believes that many of the skills she has carried through life, especially self-discipline, come from her training. "I think from sports in general, you acquire a lot of wonderful qualities that you not only apply to sports but in your relationships with people and the work that you do."

Anita DeFrantz devoted her legal career to equity in women's sports and greater opportunity for minority youths. In 1986, she became the first female official of the International Olympic Committee, where she long played a leadership role. For nearly three decades, she headed the LA84 Foundation, whose mission is supporting youth sports, initially with surplus funds from the 1984 Olympics; however, the money distributed keeps growing, and in 2015 totaled more than $225 million.

Looking back to the early years of women's rowing, Anita says, "First we had to go through that dreadful period, but finally when things changed, it changed. It's a shame there were restrictions for so long. But, okay, the river continues to flow with both men and women on it."

CHAPTERSEVEN

THE "VESPER EIGHT"

A Motley Crew Vies for
an Olympic Berth

The somewhat rumpled, sometimes unruly men who found their way to the Vesper Boat Club in Philadelphia
by 1964 shared little in common but strength, height, an incomprehensible joy in punishing their bodies, and a
beyond-burning desire to succeed. They included four men in their mid- to late 20s on loan from various branches of the
military; two students from La Salle College barely out of their teens; a 34-year-old father of six with a business to run; and
the coxswain, a 46-year-old Hungarian refugee who often muttered commands in his native language.

Their coaches? A Jew and a German, within short memory of World War II.

"Old men," "a curious crew," "a crusty bunch of adults," the press would later call them.

Regardless of their differences, they all had come together with a single purpose, matched by the determination to do
whatever it would take to get them there. Some, carrying humiliation on their shoulders, were driven by a lifelong hunger
to prove themselves. Others, battling the unhealed wounds of past defeats, ached for vengeance, for victory at last.

That is how it was for Emory Clark. He arrived at Yale in 1956, just before the university's eight-oared crew returned
home from Australia with Olympic gold medals. The cocky freshman assumed that four years later he, too, would bask in
Olympic glory. Everything pointed that way. After all, he had rowed successfully at Groton. He had captained Yale's

freshman crew to an undefeated season and had continued to pile up victories throughout his sophomore and junior years. The 1960 Rome Olympics were within his grasp.

Then came senior year. The Yale eight lost every single race. But the worst defeat, the one that replayed in an endless loop through his mind, was the crew's loss—his loss—to Harvard in the schools' annual four-mile race. The tradition went back to 1852, when the two schools squared off against each other in the nation's first collegiate competition. Emory's crew—the crew of which he was captain—crossed the finish line an ego-shattering seven boat lengths behind Harvard.

"Despair. A broken heart. A life ended in tragedy at a youthful 22," he would later write in his memoir—only somewhat tongue-in-cheek.

Boyce Budd, a fellow Yalie a year behind Clark, graduated with a similar psychic wound. As a freshman, Boyce—at 6 feet 3 inches and 205 pounds—had long searched for a sport in which his powerful body could excel. A "Clydesdale," he called himself, as compared to a thoroughbred. He was thrilled to find that he was good at rowing. So good, in fact, that he made varsity his sophomore year. Then, for reasons he never understood, he was demoted to junior varsity for the remainder of his Yale career.

"He was too big, too rough, too strong," Emory would say of Boyce, or "Big Turkey" as Emory called him. (Not that Emory, at 6 feet 4 inches and 195 pounds, was much smaller.) The coaches "weren't good enough to harness his talent."

There would be no 1960 Olympics for these men. Yet they yearned.

Boyce graduated and went to Cambridge University in England, where he kept on rowing. Emory, uncertain about what to do with his life, enlisted in the Marines. The memory of that Harvard defeat dug into him like a claw. He thought about it in Okinawa or Thailand or wherever he happened to be in Southeast Asia as Americans became increasingly involved in Vietnam.

In November 1962, Emory received a letter that would change everything. "Dear Em," Boyce wrote, "I have decided that come Hell or high water I for one am going to be participating in the 1964 Olympic Trials. . . . I sincerely hope that you and I can team up in a pair and win the whole lot. . . . It is going to take an extraordinary effort. . . . With a will and the kind of devotion that it will take, you and I could win two gold medals. . . . We must start now! What do you think, Buddy?"

Emory's heart leapt at the idea. In a dance hall in Olongapo, off Subic Bay in the Philippines, Infantry Lieutenant Clark paid no attention to the for-hire women who accosted him while he composed his letter to

Sports Illustrated calls the crew that John B. Kelly Jr. is assembling to represent the United States at the 1964 Tokyo Olympics "a crusty bunch of adults from Vesper . . . in a dilapidated old shell straight out of a Pogo comic strip." The cast of characters are (from left): coxswain Robby Zimonyi, a Hungarian refugee in his mid-40s; stroke Bill Stowe, a Cornell man who says the crew has but one purpose in common: "rowing and winning"; Bill Knecht, a middle-aged father of six; Boyce Budd and Emory Clark, two Yalies seeking revenge on Harvard; Tom Amlong, a military brat with expertise at put-downs; Stan Cwiklinski and Hugh Foley, the kids of the crew who stay out of the fray; and Joseph Amlong, who, with his brother Tom, spars with the Ivy Leaguers in the boat.

R. L. Mooney/*Philadelphia Inquirer*, Special Collections Research Center, Temple University Libraries, Philadelphia.

Boyce Budd (left) and Emory
Clark both rowed at Yale.
Both suffered humiliating
defeats and carried chips on
their very broad shoulders.
They are determined to
compete in the 1964
Olympics as a pair.

Olympic Odyssey. Courtesy of
Emory Clark.

military brass. It was filled with bravado. He was "God's gift to rowing," Clark would later quip, though he
did not exactly write those words. He was Olympic material. He asked to be sent home to train, somewhere
on the East Coast. His letter went up the chain of command in a military that honors athletes. Months later,
he got orders to transfer to Philadelphia, as good a place as any, he thought.

Emory arrived just after Labor Day 1963. That afternoon he called around to see how he could get on the
river in a single scull that day. Someone at the Fairmount Rowing Association offered him a boat that

weekend. Vesper invited him to row that very afternoon. "Come at 5—I'll call Jack Kelly," an acquaintance who belonged to Vesper told him.

"I'd never heard of the Vesper Boat Club, but I was going to pull an oar before I slept." Emory would write in his diary.

So, with its quick reflexes, the Vesper Boat Club acquired Emory Clark, and a month later, after his discharge from the Marines, Boyce Budd. The two men added to the ragtag but formidable crew that Olympian John B. Kelly Jr. was laboring to put together in his long-shot drive for Vesper oarsmen to reach the 1964 Olympics.

A Vesper crew had won in 1900 at the newly resurrected Olympic Games, held in Paris. Vesper had won again in St. Louis in 1904. After that, the spotlight dimmed for America's private rowing clubs when it came to the world's premier rowing event—the eight-oared crew. For the next 60 years, only college crews, made up of kids in their late teens and early 20s, had carried America's flag in this race. They had largely been victorious. In the 11 summer Olympics following 1904, America's collegiate eights had lost only three times—twice to Great Britain (in 1908 and 1912) and once, in 1960, to Germany. The University of California had claimed gold three times. Yale and the U.S. Naval Academy had each won twice. And the University of Washington triumphed in the extraordinary 1936 games in Hitler's Berlin.

College crews had the advantage of strapping young men whose scholastic schedules allowed for rigorous, regular practices led by talented and dedicated full-time coaches, rowing on rivers conveniently near campus. Besides their individual hunger for victory, collegiate rowers also shared an esprit de corps, seeking glory for their alma mater.

Vesper, on the other hand, had John B. Kelly Jr. A rowing celebrity, Kell had twice vindicated his father's exclusion from the prestigious Diamond Sculls competition at Henley, England. He had gone on to win a slew of medals and had competed in four consecutive Olympics, in 1948, 1952, 1956, and 1960.

By 1963, at the age of 36, Kell was nurturing, inspiring, hiring, fundraising, and throwing his significant national stature into building Vesper into a rowing behemoth.

Long a fixture at Vesper when Clark and Budd arrived was Bill Knecht, Kell's rowing partner from the 1959 Pan American Games, where the two had won gold in the double.

They had also competed in the 1960 Olympics, where they had not fared so well. But Bill was now 33, with a large family to support and a sheet metal business to run. Despite his strength, intensity, experience,

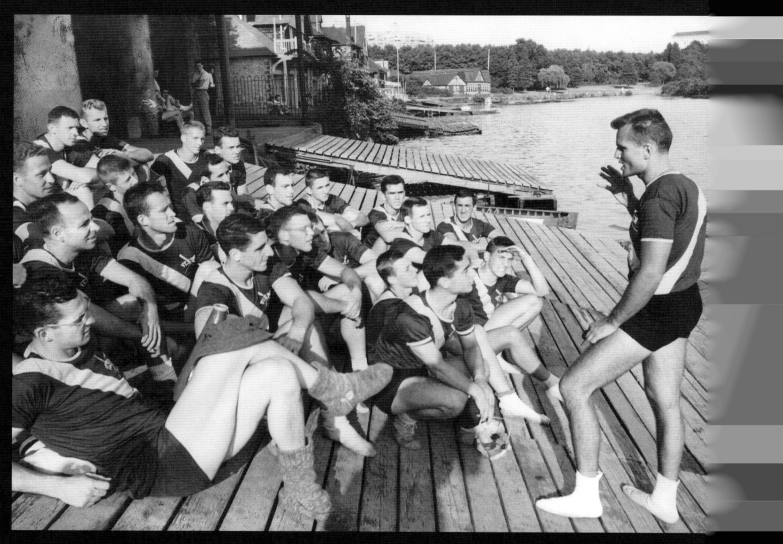

Looking to the Future

John B. Kelly Jr. (Kell), 27, briefs Vesper members about upcoming nationals. Like his Olympian father, John B. Kelly Sr., he pours love and energy into the Vesper Boat Club. Having triumphed twice in the Diamond Challenge Sculls at Henley and participated in four consecutive Olympics, winning a bronze in the single, he focuses on building a world-class Olympic crew on Boathouse Row.

Philadelphia Inquirer, July 12, 1954, Special Collections Research Center, Temple University Libraries, Philadelphia

Unretiring: Bill Knecht

Bill Knecht (left) rows with his longtime doubles partner, John B. Kelly Jr., prior to a national competition in 1954. The two later race together in the 1960 Olympics, but Kell falls ill and they finish in 15th place. In 1964, Kell, who is three years older than Knecht, retires from competitive rowing. But Knecht, at age 34, goes on to become the oldest rower in the Vesper Eight making a bid for the Olympics that year. "He had seen so much club rowing in 16 years," said crewmate Emory Clark, "that the disorganization and squabbling did not affect him one way or another."

Philadelphia Inquirer, July 17, 1954, Special Collections Research Center, Temple University Libraries, Philadelphia.

At 46, Robby Zimonyi (second from left, next to coach Al Rosenberg) is the oldest man in the Vesper eight. Just days after the 1956 Hungarian Revolution, he defected in Melbourne, Australia, along with most of his teammates, after competing in his third Olympics. John B. Kelly Jr. (who won bronze in a single in Melbourne) encouraged the 115-pound coxswain to come to Philadelphia. In 1964, he proves invaluable to Vesper where his crew jokes about his accent. "I feel nossing, boys. I feel nossing!" Robby would say, prodding on his men.

Philadelphia Evening Bulletin, Special Collections Research Center, Temple University Libraries, Philadelphia.

and focus, his vital statistics did not appear to be those of a future Olympian. Indeed, 1964—if he even got that far—was looking much like a "last hurrah."

Even older was Robert Zimonyi, a Hungarian refugee who would be a stunning 46 years old if Vesper made it to the Olympics. At the 1956 games in Melbourne, Australia—having already coxed the Hungarians to silver and bronze in two previous Olympics—Robby defected, along with 55 other Hungarian athletes. Just weeks before, the Soviet Union had crushed the short-lived Hungarian Revolution as thousands fled under barbed-wire fences. As luck would have it, Kell was in Melbourne, too, winning his first and only Olympic medal—a bronze in the single, which he gave to his sister, the newly married Princess Grace of Monaco.

Kell helped Robby emigrate to Philadelphia and set him up with a job at the family business, John B. Kelly, Inc. (Kelly for Brickworks). The Hungarian proved his worth at Vesper, where his straight steering shaved seconds off any boat he coxed.

Another pair of military men hell-bent on Olympic vindication had, by the fall of 1963, also settled in at Vesper's 90-year-old boathouse at #10 Boathouse Row. Tom and Joe Amlong had become infatuated with rowing in their mid-teens when their career Army father, stationed with the family in Liege, Belgium, sent the boys to a rowing club for exercise. Like Boyce and Emory, the Amlong brothers were chafing over past defeats. In their late teens, they had failed to make it through the 1956 Olympic trials. Four years later, they had failed again.

But in the summer of 1961—during an interlude between college and the military—the brothers had rowed in Philadelphia, winning races "that put us on the map," Joe Amlong recalled. Tom, who had rowed at the University of Virginia, had convinced Joe, who went to West Point, which had no crew, to get back in the game.

Within a year, Air Force Lieutenant Joe Amlong and Army Lieutenant Tom Amlong, ages 27 and 29, were back in Philadelphia, thanks to Kell, whose letters to military brass had convincingly argued that the Amlongs could best serve their country by training for the Olympics.

"My brother said, 'We have to go to Philly to row because that's where it's at,'" explained Joe. But without Kell, he added, "we would never have been able to get there."

**The Youngsters:
Foley and Cwiklinski**

The kids in the boat are
Westerner Hugh Foley (left)
and Philadelphian Stan
Cwiklinski, two La Salle
College students barely out of
their teens. Cwiklinski says
Coach Allen Rosenberg
motivated him to work harder,
and Dietrich Rose, their
trainer, "had a lot to do with
my maturization." Cwiklinski
bonds with the oldest rower,
Bill Knecht. Otherwise, he
says, the group "didn't have a
social life off the river."

Courtesy of *La Salle Explorer
Magazine.*

As kids in Liege, they had swooned over a sleek two-man shell
that was off limits to them as beginners. Later, that sweep boat, in
which each man rows with one oar, became their boat of choice—
the pair without coxswain. They had no interest in sweep rowing
in an eight-oared boat. They did not want to rely on anyone but
themselves.

"We didn't want anything to do with the eight. We thought it
was mathematically too difficult to win—eight men rowing together
all at the same time," Joe Amlong would later say. It was about the
only thing the Amlongs had in common with Boyce and Emory.
"One of the reasons Boyce and I were so determined to row in the
pair was that we did not want to have to count on anyone else,"
Emory wrote.

Despite that shared conviction, the preppy Yalies and the trash-
talking Amlongs roiled each other. There was no way the Amlongs were getting into an eight with those Ivy
"pussies" or anyone else, the brothers would say.

On the opposite end of the age and personality spectrum were the two youngest Olympic aspirants to
find their way to Vesper—ranch boy Hugh Foley and city-bred Stan Cwiklinski. The two "quiet ones," everyone called them.

Foley, the son of a Montana cattleman, had escaped cold and countryside to attend college in Los Angeles. Though he had never held an oar, at 6 feet 3 inches, he attracted the attention of Loyola's freshman crew
coach. After two seasons of rowing, his coach, who formerly coached crew at La Salle College in Philadelphia,
encouraged the 19-year-old, who had yet to win a race, to go East and get some experience at Vesper. That
summer, Vesper coach Allen Rosenberg was organizing a boat to compete in Japan in a pre-Olympics race.
Hugh somehow made the eight, which finished a surprising second to Germany's famed Ratzeburg crew. "As
soon as we returned from Japan, I realized that we had a real good chance for the Olympics," Hugh said.

He transferred to La Salle and never looked back. That fall, Hugh learned that a Philadelphian, Stan
Cwiklinski (*Quick-lin-ski*), was making a name for himself in La Salle crew. An all-around athlete, Stan, at

Like Herding Cats

In the fall of 1963, the crew that Kell is assembling for a bid at the 1964 Olympics has yet to fall into place. Working out (from left) are Tom Amlong, Joe Amlong, Bill Knecht, and Dietrich Rose. A German who rowed with the famed Ratzeburg Rowing Club, Dietrich brought cross-training to Vesper. But he would need to get U.S. citizenship to row for Vesper in the Olympics. The Amlongs wanted nothing to do with an eight.

Philadelphia Evening Bulletin, September 11, 1963, Special Collections Research Center, Temple University Libraries, Philadelphia.

6 feet 2½ inches, had fenced, played football, and run track at Central High School. He had also rowed out of the Fairmount Rowing Association, under the banner of Central, which had no rowing program. With Stan, La Salle's freshman eight had won the prestigious Dad Vail race, the largest collegiate competition in the country.

Hugh "encouraged me to drop everything else I was doing, including La Salle rowing," said Stan. "I was lucky to be in the right place at the right time to join the bunch at Vesper."

In the winter of 1964, as members of this random cohort each trained toward his particular goal, the group was mentored by two very different coaches: Allen Rosenberg and Dietrich Rose.

Coach-Technician: Al Rosenberg

After Vesper's eight fails miserably at the 1963 Pan American Games, Kell installs as coach Allen Rosenberg, a long time coxswain at Vesper. "Kelly made it pretty clear that Al was the coach by default," Boyce Budd says. "He had tried to recruit coaches from all over the country, and he fell back to Al." But Allen Rosenberg proves himself a remarkable technician, working closely with Dietrich Rose to train the men. "They've been on the weights for years," Rosenberg tells *Sports Illustrated*, which calls the crew "the naval arm of the Philadelphia Eagles."

Philadelphia Evening Bulletin, August 24, 1964, Special Collections Research Center, Temple University Libraries, Philadelphia.

A Vesper coxswain, Al was diminutive in size—5 feet 1 inch and 105 pounds—but large in impact. Kell had installed him as coach after the club disappointed in the 1963 Pan American games. With degrees in both pharmacy and law, Al studied the technique of rowing with the same intensity he had brought to his academic work.

"His genius was in providing unobtrusive but firm leadership, mediating the constant disputes, and gradually earning the respect of all of the team," said former Secretary of the Navy John Lehman, who trained at Vesper in 1963 and 1964. "He was a master psychologist."

The 32-year-old was also a "bundle of neuroses," said Emory in a joint interview with Boyce 50 years later.

"He had a little bit of a chip on his shoulder," added Boyce.

"He had every chip on his shoulder," piled on Emory.

"Kelly made it pretty clear that Al was the coach by default. He had tried to recruit coaches from all over the country, and he fell back to Al," said Boyce.

Born in 1936, Dietrich Rose narrowly missed serving in the Hitler Youth. "I had a uniform, but I was too young," said Dietrich, who was nine years old when the war ended. By 1963, he was one of Germany's top rowers and a member of the Ratzeburg Club, whose eight-oared crew won gold in the 1960 Olympics, breaking the hammerlock on the event that the Americans had held for seven straight Olympics. To his dismay, Dietrich had not been in that lineup. He was 27 years old, an engineer with 250 victories under his belt, "and I wanted to do something different," Dietrich explained. "A woman who worked for me said, 'You ought to see the world.' I decided I wanted to emigrate to the United States, and I needed a sponsor. Someone suggested Jack Kelly. He said 'We'd love to have you and will get you a job.'"

To Vesper, Dietrich brought the technique of "interval training," which had been refined by Ratzeburg's coach, Karl Adam. It demanded that rowers cross-train, using weights and running, to improve their lung capacity and maximize their strength. He also brought expertise in European equipment and rigging.

Drilling the Vesper oarsmen, Dietrich was encouraged by their strength compared to the Germans'. What was discouraging, though, was how out of sync they were with one another. In America, Rose observed, "Every college coach had a different style, so people all rowed differently. It was hard to put them all together to do the same thing." And ego got in the way, too, a sense of "I'm from here, I'm much better," Dietrich said.

As for tension between the Jew and the German—if it existed at any level, the two did not show it. Said Emory, "You had Rosenberg and Rose as the coaching team. And I swear you would not be interviewing us right now, this all would not have happened, had those two not formed such a perfect partnership."

"I brought something new," said Dietrich, and Al "was willing . . . to be part of the change. The main thing between him and me was to try to get along. I designed workouts. He was a very good technician coach—how to hold hands on the oars and finish the stroke. He was very good at that. I learned something from him. We didn't have any big clashes."

By November 1963, Emory and Boyce had developed a grueling routine: up six days a week at 5:30 A.M., on the river by 6:00; off to their jobs; another row in the evening, often followed by a run; dinner together in their Germantown apartment with "one can of beer in which we indulged occasionally," along with women, in which they indulged more frequently.

On November 21, Emory wrote in his diary that they rowed the course a couple times "wobbly and on port but worked hard," just missing some of the bridges, only to have their world upend the next day. President John F. Kennedy had been assassinated in Dallas. Emory heard the news while in uniform at his Marine post on South Broad Street. He felt a sense of impotence, that his own energy, competitive drive, and determination to vanquish could not prevent such tragedy. "I became sweaty thinking of my own insignificance, how history is bigger than us all, and how no matter who or how many I 'kicked the shit out of' it would not undo this unbelievable act," he wrote that night.

In December, Emory and Boyce raced on the Schuylkill together as it snowed. Through winter, when ice on the river grounded them, they kept training by running three miles, lifting weights, and doing squat jumps while clutching a 35-pound disc. "The weights were unrelieved pain, not something you want to do without powerful motivation," Emory wrote. "We had it."

By February, they were again on the river virtually every day, sometimes when it was 21 degrees and "colder than sin."

"Some dark, cold mornings my whole body seemed tired as I rolled out of bed before even starting the workout. We figured it was good for us and weren't happy unless we were exhausted. . . . We looked forward to that point of challenge, eager to meet it, to demolish it, to obliterate it."

They rowed, too, in miserable rain. "Bare feet are cold on the wet dock, wind drives through your sweat shirts as you put the boat in and rain goes down your neck. . . . Dark when we came in and still nasty. Wonderful . . . pray that the warm weather will see an end to our aches and pains."

Like the Yalies during these dark months, the Amlong brothers mostly rowed in their pair, ever resistant to the idea of collaborating in a bigger boat.

That March, Bill Knecht—a former Olympian and Kelly's longtime rowing partner, began driving the half hour from his home in Haddonfield, New Jersey, to Boathouse Row, to row with the eight-oared crew that Kelly was pulling together for the Olympics.

"He wasn't a huge guy, but a technique guy. He knew how to enter the water perfectly. You didn't have to tell him anything," recalled Dietrich Rose, noting that for an elite rower, Knecht's age, 34, was "unusual."

"We didn't have that many people to select from . . . there wasn't anybody else. He was it."

About then, Navy lieutenant Bill Stowe showed up on the dock. He was the fourth active military man, along with the Amlongs and Emory, to win dispensation to train at Vesper, thanks to Kell's intervention. Like Boyce Budd, Bill Stowe had been a big, awkward kid. He remembers the regular humiliation of always being the last one chosen for those school recess teams.

"As a non-athlete, I was pathetic and was embarrassed to try anything," he wrote in his book about the 1964 race, *All Together*. But as a neophyte rower at the elite private Kent School in Connecticut, he discovered he was no worse than others. On the contrary, he eventually became so good, he made the Kent crew that crossed the Atlantic to compete at Henley in England. Harvard knocked them out in an early round. It was "a defeat which set up for me a lifetime dislike for anything, if not everybody, to do with Harvard," he wrote.

At Cornell, as he had at Kent, Bill Stowe continued to row "stroke"—the critical "eight seat" that follows the coxswain's orders and sets the pace for the seven men seated behind him. But sophomore year, after pinching a church's crèche during a drunken fraternity party, he was suspended from rowing, only later realizing that his antic might have cost Cornell a chance at the 1960 Olympics.

A signature event of his collegiate rowing career had taken place in Philadelphia, at a memorable Independence Day Regatta in 1962. That year, Olympian Vyacheslav Ivanov and his Soviet crew competed before a crowd of anywhere from 50,000 to 100,000 people, depending on what newspaper was counting. The Soviets won by a length, followed by Vesper—and only then, Cornell. "Who the hell is Vesper?" Bill Stowe and his teammates asked themselves.

A year later, Naval Lieutenant Stowe—now using his Cornell hotel school training to run the officers' club in Saigon—began getting letters from rowing coaches, all offering to convince the Navy to bring him home to train. One of those letters was from Kell.

Rosenberg quickly seated the 24-year-old Stowe at stroke. Stowe made an immediate difference. Not only was he good at passing rhythm back through the boat, but he was powerful. "Bill pulled as much or more water than most six men," Emory instantly noted. With Bill Stowe stroking late that March, for the first time Emory began to get excited about participating in an eight. "The damn boat really moved. . . . We could win everything with that boat if they'd just get organized and not be so damn haphazard."

A test for the crew came on June 6, 1964, at the American Henley race on the Schuylkill. Emory's oar caught a "crab," sucking the blade underwater and braking the boat in mid-glide. Catching a crab is what Emory calls "an oarsman's nightmare," "the catastrophe which strikes without warning, leaving shame, tragedy, ruined dreams and lost races." The error contributed to Vesper's loss to the University of Pennsylvania by nearly a length.

The regatta also proved a critical trial for the Amlong brothers. All that winter and spring, they had refused to step into the eight, continuing to cling to their hopes in the pair. But at the American Henley, they lost to Tony Johnson and Jim Edmonds of the Potomac Club in Washington. The following Monday, Tom and Joe were in the eight, though they insisted on sitting in the five and six seats, where Emory and Boyce had long been practicing, pushing them back to three and four. "We didn't care; we knew we needed them," Emory wrote. "With Bill Stowe now firmly established in the stroke seat and Knecht at seven, Tom, Joe, Boyce and me in the engine room, there was now no weak link. Stan and Hugh, the bow pair, had yet to mature, but they had the basics, were tough, rowed hard and didn't talk."

The Amlongs, though, did not stop talking—mocking the other rowers and boasting about their sex lives (Joe had just married and would regale the men with accounts of the previous night's gymnastics and where they had taken place.) Decades later, Joe would explain that when he and Tom taunted their crewmates,

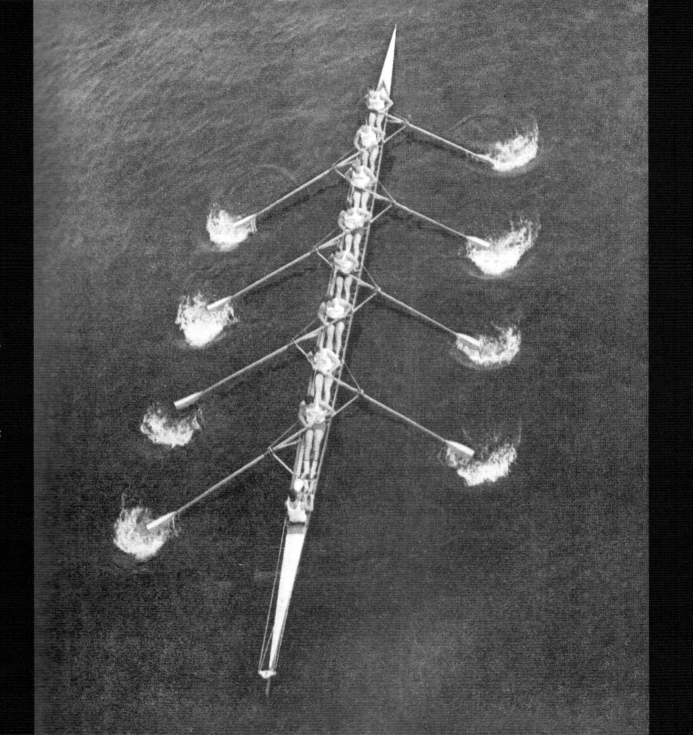

A Moment of Melding

Some kind of magic happens when the Vesper crew catch their stride and row in complete synchrony. It is what keeps them going, though otherwise they are a "kind of Monty Python's Flying Circus," says former Secretary of the U.S. Navy John Lehman, who trained at Vesper in the early 1960s and had a "ringside seat" on their antics: "Every day was some new drama or comedy. It wasn't until I got to my first Navy squadron that I ever saw anything like those ten ultra-type-A characters. What a fascinating group of individuals, every one very different and each in his own way a supreme egotist."

Vesper Eight on the Schuylkill, August 8, 1964. Philadelphia Inquirer Magazine, Special Collections Research Center. Temple University Libraries, Philadelphia.

saying things like, "You can't row your way out of a paper bag!" or calling them "pussies," it was more like teasing than animosity—a way to goad performance.

In his book *Olympic Odyssey*, Emory put his feelings about the Amlongs on paper, in words as cutting as theirs. "They were short, maybe a little over six feet, and each was a solid 200 pounds, enormously powerful with slabs of muscle everywhere—including their brains. Antagonistic and contemptuous of everyone, including each other, they were legendary for their lack of tact." And they were "crude in the extreme in sexual matters . . . one was never in doubt of either's sexual prowess."

"The four of us co-existed in the boathouse and were careful not to clash on the river where we had a good deal of respect for each other," Emory continued. Most important of all, they were very, very fast.

The youngsters, Hugh Foley and Stan Cwiklinski, largely stayed out of the fray.

"At my age, I'd follow along," Stan said, especially with Tom Amlong, who eventually sat in front of him in the eight. "He had a way of instigating. He would turn around and shout words—'do or die' kinds of things. He was a real disciplinarian."

Stan remembered how Tom would take him out in a pair-oared boat, where each oarsman sweeps with one oar. Tom would use his strength to force the boat around, testing him. "I persevered and straightened the boat. That irritated him and I gained some favor. He settled down. I had to stand up to him."

But Stan sensed the reason behind Tom's pushy behavior: "He was always trying to make me be better than I could be."

What Dietrich Rose and Allen Rosenberg were trying to do was to meld this diverse and divisive group into a well-oiled machine, where every part, every movement, every pull of the blade was in total synchrony. Not only that, but they would have to move in perfect harmony while rowing at a lung-screaming speed of up to 40 strokes a minute. It was the only way they could win.

"There were times when I felt like a wild animal trainer with a chair and a whip to get the beasts in line and to do what was needed," Al said.

Besides working out in the eight, they also trained in smaller boats. Not only was it a form of cross-training, but the Amlongs as well as the Yalies still held out hope that they could compete in Tokyo in their pairs—if the eight did not make it through the U.S. Olympic trials. And if, by some chance, Vesper did win the Olympic trials in the eight, the crew could still split up for the Nationals and even possibly the European championships.

"We rowed six days a week in all kinds of weather, and we killed ourselves," wrote Bill Stowe. When we were not rowing, we weight lifted—tortured our bodies. . . . We greeted the sun in the morning and put it to bed in the evening. . . . It was both wonderful and dreadful."

Dietrich watched as the boat began to come together. "They raced against each other; their words flying back-and-forth but it leveled out. . . . Finally they realized that maybe there was not so much difference between them, especially when you have a chance to go to the Olympics."

As haphazardly as they might row in practice, when they actually raced, something extraordinary kicked in. "There seemed to be a pent-up violence in the Vesper boat," Boyce said. "An irreverence toward all the 'nice' things about rowing—all the nice guys, the blue blazers, and all that shit. We threw all that out the window. . . . There was a savagery about it that I really loved."

On July 6, the Vesper Eight arrived at Orchard Beach, Long Island, for the Olympic trials, clear underdogs among the 16 entries. It had been six decades since a club crew (the very same Vesper Boat Club) had represented the United States in the Olympics. The University of California was unbeaten; Yale was strong; and Harvard, also undefeated and coached by Harry Parker, who had rowed under the great Joe Burk of Penn, was favored.

Worse, Vesper was told its entry had arrived late and they had been disqualified. Al Rosenberg, using his legal training, filed a protest. The dispute was finally resolved by the nation's top rowing organizations the night before the first heats.

Meanwhile, the Amlongs were waging the psychological warfare in which they were so adept. They "took special pains to strut about the dock looking muscular and mean. Tom chewed tobacco and spit disdainfully into the water as he muttered loudly about the 'pretty pussies,' referring in this case to the Harvard crew," Emory remembered.

Unlike the college crews, the Vesper men did not have practice uniforms. "We dressed in rags, our normal outfits," Stowe recalled. On a practice row, they fumbled with rigging and lamely pulled away from the dock, with only a couple of them rowing while the others talked. "The college trained oarsmen on the shore were flabbergasted at this mess called the Vesper Boat Club, but we were loving it, throwing them off. It was a fun psych job."

To everyone's surprise, Vesper survived the semifinals. But in the finals, with Yale and California also contending, Harvard got off to its best start of the year, Coach Parker would later say. On the other hand, Vesper's start was terrible. Their plan had been to keep a steamy pace of about 37 strokes per minute to the halfway mark of the 2,000-meter race, then pour more on. But being behind so early in the finals "made me mad," Emory wrote. "I wanted to row them down and then blow them away. I wanted to crush them. I know Boyce felt the same way—he had never beaten Harvard in four years at Yale." Bill Stowe was also seeking his Harvard revenge.

Robby finally ordered the oarsmen to execute a "power ten." He timed the order to come right after Harvard's men had exhausted themselves with their own ten big strokes. Vesper shot ahead to win the race, with open water between them and Harvard. In a further assertion of Vesper's prowess, the crew continued to row past the finish line as the Harvard men collapsed over their oars.

"The destruction of Harvard was total and complete, and if I derived from it a kind of obscene pleasure, a vindictive catharsis, may God forgive me," Emory wrote.

Al told *Sports Illustrated*, "A boatload of men will beat a boatload of boys every time" (July 20, 1964). Kelly credited the win to the intense dedication of the Vesper crew, along with interval training, including rowing in small boats; this makes the big shell feel lighter, like a baseball player swinging three bats before going to the plate.

In August, the eight split up to race in the Nationals. Emory and Boyce won in the pair with cox, and the Amlongs won in the straight pair, earning the right to represent the United States in the European competition. The remaining Vesper rowers—Bill Stowe, Bill Knecht, Hugh Foley, and Stan Cwiklinski, racing in a four, came in second, but the winners did not have the money to go to Europe. So America's Olympic contender for the eight-oared crew made the unprecedented decision to break up and compete in little boats in Amsterdam. Only the Amlongs made it to the finals, though, finishing fourth. It was, perhaps, a sign that Vesper's strength lay with them united in one big boat.

While in Amsterdam, the men of Vesper had watched Germany and the Soviet Union fiercely compete in the eight. They returned home awed and anxious, knowing what they would be up against. They also worried whether Dietrich could come with them to help coach, since he was not yet an American citizen and Vesper would have to pay his way. (Kell had previously tried to convince him to marry an American to get his papers so he could actually row in the boat, but Dietrich had declined the ploy.)

Their prospects seemed even more ominous in early October, when the crew arrived in Tokyo. Burly Boyce Budd, felled by mononucleosis, was just recovering, and Stan Cwiklinski, hit by the flu and shaking with fever, was quarantined for two days in the Olympic Village infirmary.

The "Old Men" Best the Boys

Exuberant at their win in the Olympic trials in
Orchard Beach, New York, the "old men" of the
Vesper crew toss coxswain Robby Zimonyi into
the water, a tradition of victorious crews. Vesper
defeats Harvard by a satisfying 1¼ lengths. "The
colleges had this arrogance about them," Boyce
Budd recalled. "When we went up to Orchard
Beach to race in the trials, I remember reporters
calling me up and saying, 'What's Vesper? Who's
Rosenberg? There was just an unspoken
superiority you get out of the Ivy League."

Philadelphia Inquirer, July 12, 1964, Special Collections
Research Center, Temple University Libraries,
Philadelphia, PA.

Onward, Excelsior!

A proud hometown newspaper produces a double
spread on its Olympic contingent heading for Tokyo.
From left: Allen Rosenberg, coach; Robert Zimonyi,
coxswain; Bill Stowe, stroke; Bill Knecht, Tom Amlong,
Joe Amlong, Boyce Budd, Emory Clark, Hugh Foley,
Stan Cwiklinski (bow).

*Vesper Boat Club Eight, August 8, 1964. Philadelphia
Inquirer Magazine*, Special Collections Research Center,
Temple University Libraries, Philadelphia.

But after days of working out with substitutes, Boyce's strength was returning. Stan was able to breathe deeply again. And thanks to Kell's fund-raising drive, Dietrich was unofficially with them, riding his motorbike up and down the Toda Canal to check out the other crews' strategies.

Fourteen countries had sent eights. They would be whittled down to the final six through a series of heats. Germany's Ratzeburg Club, whose crew won the 1960 Olympics, was the biggest threat. Through a draw, the crews were divided into three groups of five, five, and four. The three winners of these heats would go straight to the finals. The rest would have to race again in a "repêchage" heat to yield the remaining three contenders.

Of course, it is better to win right away and rest, rather than having to race twice before the final. Which very well might not happen for Vesper, which had known for a week that it was racing against Ratzeburg in the first heat on October 13.

Emory vowed, "If we were to lose, as I thought inevitable, it would not be because I had anything left. . . . I would put in the absolute ultimate effort . . . welcome the pain."

With arms turning to cement, thighs burning, and lungs gasping, Vesper raced what felt like an endless 2,000-meter row; it lasted only 5 minutes and 54.30 seconds. Germany won. But only by $^{28}/_{100}$ of a second, coming in at 5:54.02.

As the Philadelphia crew dejectedly rowed back to the dock and carried their boat out of the water, they were met by Kell, who was ecstatic. The Vesper men were exhausted, but the Ratzeburg boys were wiped. They had continued to sit in their shell for 15 minutes after the race and some "were lying on the dock writhing."

In their bones, now, the Vesper oarsmen knew they had a chance. As Emory put it, "With the exception of Hugh and Stan, each of us had been training for a long time, each had dreamed and been disappointed, for each this might well be his last try, and no weak-willed pussy was going to get in the way of the goal."

Vesper easily won its repêchage the next day against Japan and Korea.

The final race for Olympic gold came on October 15, a windy day on Japan's Toda Canal, so windy that racing was halted. It was nearly nightfall when the motley crew of the Vesper Eight set out against the Soviet Union, Yugoslavia, Czechoslovakia, Italy—and Ratzeburg of Germany. Dietrich, checking the Vesper boat shortly before the race, found a partially broken ball joint and replaced it. Some later described it as sabotage, but Dietrich said it was "in no way malicious, just wear."

To the shock and consternation of the Vesper Eight, flares explode in the darkness of early evening as they near the finish line of the Olympic finals. Had another crew won? The Vesper men can recall every moment: the long, wind-delayed wait for the race to begin. Their surprisingly flawless start as darkness falls. The silently spoken prayers as Emory's oar slaps the water instead of dropping in. Flares suddenly exploding. And Robby Zimonyi screaming, "Vee are vinning!"

US Winning Eight-Oared Shell Race at the Summer Olympics, October 15, 1964. Photograph by George Silk/The LIFE Picture Collection/Getty Images.

Then they were at the starting line. Boyce was wondering, "What am I doing? . . . I wasn't ready. . . . I had lost control of my life." Robby Zimonyi, all 115 pounds of him, was anxious to win for his adopted country. Joe Amlong, who as a younger rower might once have been asking God to get him through the excruciating pain ahead, now was thinking that only over his dead body would anyone pass him.

"*Êtes vous prêt? . . . Partez!*"

Their start was perfect. "The best start ever," Boyce would recall, with "hardly any of the usual smacking of puddles with water flying all over the place. . . . I remember thinking we finally got this old ship rocking."

Sixty seconds into the race, as they were rowing at a comfortable 36–37 strokes a minute into a headwind, Robby announced in his megaphone: "Vee are in third place."

By the 1,000 meters, they had passed the Soviets and were within five feet of the Germans, closer than they had been at that point during the first heat. After a "power 20," they were a boat length ahead of Ratzeburg. Just then, Emory's blade "slapped a wave on the recovery and spun in my hands" and was backwards when he got to the catch, the moment at which he should have been dropping it back into the water. Would this miss result in disaster for himself and the entire crew?

Never having experienced that precise misadventure before, I did not know precisely what to do. Since we were rowing at 37 strokes a minute there was not a lot of time for mental debate. But I alertly concluded it would be unwise to put the oar in the water. So I pulled what the British call an "airshot" and frantically twisted the oar handle round properly. . . . On my next trip up the slide, I decided the others could row it in. I was going to make sure I did not mess up, catch a crab or do something equally catastrophic. It was so dark I did not think anybody noticed—the boat kept on churning. But Robby said he saw it and Boyce claims he started to pray after sensing the missed stroke.

With the finish line still 500 meters away, suddenly "there was a bright explosion and another, and I had something else for my ravaged brain to focus on," Emory wrote. "Could we have passed the finish line? Had I so miscalculated?" Boyce remembers just going up and down the slide, doing what he was trained to do but wondering whether the burst of light he was seeing was really his exhausted brain in some kind of meltdown.

Young Hugh Foley, in the two seat with his back to the wind, remembered thinking that the race was over and Vesper had gotten third. He was rowing without his heavy horn-rimmed glasses and could not see.

Vesper Victorious

Vesper finishes in six minutes, 18.23 seconds, defeating its most feared rival, the Ratzeburg club of Germany by five seconds, and Czechoslovakia by nearly seven seconds. Vesper's victory is the first time in 60 years that an American club eight, rather than a collegiate crew, wins gold at the Olympics. It also proves to be the last time that an American club eight will row together in an Olympics because crews are now chosen through a national camp system.

Courtesy of the International Olympic Committee, October 15, 1964.

"Fortunately I did not stop rowing because we still had a minute left to row to the finish line." Robby was saying something but he had lapsed into Hungarian again, and I couldn't hear him anyway because of the now intermittent explosions."

Stan heard Robby yelling, "Let's go boyz!! Vee are vinning!!" but did not believe him and rowed harder. "I was not sure what was happening but assumed that exhaustion was eating into my senses."

Under flares bursting to light the way, Vesper streaked across the finish five seconds ahead of the Germans. The interminable months of workouts and weights and worry were over in 6 minutes, 18.23 seconds, clinching gold for Philadelphia and the United States. The "old men" had defeated the best in the world by 1¼ boat lengths.

Winning gold medals at the 1964 Tokyo Olympics became the highlight of many of the Vesper oarsmen's lives. Bill Stowe and Emory Clark wrote books about their experience. Every four years, with another summer Olympics approaching, schools and organizations would ask the men to bring out their medals.

John B. Kelly Jr.—Kell—who devoted so much of his life to rowing—was elected president of the U.S. Olympic Committee in February 1985. A month later, at age 57, he collapsed and died of a heart attack while jogging near the drive now named for him.

In a way, the 1964 Vesper crew, which Kell recruited, drawing as it did from the best rowers from all over the country, became the model for the national training camp system that the USOC now uses to select America's Olympic contenders.

Kudos from Kell

John B. Kelly Jr., himself an Olympian, admires the medal worn by the diminutive Vesper coxswain Robby Zimonyi, after the crew's stunning victory. Towering over him and Coach Allan Rosenberg are oarsmen Hugh Foley, Bill Knecht, and Stan Cwiklinski.

Philadelphia Evening Bulletin, October 27, 1964, Special Collections Research Center, Temple University Libraries, Philadelphia.

Their Patron Departs

John B. Kelly Jr. walks off the dock at the Vesper Boat Club after a morning row, five months before he collapses and dies while jogging along Boathouse Row. In his diary, Emory Clark writes a remembrance of the man who "gave of his time, his energy, his money and his name. Shameless and brash in using that name to get what he wanted, such as amorous favors from young women, he was unselfish in sharing the influence generated by it if it would help an oarsman, a crew, the sport of rowing, or amateur athletics."

John Paul Filo/*Philadelphia Inquirer*, October 1984.

OLYMPIC MEDALISTS OF BOATHOUSE ROW

st of men and women who trained on Boathouse Row before winning Olympic
owing began in 1976.

od, Edward Marsh, Edward Heley, William Carr, John E. Geiger, James B.
ecke, John O. Exley, Louis G. Abell (Vesper Boat Club), coxed eight.

Michael D. Gleason, Frank A. Schell, James S. Flanagan, Charles E.
Lott, Joseph F. Dempsey, John O. Exley, Louis G. Abell (cox) (Vesper),

(Vesper), single sculls.

per), single sculls.
Paul Costello (Vesper), double sculls.
hmidt, Kenneth Myers, Eric H. Federschmidt, Carl O. Klose, Sherman Clark
e Club), coxed four.

Paul V. Costello (Vesper), double sculls.
ore (Bachelors Barge Club), single sculls.
Harold C. Wilson, Edward T. Jennings (Pennsylvania Barge Club), coxed pair.
Edward P. Mitchell Jr., Robert B. Gerhardt, Sydney Jellinek, John G.
Barge Club), coxed four.

Garrett Gilmore, 1924, 1932

Courtesy Bachelors Barge Club.

Dan Barrow, 1936

1928

Gold: Paul Costello, Charles McIlvaine (Pennsylvania Athletic Club), double sculls.

Silver: Kenneth Myers (Bachelors), single sculls.

Silver: Ernest Bayer, George Healis, Charles Karle, William G. Miller (Penn Barge), coxless four.

Bronze: Paul McDowell, John Schmitt. (Penn Barge), coxless pair.

1932

Gold: Charles M. Kieffer, Joseph A. Schauers, Edward F. Jennings (Penn Barge), coxed pair.

Gold: W.E. Garrett Gilmore, Kenneth Myers (Bachelors), double sculls.

Silver: William G. Miller (Penn Barge), single sculls.

1936

Bronze: Daniel H. Barrow Jr. (Penn AC), single sculls.

1956

Bronze: John B. Kelly Jr. (Vesper), single sculls.

1964

Gold: Joseph B. Amlong, Hugh M. Foley, Stanley F. Cwiklinski, Thomas K. Amlong, Emory W. Clark, H
     Boyce Budd, William J. Knecht, William A. Stowe, Robert Zimonyi (Vesper), coxed eight.

1972

Silver: Eugene Clapp (College Boat Club/University of Pennsylvania), coxed eight.

1976

Silver: Michael Staines, Calvin Coffey (Vesper), coxless pair.

Bronze: Gail Ricketson (College/U. of P.), Anita DeFrantz (Vesper), coxed eight.

1984

Gold: Carol Bower (Vesper), coxed eight.

Silver: Edward A. Ives, Thomas N. Kiefer, Michael Bach, Greg T. Springer, John S. Stillings (Vesper),
     coxed four.

Silver: Phillip Stekl (College/U. of P.), coxless four.
Silver: Bob Jaugstetter (St. Joseph's University), coxed eight.

1988
Silver: David Krmpotich, Thomas R Bohrer, Richard B Kennelly, Raoul Rodriquez (Penn AC), coxless four
Bronze: Mike Teti (St. Joseph's University), Jeffrey McLaughlin (Penn AC), John Pescatore (College /U. of P. and Vesper), coxed eight.

1992
Silver: Thomas Bohrer, Jeffrey McLaughlin, Doug Burden, Patrick Manning (Penn AC), coxless four.

1996
Silver: Teresa Bell (Crescent Boat Club and Fairmount Rowing Association), lightweight double sculls.
Silver: Timothy Young (Undine Barge Club), quadruple sculls.
Bronze: Bill Carlucci (Vesper), Jeff Pfaendtner (College/U. of P. and Vesper), lightweight coxless fours.

2000
Bronze: Sarah Garner (Penn AC), lightweight double sculls.

2004
Gold: Dan Beery (Penn AC), Peter Cipollone (St. Joseph's Preparatory School), Jason Read (Temple University), coxed eight.

2008
Bronze: Micah Nathan Boyd and Matt Schnobrich (Penn AC), Steven Coppola Jr. (Vesper), Josh Inman (Vesper), Marcus McElhenney (Msgr. Bonner High School), coxed eight.

2012
Bronze: Glenn Ochal (Roman Catholic High School/Crescent), coxless four.

Sarah Garner, 2000

Courtesy Pennsylvania Athletic Club.

CHAPTER EIGHT

EDWARD T. STOTESBURY

The Forgotten Forces of High School Rowing

Wedged into a sliver of space at the bottom of Boathouse Row, between the Fairmount boat club and Lloyd Hall, where people now stop for ice cream or to rent bikes, is a narrow boat shed and a dock. This is home to the newest group on Boathouse Row—Philadelphia City Rowing (PCR).

Here, teenagers from public city high schools with no crew program and no rowing tradition come to work out on rowing machines, jump on and off balance beams, do push-ups, and get out on the river. Some live a stone's throw away, like many of the early rowers who banded together to establish private clubs. Others travel after school by bus and subway from far-flung sections of the city.

For most of the 130 or so youths from several dozen city schools who row each season with PCR, the sport of crew is alien to any they have known. That's how it was for Daekwon Smith, 17, who was urged to pick from a list of rigorous programs geared to at-risk youths as a way to channel the anger he was expressing after his grandmother's death. He chose rowing because he likes to try new things.

A year later, he loves the challenge of it, the physicality of it. "I never experienced anything that was as much mental work as it was physical work and just shear technique all at once," he said. Crew also requires exquisite synchronicity with

Daekwon Smith, 17, lofts
a shell at Philadelphia City
Rowing, the latest effort to
engage more Philadelphia
kids in rowing on the river in
their backyard. Without
more exposure to crew in the
public schools, he says, the
sport will not get traction. "A
lot of kids know how to be in
a pool, but they don't know
how to actually swim."

April Saul.

"an entire team of people with different personalities, different mindsets, different interests." It has taught him better ways to deal with conflict. "Like you have to put a rein on your own anger, because if you're in the middle of the river, you can't just freak out."

He wishes more of his friends were involved. He hopes to interest his younger brother. Doing so may be a challenge.

"The generation ahead of us, like our parents, uncles, aunts, didn't have the exposure," said Daekwon, who is African American, "so there's no trickle-down effect."

Not Just about Rowing

PCR draws students from more than three dozen Philadelphia public and charter schools, who would otherwise never row or know one another. Rowing demands discipline, dedication, and teamwork, challenging students to meld into a smoothly synchronized crew despite their distinct personalities, backgrounds, and egos. From left are Tylidia Garnett, Michaela Kelly, Saniya Robinson, Cameron Lightsey, and Jessica Hobbs Pifer.

April Saul.

In his neighborhood of West Philadelphia, there are football fields, basketball courts, and recreation centers, but no public schools offering crew. "So a lot of the kids end up playing football, or they learn to box or run track. They do what's normal and near them and around them." Plus, he said, a lot of his friends can't swim.

Although Philadelphia is home to the Stotesbury Cup Regatta, the largest high school rowing competition in the world, rarely over the last century have its public school children had the opportunity to participate.

But if there is one way that Boathouse Row holds a mirror to America, it is in its slowly changing complexion, one that started out to a great extent with the dominance of white men of means, expanded with working men and immigrants, and finally exploded with the much-delayed inclusion of women. The children of Philadelphia's impoverished public school system, most of whom are now African American, Latino, and Asian American, are the last to show up on the dock.

Ironically, for a brief time, Philadelphia's public school students were among the first to row. Central High students were already on the river at the dawn of Boathouse Row. Thomas Eakins, who famously painted scullers on the Schuylkill, himself rowed while attending Central High in the early 1860s. So did his classmate, the future champion rower Max Schmitt. For that matter, Eakins' chemistry professor at Central, Dr. Benjamin Howard Rand, was president of the Undine Barge Club.

Central High opened in 1838 as the first public high school in Philadelphia and only the second one in the United States. The all-male school was conceived as a "free academy," essentially a publicly funded private school for the city's brightest middle- and lower-middle-class boys. Its rigorous classical education would give them the chance to go into business or on to college, like the more privileged students who attended the city's private academies, such as William Penn Charter, Episcopal Academy, and Friends Select.

Rowing, along with golf and track and field, was a signature of Central's elite status, as it was for some of America's earliest private secondary schools, which adopted the upper-class English tradition. In 1852, students at St. Paul's School in Concord, New Hampshire, were racing, as were those attending Phillips Exeter, in Exeter, New Hampshire, a decade later. By 1882, Episcopal Academy, then located at Juniper and Walnut Streets in Philadelphia, was buying rowing machines.

It was fitting that Central High would want to compete in the same sports as its private-school peers. With its selective admission and rigorous curriculum, it touted itself as offering all the advantages of a private secondary school—"advanced instruction and social exclusiveness" without tuition.

Sports had its place in that education, built on the growing conviction that a healthy body was key to a critical mind. The discipline of sports was also seen as building character. More than a century later, that same thinking led to the founding in 2009 of Philadelphia City Rowing: namely, that a rigorous sports program—one that demands discipline, commitment, and teamwork—can alter the trajectory of a student's life.

"Our mission is to empower youth through the sport of rowing," explained PCR's executive director, Terry Dougherty. "That means you're responsible for you."

As high school became an expectation rather than a privilege in the late 19th century, Philadelphia became a pioneer of sports leagues, which often included rowing. Its private schools organized the nation's first scholastic athletic conference in 1887—the Inter-Academic Athletic Association, or InterAc as it is called today. A Friends league quickly followed. Then, in 1897, the city's private and public schools joined to form a purely rowing association called the Interscholastic Rowing League. It included two public city high schools—Central High, whose formal crew program was spurred on by two faculty members, and Central Manual Training. Also in the league were William Penn Charter School, Episcopal Academy, Germantown Academy, Eastern

Academy, and Friends Central School. Rowing, too, were students at Roman Catholic High, which had opened in 1890 as the first free Catholic high school for boys in the United States.

In 1897, *Harper's Weekly* praised Philadelphia's private boat clubs for supporting the InterAC and promoting schoolboy rowing. "Last spring the Bachelor club conceived the idea of a junior membership, recruited from certain worthy schools, which should pay no dues, and yet, under a coach, have the use of the club's boats. Other clubs quickly saw the possibilities of such a recruiting field and today the majority of the clubs on the Schuylkill at Philadelphia offer the splendid facilities of their iconoclastic houses and the best of their boating equipment to any pupil of a certain number of schools."

Given crew's expensive equipment, such collaboration was indispensable to the high schools. At a time when a year's college tuition was $150, a shell cost nearly $400 (about $9,500 today). In 1878, for example, Harvard freshmen rowers tried to raise $1,500 by soliciting $25 (about $580) from each "wealthy man in the class."

In its first year of competition in the new rowing league, the public Central High lost to the private William Penn Charter, but Central triumphed in 1898. That year, too, Central was the only high school to compete against the clubs of Boathouse Row in the People's Regatta (now the Independence Day Regatta), winning the junior four oared gig race. For the next two years, Central also dominated the Interscholastic Rowing League, defeating the private schools.

Rowing proved so popular at Central that, despite the "long and severe training," 60 to 70 students would come to tryouts on rowing machines. The next two decades would be the golden years of crew at Central, underscored by its defeat of Naval Academy freshmen in Annapolis on May 2, 1914. But crew in Philadelphia's public schools would be short lived. The less costly sports of basketball, invented only in 1891, and baseball had caught fire. And World War I, like every war, bled the coffers of the high schools' rowing godfathers—the clubs of Boathouse Row. By 1919, Central High was the only public Philadelphia school that still had a crew program. It soon floundered, unable to row against the tide.

Edward T. Stotesbury was 78 years old in 1927 when he decided to underwrite a high school rowing cup. Little did he know that this small gesture would prove to be his life's greatest legacy, setting the course for a legendary high school regatta.

Called "Philadelphia's first citizen," and a "banker's banker" by newspapers and civic leaders of his time, "Ned" Stotesbury was one of the richest men in the nation, with a net worth of more than $100 million (nearly $1.4 billion today). A widower for many years, at age 62 he married a socialite and built her Whitemarsh Hall, a 100,000-square-foot mansion on 300 acres in suburban Wyndmoor, Pa. With 147 rooms, 28 bathrooms, and 24 fireplaces, it was described as the "Versailles of America." The couple summered and wintered in their other palatial retreats in Bar Harbor, Maine, and Palm Beach, Florida, where they entertained the likes of Henry Ford, Will Rogers, and the crown prince of Sweden.

The son of a Quaker mother and Episcopalian father, Stotesbury had worked his way up from a clerk's position at Drexel & Company to become senior partner of the banking behemoth. He was also a partner in J. P. Morgan, finance chairman of the Reading Company, and a top fundraiser for the Republican presidential campaigns of Theodore Roosevelt and William Howard Taft. With his economics acumen much in demand, he was recruited to the boards of nearly three dozen banking, rail, and coal companies, and helped open the doors to China trade by negotiating a major loan to its railroads. He was also a trustee of both the University of Pennsylvania and the Drexel Institute (now Drexel University).

Civic-minded as well, for 26 years he served as president of the Fairmount Park Commission. He also chaired the American Red Cross' local chapter during World

TWO MILLIONAIRES' EXCLUSIVE OTHER CLUB

Two of the wealthiest men to leave their mark on Boathouse Row were also members of Philadelphia's most rarefied clique: the Farmers' Club of Pennsylvania. Dating from 1847, the club, with about a dozen members, admitted only men who owned large tracts of land. By 1912, among them were Effingham Morris, who in 1872 had founded the University of Pennsylvania's College Boat Club, and Edward T. Stotesbury, who had joined Bachelors Barge Club in 1878. The two were also banking giants: Morris was president of the Girard Trust Company; Stotesbury was senior partner of Drexel & Company.

The Farmers' Club men dined monthly at their city mansions or country estates to discuss "the problems and pleasures of farming." Morris owned the 525-acre Bolton Farm, four miles from Bristol, Bucks County. Stotesbury, at whose Rittenhouse Square townhouse at 1925 Walnut Street the club often met, owned a 40-acre horse farm in Springfield Township, where he raised prize-winning trotters.

Often their many guests, including governors, senators, judges, and other dignitaries, would be transported to the dinners from New York, Harrisburg, or Washington in sumptuously furnished private rail cars.

Although Stotesbury was seven years older than Morris, their career paths continually crossed through the prosperous worlds of banking and railroads in the early 20th century. Between 1901 and 1918, both served together on boards or committees of the Pennsylvania Steel Company of New Jersey (which sought Cuban ore to benefit American railways); Franklin National Bank at Broad and Chestnut; the Cambria Steel Company in Johnstown, Pennsylvania; the Pennsylvania Fire Insurance Company; and the United Gas Improvement Company of Philadelphia. Both also were trustees of the University of Pennsylvania.

But their boathouse club paths diverged. Morris soon left the College Boat Club he had founded. Not so Stotesbury, who remained a member of Bachelors to his dying day.

Stotesbury's "Versailles"

Stotesbury's over-the-top mansion, Whitemarsh Hall, is completed in 1921 at a cost then of $3 million, plus $3 to 5 million more in interior decorating, not counting the artwork—more than $80 million in total today. French landscape architect Jacques Greber designed the English park–style gardens. The building itself (with three stories under ground with wine cellar, a 5,000-square-foot kitchen, and a movie theater) was designed by noted Philadelphia architect Horace Trumbauer. This "Versailles of America" fell into ruin after Stotesbury's death in 1938 and is now the site of Whitemarsh Village homes.

Aerial View of Whitemarsh Hall by Horace Trumbauer, Residence for E. T. Stotesbury, Springfield, PA, 1919. Free Library of Philadelphia, Print and Picture Department.

The First Stotesbury Cup

The Stotesbury Regatta, today the largest high school competition in the world, started out in 1927 as a single race, with this silver cup. West Philadelphia Catholic High School retired the trophy after winning it three years in a row. With insufficient interest, the school's crew program ended in the 1980s.

Stotesbury Cup, May 17, 1927. Philadelphia Evening Bulletin, Special Collections Research Center, Temple University Libraries, Philadelphia.

War I, helping to raise $3.5 million and winning the gratitude of the French, who honored him as a Chevalier of the Legion of Honor.

If his now-forgotten achievements went on for pages, so did his membership in clubs and societies, through which he sought recognition and connections, as did so many Philadelphians of his time. The Social Register of 1901 lists Stotesbury's membership in nine clubs before ending its entry in "etc." These included the Rittenhouse Club, the Art Club, the Philadelphia Cricket Club, the Radnor Hunt, the Germantown Cricket Club (vice president), the Union League (president), and the Racquet Club (president).

In his acerbic look at Philadelphia society, *The Perennial Philadelphians: The Anatomy of an American Aristocracy*, Nathaniel Burt attributes Stotesbury's social reach to his not quite blue blood. Stotesbury, he writes, was "fairly definitely not an Old Philadelphian, despite a good old-fashioned semi-Quaker family and so his social row was harder to hoe than that of his predecessors."

It may be one reason why in 1887, the aspiring Stotesbury, still in his 30s, decided to join the Bachelors Barge Club, though not as a rower. He valued the camaraderie of the club on Boathouse Row, whose members were of the highest pedigree. Only a social member, the slim, jocular financier dined at the Bachelors' upriver club, the Button, with men with names like Burpee, Clothier, Lippincott, and Wyeth. There, members would address Stotesbury by his one-syllable nickname, a Bachelors tradition that continues today. Stotesbury, who had a quirky sense of humor, was "Brother Gum," perhaps deriving from a song he liked to sing about a shared family toothbrush, "all covered with slime."

Bachelors' use of nicknames was "a leveling" of the men's real-world status, explained Henry Hauptfuhrer, a member who has studied the club's history. "Once you walked in, you left behind your social standing."

One day in 1927, "Brother Gum," now 78, was approached by 32-year-old "Brother Loft"—high-flying rower Garrett Gilmore, who three years earlier had won Olympic silver in the single scull. Gilmore wanted to see a blossoming of schoolboy crew, which had so faded after the war. He asked Stotesbury to fund a silver trophy cup for a new eight-oared race on the Schuylkill.

Along with Gilmore, another Olympian, John B. Kelly Sr., was also trying to lure more teenagers into crew and had begun recruiting students at West Philadelphia Catholic High School for Boys to build bench strength for his club at the time, Penn AC.

Six weeks after the West Catholic boys began practicing with Penn AC's storied coach Frank Muller, its crew won the very first Stotesbury Cup race, on May 30, 1927. Its competitors did not include a single public

Garrett Gilmore, one of
the greatest racers of the
Bachelors Barge Club and the
Row, wins silver in the single
sculls in the 1924 Olympics
after edging out John B. Kelly
Sr. in the Olympic trials
(which is why Kelly competed
in a double that year).
Gilmore goes on to win gold
in the double sculls with Ken
Myers in 1932. Like Kelly,
Gilmore realizes that the
future of rowing lies with high
school youths and works to
create both the Stotesbury
Regatta and the Schoolboy
Rowing Association of
America. Its name changes
to the Scholastic Rowing
Association of America in
1976 after the addition of
women in 1974.

Courtesy of the Bachelors
Barge Club.

school. All were private or parochial: Germantown Academy, La Salle College High School, St. Joseph's Preparatory, and the former Brown Preparatory. Under Ned Stotesbury's rules for his Grecian vase–style silver
trophy, any school winning the race three times could keep it. Which is what West Philadelphia Catholic
immediately did. So Stotesbury bought a second silver cup, which West Philadelphia again retired. Buying a
third cup, Stotesbury insisted it henceforth be passed from winner to winner.

In 1935, Gilmore expanded the Stotesbury cup race into a full-fledged regatta, attracting a growing number
of high school crews from around the country. That year, too, he started the Schoolboy Rowing Association of

America, in which the top crews, determined in part by the Stotesbury Regatta, competed for national honors. (After the addition of girls in 1974, Schoolboy Rowing was renamed the Scholastic Rowing Association of America.)

Statistics from the Stotesbury show the growing popularity of high school crew. In 1945, 106 youths from six schools competed. By 1980, participation, now including girls, had grown tenfold, to 1,100 kids from 57 schools. In 2016, more than 5,700 students from 191 schools traveled to Philadelphia from around the United States and Canada, making the Stotesbury the largest high school regatta in the world. By then, 41 high schools in Philadelphia and its seven suburban counties were turning out for crew. Only one, however, was an individual Philadelphia public school—Boys Latin, a charter school.

As for the man behind the race, Ned Stotesbury, the Bachelors Barge Club elected him president in 1927, a post he held until his death in 1938 at age 89. The news of his passing brought the chatter at the city's private luncheon clubs to a halt as Philadelphia society paid tribute with a moment of silence. Police were called out to direct a mile-long line of traffic as the curious queued up to drive by palatial Whitemarsh Hall, and numerous dignitaries traveled in from New York and Washington, DC, for his funeral.

Yet, in the several days of front-page coverage of Edward T. Stotesbury's death and legacy, not a single mention was made of his half century of membership in the Bachelors Barge Club nor of the event named for him, the Stotesbury Cup Regatta.

———

Rowing was not anything that Tony Schneider had ever imagined for himself, if he ever thought of rowing at all. He was in his 50s when his daughter got into the sport at the private Shipley School in suburban Philadelphia. Her high school crew was racking up one victory after the next, and Schneider got caught up in her excitement.

The Vesper Boat Club welcomed Schneider in 2001, as part of a wave of active Baby Boomers discovering the sport. While Vesper's primary goal was to recruit young, talented rowers who might reclaim the club's fabled status, that cohort could not pay the bills. Rather, it cost the club money to support elite athletes aiming for international competition, with equipment and coaches. It also was seeking mature members such as Schneider to help fund desperately needed repairs and renovations.

THE CATHOLIC CURRENT

Private Catholic and archdiocesan high schools in the Philadelphia region boast champion crew organizations, in part because of efforts made by John B. Kelly Sr. and others to develop bench strength for Boathouse Row. Starting in the 1920s, they turned to students at such schools as West Philadelphia Catholic, Roman Catholic, and North Philadelphia Catholic, which opened in 1926 as Philadelphia's parochial school system was expanding to become the largest in the country. Many were the children of immigrants, driven to do whatever it took to succeed in a nation that had yet to overcome its Catholic antipathy.

"They had tremendous work ethic," explained Bill Lamb, crew coach from 1981 to 2001 at St. Joseph's Preparatory School, an elite private Jesuit school. "The values of rowing fit well into the values of Catholic education."

By the 1920s, Philadelphia's Catholic community had established its own hospitals, schools, business groups, athletic clubs, and more. They were a parallel universe to the Protestant majority, the result of a long history of anti-immigrant, anti-Catholic bigotry.

As Kelly's recruits from West Catholic High School graduated and continued training at Penn AC, the club almost overnight became an international juggernaut. From 1929 through 1931, its "Big Eight" crew was arguably the best on the planet, setting a world record along with winning three national championships, the Canadian championship, and 31 straight victories. Among the boys in the boat were West Catholic's Dan Barrow, who would go on to win singles bronze in the 1936 "Hitler Olympics;" John McNichol, who would later coach at West Catholic, Penn AC, and the 1936 Olympics; and Tom Curran, another Olympian who would coach La Salle College rowers to victory year after year in the 1950s and 1960s.

Restoring the Ranks

In the winter of 1945, John B. Kelly Sr. breaks up the ice at Penn AC, where he is coaching La Salle College High School students. The need for new recruits to rowing is especially acute after World War II, when boathouse membership plummets with the loss of so many men.

John Kelly and La Salle College Team Breaking the Ice. Historical Society of Pennsylvania.

So many Catholic kids were being turned on to the sport in high school, thanks to Kelly and his protégés and Garrett Gilmore's expanding School boy Rowing program, that colleges were feeling pressure to start crew programs. In 1946, La Salle became the second college in the Philadelphia area with a racing program. For nearly seven decades, the University of Pennsylvania alone had held that distinction. The Drexel Institute and St. Joseph's University had varsity crews by 1959, with George Mattson—West Catholic High's 1927 captain—playing a role in St. Joe's launch. Mattson, who rowed in Penn AC's coxless four in the 1932 Olympics (finishing fourth), coached at Monsignor Bonner High School from 1958 to 1970.

Kelly went beyond the Catholic community to be "very, very supportive of all youth rowing," said Lamb. "He also had the political savvy to recognize that this was a great way to make sure that Fairmount Park would be open to more than just the members of the clubs."

From "Big Eight" Rower to Coach

Charley McIlvaine, who garnered fame as a member of Penn AC's celebrated "Big Eight" of the early 1930s, coaches La Salle College High students in their first spring practice of 1947 in hopes of a repeat of the previous year, when La Salle's junior and senior varsity eights swept the Stotesbury. Sitting in the six seat (third from coxswain) is 17-year-old Bill Knecht, who will go on to become an Olympian in the 1964 Vesper Eight.

Philadelphia Evening Bulletin, Special Collections Research Center, Temple University Libraries, Philadelphia.

La Salle College High School, 2015

La Salle College High School rowers on their dock at the Crescent Boat Club finish up a practice. First established in 1918, La Salle's high school crew was revived in 1945 by Jack Kelly. Its boys' senior and junior crews both immediately won the Stotesbury in 1946, 1947, and 1948.

April Saul.

"I was not athletic. I'd never done anything like this in my life," said Schneider, a real estate developer who is founder and president of the Glenville Group, president of the Anti-Defamation League Foundation, and on non-profit boards from the Philadelphia Mural Arts Program to the Wistar Institute.

Schneider was starstruck. He could not believe he was sharing the locker room with elite rowers training for international races. Timid at first, he quickly found contagious their passion for hard work, excellence, and the heady excitement of racing. He began to share their dream as he, too, began competing in—and to his shock, winning—masters races. In 2006, racing in his single scull, he won first place in the masters world championship in his 55–59 age category.

And then he had another dream: Was there a way to combine his new passion for rowing with his long-standing concern about what he calls the "under education of urban youth"? Despite all the kids he saw on the river, he was dismayed by the absence of Philadelphia public and charter school children. Maybe the rigors of rowing, the teamwork it demands, and the self-discipline it inspires could help direct the lives of some at-risk children.

After World War II, Philadelphia public school youths had only occasionally had crew programs, usually when one of the selective schools, Central High or Masterman, had a swell of interest. Even some of Philadelphia's archdiocesan high schools, which had produced champions in the early days of the Stotesbury, had abandoned crew as their demographics underwent a seismic shift.

Brother Tim Ahern, a former athletic director and president of West Catholic, watched its legendary crew program wither during his tenure from 1971 to 2012 as the student population, once mostly Irish, Polish, Italian, and German, became increasingly African American, Latino, and Asian American. At the same time, other sports such as basketball thrived. Contributing to the disappearance of crew, Ahern said, was its expense as well as its "upper-class Ivy League image, similar to golf and tennis—sports which students are not exposed to." In 2007, Brother Tim tried to restart crew, but the allure was alien to West Catholic's 21st-century student body. Plus, he said, few of the 15 students who showed up knew how to swim.

Excitement about crew had migrated to the suburbs, moving out with families who had left the city. Almost immediately after the Archdiocese of Philadelphia in 1953 built Archbishop Prendergast High School to meet the demands of newly suburban Catholic families, a parent advocate, Manuel A. Flick, organized a crew program for the school. Soon, he expanded it to an area-wide weekly regatta, the Manny Flicks, to assure high school kids had enough opportunities to race.

With only a handful of races geared to high school students—including the Stotesbury, the City Championships, and the scholastic nationals—the Flicks were "a chance for the kids to do scrimmage racing," said Paul Horvat, who raced for St. Joseph's Prep in the 1970s. At the time, more and more suburban high schools—public, private, and parochial—were offering crew and transporting their students to the Schuylkill to train. He could not help but get involved. His father, Don Horvat, a former Olympian for Yugoslavia, was committed to youth rowing, and the Flicks would be renamed the Manny Flicks/Horvat Series.

**College-bound:
St. Joe's Prep Rowers**

High school seniors rowing crew at St. Joseph's Preparatory in 2006 wear the T-shirts of the colleges that they will be attending, almost all in the Ivy League. Their coach, Bill Lamb, says parents open their wallets for crew, knowing the benefits it may have for their children. Gaining an advantage for college admissions is one reason crew flourished early on among the Catholic schools.

Courtesy of Bill Lamb.

The wave of interest became a torrent when high school girls began pouring into the sport after the passage of Title IX in 1972, which barred schools receiving federal dollars from discriminating based on sex. In the era of women's lib, with a new aesthetic that appreciated independent, determined, and physically strong women, high school girls relished proving themselves in this once all-male universe.

Savvy parents were also encouraging their children to take up crew, having discovered that colleges were rewarding rowers with preferential admissions, if not scholarships. They were also opening their wallets. "Parents started to see opportunities," said Bill Lamb, for many years the crew coach at St. Joseph's Preparatory. "'My kid's really good; he can go to Penn instead of St. Joe's; he can go to Harvard instead of Georgetown.' All of a sudden parents were, 'What do we need to be really good? We need new boats? Here's some money, go buy a boat.' Here's what I learned in 30 years of coaching high school kids: I don't care if a parent has means. I don't care if a parent's on food stamps. If they feel or perceive that they can create an advantage for their child by writing a check, they will write the check."

Where once the boathouses supported high school rowing, now the high schools—and parents—were supporting the cash-poor boathouses. Not only were the clubs struggling to pay for major long-deferred repairs, but the once all-male clubs were also seeking funds to renovate their locker rooms to accommodate the influx of women. More and more colleges and high schools began paying the clubs for a place to house their crew programs, something the Philadelphia School District could not afford.

Lamb recalled roughly what it cost St. Joe's Prep to row out of Penn AC in 2000: about $25,000 a year in rent, plus $100 for every student. With 120 students rowing, that meant another $7,000. Plus $1,000 for every boat rack it used—another $12,000. "And that's before we ever put gas in the launch, paid a coach, or bought a boat," he said; which is one reason why St. Joseph's University and "the Prep" in 2002 built their own facility, the Gillin Boathouse, about a mile upriver from the Row.

This was largely the picture of high school rowing that Tony Schneider saw as he began pondering ways to bring crew to youths in Philadelphia's underperforming, underfunded schools. Investigating what had been tried before, he learned of the well-meaning initiatives that Boathouse Row had undertaken over the years. Most had come and gone, plagued by insufficient capital and insufficient participation.

In the early 1970s, Chuck Colgan started a summer camp, called Dimensions, for children from low-income families. It was one of a number of initiatives he tried, to open crew to minorities and the disabled, earning him recognition by USRowing. John B. Kelly III had worked with Benjamin Franklin High School for a while. The Malta Boat Club coached students from a neighboring parochial school. Various boathouses had offered, and were still offering, summer learn-to-row programs for students, though not all were free. Even the Philadelphia School District, under Superintendent Paul Vallas in the early 2000s, had tried to get crew underway but had been stymied by union issues around coaching, among other obstacles.

Then Schneider learned about Row New York, a program in New York City that was transforming the lives of teenagers through rowing combined with a lot of academic support. Why not try something like that here? Schneider thought. He quickly discovered elite coach and rower Libby Peters, who had medaled in North American and international races; she was similarly passionate about the possibility of an urban crew program.

They approached city officials to see if they could wrangle space on the Row and an agreement with schools and the teachers union. Philadelphia, which had long-standing concerns about the private clubs' monopoly of Boathouse Row, was eager to collaborate. The school district gave Schneider and Peters used boats and oars, which it had bought from Princeton University and kept in storage since the Vallas years.

An early thought of situating PCR downstream at Bartram Gardens was quashed, said Robert B. Coleman, then the school district's executive director of athletics. "I kept seeing it as the back of the bus. We were so far past this." Instead, the Fairmount Park Commission turned over to PCR a narrow slice of land between Lloyd Hall and the Fairmount Rowing Association, at #2 Boathouse Row. And the district cut through its own red tape. "We started doing what was right for the kids," Coleman said.

PCR began slowly in 2010, with Peters recruiting students and coaches. "There was no road map," Schneider said. "We were creating all the relationships." The money for its tiny paid staff, office rent, and expenses came almost entirely from Schneider and three loyal friends. The clubs on the Row offered little financially, he said, but were welcoming and helpful with facilities. Volunteers stepped up to coach the novice rowers

One of Many Efforts

Dimensions, a summer program started in the early 1970s by coach and Vesper member Chuck Colgan, encourages students from Germantown, East Falls, South Philadelphia, West Oak Lane, and West Philadelphia to learn to row. It ends after a few years. Later, Colgan laments to the *Philadelphia Inquirer*, "There's not two dozen black rowers on Boathouse Row. It's a shame. I think it's obvious that we have to do something."

Philadelphia Evening Bulletin, July 1971, Special Collections Research Center, Temple University Libraries, Philadelphia.

Tony Schneider: Sharing His Passion

Tony Schneider, a generous supporter of programs that can change the lives of at-risk youth, hangs at the dock of Philadelphia City Rowing with some of its high school students. Schneider was inspired to bring rowing to urban youth by his daughter, who became enamored of rowing at the private suburban Shipley School.

April Saul.

and tutor them when needed. By 2016, the program had expanded exponentially to 80 students from two dozen high schools and another 48 students from 19 middle schools, who were also getting swimming lessons. Almost every afternoon and Saturdays, spring and fall, they practiced on the river, competing in the Flicks against the private and Archdiocesan schools and suburban publics. In winter, they worked out with weights and on rowing machines. All the participants were graduating high school, and virtually all were going on to college.

PCR's success began attracting some grant money, critical to its survival. Its presence also has prompted scholastic rowing organizations to rethink their age-old rules, which limit competition to individual high

PCR Rower Jacob Harris

Jacob Harris, 15, who has little social contact with other youths in his Philadelphia cyber high school, enjoys the team aspect of rowing, where "it's nice to know what you're doing helps the team." But, he says, "you have to commit to it. It motivates you. You have to get your work done so you can row." Also, "It hurts a lot. It's singlehandedly the most painful sport. You have to be mentally prepared for pain."

April Saul.

A Moment of Mirth

Laughter overtakes a crew from Philadelphia City Rowing as they prepare for a row on the Schuylkill River. In 2016, PCR for the first time received permission to row in the Stotesbury Regatta. Despite the rigorous workouts and practices, or perhaps because of them, the students who stick with it are thriving, and virtually all go on to college.

April Saul.

school crews. On the one hand, because PCR rowers come from many schools within the school district—a potentially large talent pool—it could have an unfair advantage, went the argument against rule change. On the other hand, it seemed unfair to bar from competition children whose individual schools could not afford the sport. In 2016, both the Schuylkill Navy, which runs the Stotesbury Regatta and the Philadelphia Scholastic Rowing Association (with about 75 member high schools), which runs the City Championships, gave PCR an "exception," allowing its students to race as the groups undertook a review of their rules.

Schneider, board chairman of PCR, while negotiating to get his rowers full standing in those meets, had a broader vision of its purpose.

"Winning medals in races is something we would love to do but it's a byproduct. It's a byproduct of helping kids change their lives. It's a byproduct of kids understanding that they have to commit themselves to something. And they do, because a lot of the kids are lost. . . . And it's a place for them to feel wanted."

Philadelphia Public School students row home past Sedgeley and the lighthouse.

April Saul.

———

As he dug in to meet the program's demands, Daekwon Smith discovered that he had a wellspring of resilience and a new willingness to look beyond himself. "I find myself able to push through things easier simply because our coaches build you up so that no matter what you're doing, you can't give up. So I have translated that into other efforts in my life," he said.

When he is "annoyed at home," helping out with his younger siblings, or bored at his fast-food job and wanting to leave, he thinks about being on the river with his crew. "If we're doing a 2K and you're halfway through it, I can't think, 'Okay, I'm tired, I'm done,' and let go of the oar. You have to finish. If I'm on the water with my teammates, they depend on me. I can't just screw them over because I'm tired."

The total concentration needed for rowing temporarily frees him from the worries of his life. "If I'm having a bad day at home or at work or at school, once I'm on the water, nothing else matters. I don't have my phone. I'm not around the people I have problems with. You're in the middle of the river. All I have to worry about is the next stroke, and that's the greatest part."

He feels he has grown socially, working so intensely with teenagers from all over the city. "I just had to learn to adapt with how people are, for who they are and go on about it."

Daekwon hopes his enthusiasm can infect others in a city bounded by a river that can seem so distant. "You can't get involved with something if you don't know what it is," he said. "The only way for anything to grow is for more people to get involved, because if the same people or the same type of people keep rowing, it's only going to keep that cycle going."

EPILOGUE

In the research and writing of this book, I have been haunted by a coincidence so strange and otherworldly that I must share the story.

It starts in the year 1900, when my great-grandfather, a doctor in Vienna, Austria, received a gift—a large, ornate silver bowl—from "a grateful American patient." That is all my mother knew about this "presentation bowl" when she gave it to me several decades ago.

Turning it over at the time, I was dumbstruck to find the mark of Bailey, Banks and Biddle, the venerable jewelry firm dating from 1832. Imagine: a bowl that is crafted in Philadelphia, shipped to Vienna at the turn of the last century, carried during World War II by emigres to New York, only by sheer coincidence returns to its place of origin!

I was dumbstruck.

So, who was this grateful patient? The engraving read, "from Mrs. Fairman Rogers." I quickly learned that my great-grandfather's patient was not Mrs. Fairman Rogers, but likely her husband, who died in Vienna on August 22, 1900, presumably well cared for—or why else would his widow have sent such a magnificent thank you?

If the bowl's return to Philadelphia was not coincidence enough, another struck years later when editor Micah Kleit of Temple University Press approached me with the idea for this book. While researching the history of Boathouse Row, I discovered that Fairman Rogers was a patron of Thomas Eakins and Frank Furness, both of whom figure prominently in its story.

Rogers was a Renaissance man of 19th-century Philadelphia—the chair of engineering at the University of Pennsylvania, on the boards of Jefferson Medical College and the Pennsylvania Academy of the Fine Arts (PAFA), a founder of the Union League and more. As the head of the building committee for PAFA, in 1871 he selected the young avant-garde architect, Frank Furness, to design it. (It also did not hurt that Furness' brother, Horace, was married to Rogers' sister.) Later, Furness would design the most eclectic boathouse on the Row—the Undine Barge Club.

Rogers was also connected to Thomas Eakins, whose realism was grounded in his studies of perspective and anatomy. This led Rogers to recruit Eakins in 1876 to teach at PAFA (though by the time Eakins scandalized Philadelphia by exposing female students to a nude male model, Rogers had left the PAFA board).

Eakins and Rogers, an avid equestrian and coachman, also shared an interest in the potential of early cameras to capture motion. In his rowing series, Eakins had broken new ground in his efforts to depict motion on canvas. Both Eakins and Rogers corresponded with photographer Eadweard Muybridge in California, who was trying to prove what was unseen to the naked eye—that a running horse momentarily lifts all four legs off the ground. Eakins used Muybridge's insights in his painting *The Fairman Rogers Four-in-Hand*, which hangs in the Philadelphia Museum of Art.

Although Viennese newspapers noted Rogers' death in Vienna, at age 62, I have not been able to learn more about what prompted the gift of a costly silver bowl. But the thought that, once upon a time, my great-grandfather in Vienna held the hand and touched the brow of a man who so unexpectedly I have come to know still gives me shivers.

THE SCHUYLKILL NAVY AND
THE CLUBS OF BOATHOUSE ROW

The Schuylkill Navy

Among Philadelphia's many milestones of history is the formation of the nation's first amateur athletic governing organization: the Schuylkill Navy. Nine boat clubs banded together on October 5, 1858, to create an association one might regard as the United Nations of Boathouse Row. Its purpose then, and now, was to mediate disputes between the clubs, protect and pursue the clubs' shared interests, organize regattas, and set rules of conduct.

Most urgently, the Schuylkill Navy was determined to make sure that the sport of rowing maintained the standards of amateur competition at a time when the high-stakes gambling and foul play of professional races threatened to sully the noble sport.

Its initial rules defined an amateur oarsman as someone who does not race for money, whether it be a "stake," or "admission money" and who does not compete "with or against a professional for any prize." It even barred paid coaches from consideration as amateurs, a rule that was eliminated over time. Fourteen years later, rules of the new National Association of Amateur Oarsmen (now USRowing) mirrored the Schuylkill Navy's amateur definition.

Besides setting amateur standards, the Schuylkill Navy—made up of representatives of each boat club—organized annual pageants and regattas on the river, with huge crowds turning out to watch the club boats parade in formation and

FRANK LESLIE'S
ILLUSTRATED
NEWSPAPER

Entered according to the Act of Congress, in the year 1878, by FRANK LESLIE, in the Office of the Librarian of Congress at Washington.

No. 1,180—Vol. XLVI.]   NEW YORK, MAY 11, 1878.   [PRICE 10 CENTS. $4.00 YEARLY. 13 WEEKS, $1.50.

PENNSYLVANIA.—PRESIDENT HAYES AND MEMBERS OF HIS FAMILY AND CABINET ATTENDING A REVIEW OF THE SCHUYLKILL NAVY AT PHILADELPHIA, APRIL 24TH.—SEE PAGE 167.

A Dire Need to Dredge, 1934

With silt constantly accumulating above the Fairmount Dam, a critical and ongoing mission of the Schuylkill Navy is to lobby for dredging. In 1934, the area just above the dam appears to be more mud than water. Dredging in 1953 restored Peter's Island (above Girard Avenue Bridge), which had become attached to the river's west bank. The Schuylkill was dredged again in 1969 and again in 1990, when the depth of the river along Boathouse Row docks was just six inches. In 2016, silt had again piled up, threatening the ability of some clubs to launch boats.

Schuylkill River, March 27, 1934. Philadelphia Evening Bulletin, Special Collections Research Center, Temple University Libraries, Philadelphia.

Saluting the Commander-in-Chief

Besides setting amateur standards for the clubs on Boathouse Row, the Schuylkill Navy, from its very start in 1858, held regular Navy Reviews, with the clubs parading on the river in full dress code. On April 24, 1878, at 6:00 P.M., the Navy saluted U.S. President Rutherford Hayes.

President Hayes and Members of His Family and Cabinet Attending a Review of the Schuylkill Navy at Philadelphia, May 11, 1878. Leslie's Illustrated Newspaper, The Library Company of Philadelphia.

race one another. It still organizes four regattas on the Schuylkill: the Stotesbury Cup Regatta, the largest high school regatta in the world, with over 5,700 rowers; the Schuylkill Navy Regatta, one of the oldest regattas for clubs, high school youth, college students, and elite rowers; the Independence Day Regatta, the country's largest summer club regatta (called the People's Regatta until its name was changed over 1950s era concerns about a communist-sounding label); and the Philadelphia Youth Regatta, which culminates summer rowing programs for high school rowers. The Schuylkill Navy also supports other regattas, including the collegiate Dad Vail, Head of the Schuylkill, and the Navy Day Regatta.

The regattas, which put a spotlight on Philadelphia and bring revenue to the city, require the involvement of hundreds of volunteers and collaboration with city departments to facilitate parking, traffic, vendors, and more.

One argument the Schuylkill Navy has consistently made on behalf of the clubs is to keep large motorized vessels off the river in the three-mile stretch between Boathouse Row and the Falls Bridge. In the 19th century, steamboats and other large-wake boats would swamp the fragile, unstable sculls. The clubs have long maintained logbooks to record the daily mileage of each rower as proof of their utilization of the river.

A critical, ongoing concern has been the silt that accumulates above Fairmount Dam. Every 10 or 20 years, when the river becomes so shallow that some clubs can barely launch and racing lanes are threatened, the Schuylkill Navy must lobby for costly funding to dredge. "There's no permanent solution," said Margaret Meigs, former commodore of the Schuylkill Navy. "The river wants to silt."

A goal of the Schuylkill Navy is to open up rowing to more people, especially the young. As early as the 1930s, it began supporting what was known as "schoolboy rowing" and youth regattas. More recently, in negotiations with the School District of Philadelphia, the boat clubs, and Fairmount Park, it found space on tightly packed Boathouse Row near Lloyd Hall for city youths to row. Philadelphia City Rowing, a non-profit, coaches more than 140 students a year from Philadelphia public and charter schools.

Construction of a community boathouse is another goal. The city lost a public place to row when Plaisted Hall was declared a hazard and closed in 1994. Today, the Schuylkill Navy and others are once again trying to site and fund a public boathouse for Philadelphia, something other cities on rivers offer their residents.

Lloyd Hall

#1 Boathouse Row

Although the address of Lloyd Hall places it on Boathouse Row, it does not have facilities for rowing. Lloyd Hall stands on the former site of Plaisted Hall, which used to offer the public a place to row. Plaisted Hall, built in 1881 and condemned in the early 1990s, was named for Fred Plaisted, a talented professional rower who later coached on the Row. In 1998, Philadelphia built Lloyd Hall, with a café, public basketball courts, and other recreational activities.

Lloyd Hall, built in 1998, replaces what was once a public boathouse with other public facilities, including a basketball court. Outside, adjacent to its café, is a prefab boathouse and a dock that are the home of Philadelphia City Rowing, a nonprofit which engages Philadelphia public and charter school students in the sport of rowing.

April Saul.

Fairmount Rowing Association

#2 and #3 Boathouse Row

The Fairmount club was started in 1877 by a group of men who carried their heavy boat from their Fairmount neighborhood six blocks to the river. In 1881, Fairmount acquired the Pacific Barge Club's half of one of the oldest buildings on the Row at #2 Boathouse Row. In 1904, it won permission from Fairmount Park to replace that stone building with a Georgian Revival boathouse built in Flemish bond brick style, unlike anything on the strip. In the 1930s, as the adjacent Quaker City Barge Club became inactive, Fairmount absorbed it as well, thus merging one of the oldest buildings on the Row into the newest.

The Fairmount Rowing Association occupies both halves of one of the first stone houses built on Boathouse Row in 1860–1961; the original structure, on the right, is overshadowed by the 1904 construction.

All in the Family

Amerigo Sonzogni, 74, a retired tile layer, takes his daily six-mile row along the Schuylkill River in 1986. He began rowing in 1930 with his brothers, who all lived in the Fairmount section and all worked with their hands. In 1941 and 1947, Amerigo teamed up to win the national lightweight doubles championship.

Michael Mercanti/*Philadelphia Daily News.*

Fairmount has long regarded itself as a club of blue-collar men, and its minutes from the turn of the century support that, with membership including a carpenter, blacksmith, brew master, bricklayer, weaver, electrician, machinist, and linotype operator. It admitted women in the 1990s.

Over the years, the club has won many national championships. Single sculler James Castellan represented the United States in the 1976 Olympics. In 1996, Teresa Z. Bell won an Olympic silver medal in the lightweight women's double.

Today, Fairmount has a strong, competitive masters program and hosts the Quaker City Masters Regatta, drawing hundreds of rowers aged 21 and over, from the mid-Atlantic region. Fairmount also encourages junior rowers through its high school summer program. Year-round, it hosts the rowing programs of La Salle University, Episcopal Academy, and the Wharton Graduate Association.

Pennsylvania Barge Club

#4 Boathouse Row

Within a decade of its founding in 1861, the Pennsylvania Barge Club was basking in the victories of rower Max Schmitt, famously painted by Thomas Eakins in *The Champion Single Sculls*, now hanging at New York's Metropolitan Museum of Art. Eakins himself had a close association with the club. Pennsylvania Barge was among the most competitive racing clubs in the country during the 1920s, sending rowers to each Olympics between 1920 and 1932, and returning with six medals. Among them was Ernest Bayer, who won silver in 1928 in the four without cox. His wife, Ernestine Bayer, later founded the Philadelphia Girls' Rowing Club.

Faltering from the loss of members in World War II and the Korean War, the Pennsylvania Barge Club ceased as a rowing club in 1955 and leased its house to the Schuylkill Navy, the National Association of Amateur Oarsmen (now USRowing), the Dad Vail, and other rowing organizations. It also renamed #4 Boathouse Row "Hollenback House" for the former president of U.S. Rowing, William M. Hollenback Jr.

But unwilling to let a storied boat club fade into history, a half century later, in 2008, the club began rebuilding membership and raising money to rescue the historic boathouse. Today the Pennsylvania Barge Club is once again humming with active rowers who compete in regattas such as the Head of the Charles as well as national and international masters competitions. Each November the club sponsors the Philadelphia Frostbite Regatta.

Its spacious, renovated boathouse is also home to the Adaptive Rowing Association and La Salle College High School. The Schuylkill Navy meets monthly in its elegant boardroom.

The Pennsylvania Barge Club, with its major 2009 renovation and reinvigorated rowing program, is also the meeting venue for the Schuylkill Navy and home to the Philadelphia Adaptive Rowing, the oldest rowing program for disabled athletes in the country. In 2008, adaptive rowing was included in the Paralympics for the first time.

April Saul.

Crescent Boat Club

#5 Boathouse Row

The merger of the Iona and Pickwick barge clubs in 1867 gave birth to the Crescent Boat Club. It immediately built a stone boathouse with the Pennsylvania Barge Club. Each club occupied half the structure. In 1871, Crescent expanded its boathouse from two boat bays to three, innovatively using steel beams to span the bay. It also decided to place its entrance off center in an effort to be more picturesque than earlier boathouses. Twenty years later, Philadelphia architect Charles Balderston added Victorian Gothic details while raising the roof and building a fourth boat bay.

The club remained competitive until World War II, after which it was hard hit by declining membership. In 1951, it turned its building over to one of the strongest collegiate rowing organizations of the time—the La Salle (College) Rowing Association, which stayed until 1960. Under the leadership of John Wilkins, whose wife was a founder of Philadelphia Girls' Rowing Club, it reclaimed the house and in the late 1970s began rebuilding membership as well as restoring the much deteriorated boathouse. "The third-floor wall facing the river is bulging so much that it feels as if the entire wall is about to heave out. The sky is visible through sections of the rotting roof. Ceilings on the second and third floor are falling in," the *Philadelphia Inquirer* reported on October 4, 1988.

Since then, the building has been restored and reinvigorated through novice, junior, and masters rowing programs. The Crescent Boat Club hosts crew programs from Roman Catholic High School and Archbishop Prendergast.

Bachelors Barge Club

#6 Boathouse Row

Formed in 1853 and today the oldest rowing club in continual existence in the United States, the Bachelors Barge Club is rich in tradition. It initially required that all new members be bachelors; once married, they lost voting rights. Each initiate would get a single syllable nickname in a naming ceremony, a ritual that continues today. And members still gather regularly for dinners at their upriver social house in East Falls, the Button, dating from 1883.

The Crescent Boat Club (right) was constructed in conjunction with the Pennsylvania Barge Club in 1869–1871. Crescent added a second story in 1891. After difficult post–World War II years, the club regrouped, placing a focus on youth rowing.

The Bachelors Barge Club is the oldest continually operating rowing club in the United States, though it has gone through a succession of buildings. Its current house was built in 1893 by Samuel Huckel and Edward Hazelhurst, who had worked in Frank Furness' studio.

While the club is old, its current boathouse, built in 1893, broke new ground architecturally. After decades of insisting that the boathouses be built of stone, the Fairmount Park Commission approved Bachelors' plans to rebuild in brick. Bachelors boathouse is easily distinguished by its wide Italianate balcony facing Kelly Drive.

Among its most noteworthy rowers was W. E. Garrett Gilmore who, in 1932, with Kenneth Myers, won Olympic gold in the double sculls. Dozens of Gilmore's trophies are displayed in Bachelors' boathouse. But a more lasting legacy is the result of his dedication to youth rowing. With the backing of longtime club member and president Edward T. Stotesbury, Gilmore turned a single cup race into the largest high school competition in the world, the Stotesbury Regatta.

Today, Bachelors prides itself on being an incubator for new rowers, offering learn-to-row classes to anyone interested. Drexel University's crew became the club's lead tenant in 2008.

University Barge Club
#7 and #8 Boathouse Row

Tired of renting boats for jaunts on the Schuylkill River, a group of University of Pennsylvania undergraduates banded together in 1854 to form the University Barge Club (UBC). It shared an early boathouse with the former Philadelphia Barge Club, and in 1870, the two clubs constructed a double boathouse at #7 and #8 Boathouse Row, with a distinctive green serpentine stone, echoing a material also used in College Hall on the Penn campus. During the Depression, UBC absorbed the Philadelphia Barge Club and now occupies both sides of the double boathouse.

UBC founder John Thayer, on the club's 50th anniversary, described UBC as "the dawn of organized athletics" at the University of Pennsylvania. However, in 1872, a new generation of Penn undergraduates formed the College Boat Club at #11 Boathouse Row, which is Penn's competitive boathouse.

UBC is responsible for creating the Thomas Eakins Head of the Schuylkill Regatta, one of the largest rowing events in the country, open to anyone from novice to Olympian. The idea started small in 1968, when a group of club rowers who had graduated from college, seeking more opportunities to compete, established the Graduate Sculls Regatta. Now called the Head of the Schuylkill, it is still largely run by volunteer UBC

The University Barge Club proudly touts its role as the founder of the Head of the Schuylkill Regatta. If the house looks like a twin, it is, having started out as home as well to the long defunct Philadelphia Rowing Club. UBC now occupies the entire structure, built in 1870 using an unusual green serpentine stone.

April Saul.

TLC at UBC

UBC officer, rower, coach, and skilled craftsman Bruce LaLonde repairs a wooden racing shell in the club's boathouse workshop. His is a dying art. Today's boats, more often built of tougher, synthetic materials that require less maintenance, have facilitated the explosion of collegiate and high school rowing.

members. The two-day event brings more that 8,000 competitors to the Schuylkill for a weekend each October. It also features a $10,000 elite "Gold Cup" race.

UBC's boathouse has undergone several renovations. In 1990, it reconfigured its locker rooms to make room for women. Both boys and girls at Springside Chestnut Hill Academy row from UBC. The club, said President Bart Isdaner, seeks to provide "a congenial environment" for masters rowers "bound together by ties of friendship and a love of the river."

Malta Boat Club

#9 Boathouse Row

The Malta Boat Club, founded in 1860, is the only club on Boathouse Row to start out on the Delaware River. Its original seven members belonged to the Minnehaha Lodge of the Sons of the Knights of Malta, from which the club derives its name, though the only remaining connection is the white Maltese cross on the blades of its blue oars. Four of the original members were Illmans, a family that owned the largest printing plant in the country.

Malta moved to George Popps' Park Boat House, a floating rental facility on the Schuylkill in 1863 and two years later to its current site, having bought the house of the Excelsior Boat Club. Malta and the Vesper Boat Club together built a double house in 1873, though the clubs soon went their separate ways architecturally. In 1901, George and William Hewitt, disciples of Frank Furness, took a cue from city architecture and raised Malta up to three stories, the tallest on the Row. Also distinguishing Malta is its decision to remain the Row's only all-male club. (Philadelphia Girls' Rowing Club is all women.)

Malta has traditionally been a club of scullers. Its current focus is to provide access and support for its members to the sport of rowing across the spectrum of their lives, from juniors to masters rowers. It starts the process early, supporting a learn-to-row program for the children at St. Francis Xavier School in Fairmount, often succeeding in bolstering the students' academics and attitudes.

Malta also hosts rowers from Father Judge High School in Philadelphia as well as a girls' crew from Merion Mercy Academy.

Vesper Boat Club

#10 Boathouse Row

If there is one club on Boathouse Row whose name is known internationally, it is the Vesper Boat Club, the only private boat club in the nation to win gold in three Olympics with its eight-oared crew: 1900, 1904, and 1964. Its 1964 victory was the last time any eight-oared private club crew has represented the United States in an Olympics; rowers are now chosen at a national camp, mashing up the best rowers in the country.

The Malta Boat Club remains the only all-male club on Boathouse Row. Its third-story addition, by former Furness architects George and William Hewitt, also makes it the largest. Barely visible on the right is its adjoining neighbor, Vesper.

April Saul.

The Vesper Boat Club boathouse was built in 1873 along with Malta, but each has developed its own personality and architectural character over the last 150 years. Vesper's focus has long been to train athletes for national and international competition.

Vesper, dating from 1865, prides itself on its racing tradition, and two of its rowers so distinguished themselves that their names have become part of the landscape of the river: John B. Kelly Sr., a statue of whom is positioned near the grandstands, and his son, John B. Kelly Jr., for whom Kelly Drive is named.

In the late 1960s, Vesper was among the first all-men's clubs on the Row to admit women, and they have thrived there. In Montreal in 1976, the first Olympics with women's rowing events, six of the women on the U.S. team were from Vesper.

In recent years, Vesper has developed a collaborative approach with other clubs on Boathouse Row to train elite rowers for national and international competition, including the 2016 olympics. The hope is not only to support individual athletes but also to assure that Boathouse Row remains a destination for national talent. At the same time, its masters rowers compete internationally.

The club has long recognized the importance of attracting high school rowers to the sport, dating back to World War II, when it nurtured crew at La Salle College High School, among others. More recently Vesper members have offered leadership to the newest city youth rowing organization, PCR, along with a variety of learn-to-row programs. It also seeks to support needs of the broader community and opens its boathouse to several non-profits for fundraising activities. For these kinds of efforts, the Vesper Boat Club in 2014 was named USRowing "Club of the Year."

College Boat Club of the University of Pennsylvania

#11 Boathouse Row

The University of Pennsylvania rows out of what is historically called the College Boat Club. The club was formed by a small group of underclassmen in 1872 at a time when most Ivy League schools were already competing in crew. Sports were not yet supported by Penn, and students sought help from alumni to build a boathouse and to buy boats and equipment.

The start of Penn's crew may have been slow, but it caught up fast. In 1879, it won its first intercollegiate regatta, defeating Princeton and Columbia. Over the years, under a series of dynamic coaches, including Ellis Ward, Rusty Callow, Joe Burk, Ted Nash, and Stan Bergman, its elite rowers have routinely competed at an international level. For instance, between 1936 and 2012, Penn rowers represented the United States in every Olympics with the exception of one year, 2004.

Like virtually all the boathouses on the Row, the College Boat Club quickly outgrew its original structure, though when it was built in 1874, it had the most spacious boat room on the Row and a trend-setting upstairs lounge. Where once it had one large boat bay, by 1920 it had three; today it has four.

Penn women in the 1930s got a shot at intramural crew, but it was only in the early 1970s that the university began training women for intercollegiate competition.

The College Boat Club was built by University of Pennsylvania students in 1874–1875, producing one of the most luxurious boathouses of its time, though demand for additional boat bays prompted expansions that now dominate the original structure. In a father–son story largely unknown on Boathouse Row, the College Boat Club was started by Penn undergraduate Effingham Morris, a generation after his father, Israel W. Morris, founded the Bachelors Barge Club.

April Saul.

Penn AC, as it is widely known, initially got its start in 1924, when a downtown athletic club of the same name took over what was formerly the West Philadelphia Boat Club. In part to accommodate space for women, in recent decades the once all-male club added a very un-Victorian utilitarian wing (white addition). It was built by its own members, some of whom are in the construction trades.

April Saul.

Architectural historian James O'Gorman calls the northwestern wall of the Undine Barge Club "one of the most memorable vignettes in 19th-century American architecture." He points to its "plant like chimney," rubble stone wall, and wooden balconies accented by double eave gutters. The building, designed by Frank Furness, satisfied Undine's two major needs: a massive utilitarian space for boats and a gracious parlor upstairs for entertaining.

Pennsylvania Athletic Club (Penn AC)

#12 Boathouse Row

The roots of the Pennsylvania Athletic Club Rowing Association, known as Penn AC, go back to 1871, when a group of men from West Philadelphia started a club below the Fairmount Dam at Grays Ferry. The West Philadelphia Boat Club struggled to raise money to build on Boathouse Row, which they did in 1878. The new boathouse's second-floor covered porch, which looks out onto the river, was a first for the Row, adding a social element where members could relax and take in the boating scene.

In 1924, the Pennsylvania Athletic Club, based on Rittenhouse Square, sought to have a rowing venue and, offering investment, merged with West Philadelphia, changing the boat club's name. John B. Kelly Sr., disgruntled with the Vesper Boat Club, was a leader in that transaction. Penn AC, with Kelly on board, quickly became one of the most competitive clubs on Boathouse Row. Its "Big Eight" won 31 straight victories from 1929 to 1931. Among those who trained at Penn AC was Joe Burk, Philadelphia's national rowing phenomenon of the late 1930s.

Although Kelly abandoned Penn AC for the Vesper Boat Club during World War II, Penn AC rebounded in the 1980s and has continued to attract highly competitive rowers and coaches, including Mike Teti and Ted Nash, who both have coached U.S. rowing teams at numerous Olympics.

To accommodate its growing membership, in the 1960s Penn AC expanded with an unimaginative addition, adding women's lockers and boat bays. Today, its focus remains on competition, sending elite rowers to international competitions while training youth to follow in their stead.

Undine Barge Club

#13 Boathouse Row

Designed by Frank Furness in 1882, the Undine Barge Club, with its many balconies, turrets, and playful use of geometric forms, is architecturally the most dramatic on Boathouse Row. But the club itself predates the building by decades. Undine, among the earliest clubs still active on the Row, was formed in 1856 with the object of "healthful exercise, relaxation from business, friendly intercourse, and pleasure."

It quickly adopted an elaborate uniform, typical of the clubs of the time: a red shirt trimmed with blue, black pants, white belt, and straw hat for summer with "Undine" in gilt letters on a black ribbon.

In 1875, Undine hired Frank Furness to design Castle Ringstetten, a social clubhouse in East Falls, thus beginning a trend among the boathouses to build similar upriver cottages for rowing destinations and dinners. (Two of those remain in use today along Kelly Drive just above the Falls Bridge—the Castle and Bachelors Barge Club's "Button.")

After a century of hard use, Undine's boathouse underwent a major renovation in the late 1990s with the help of foundation funding and experts familiar with Furness' work. The club is proud not only of the architecture it has preserved, but also of its tradition of producing competitive rowers at every level—scholastic, junior, elite, and masters—many of whom have gone on to national and Olympic titles.

Philadelphia Girls' Rowing Club

#14 Boathouse Row

The Philadelphia Girls' Rowing Club (PGRC) is the oldest continuously competitive women's rowing club in the nation, occupying one of the Row's oldest buildings—the Philadelphia Skating Club, completed in 1861.

It is also the newest rowing club on Boathouse Row, finally breaking into the once all-male venue in 1938. After its launch by a group of bookkeepers and secretaries, PGRC began a many-decades campaign to win recognition of women's crew on the national and international levels. Among them was Joanne Iverson, an organizer of the National Women's Rowing Association, which in 1963 set a framework for women's rowing meets. (It is now part of USRowing.) A major breakthrough took place in 1967, when a crew from PGRC competed in Vichy, France, as the first women to represent the United States in European competition. In 1984, PGRC's Carol Bower was a member of the women's eight, which won gold at the Olympic Games.

Today as in the past, PGRC is open to women of all sizes, shapes, and ages who want to row. Members range from their teens to their 80s. The club offers a ten-week coaching program for beginners, followed by mentoring by experienced rowers. Club president Sophie Socha, who rowed in Vichy, says the club is as much focused on the often life-changing benefits of rowing to the mind and body as it is to putting racing crews on the water, though that option is always there.

The Philadelphia Girls' Rowing Club celebrates two claims to fame: it occupies one of the oldest houses on Boathouse Row, and it enjoys the stature of being the oldest women's rowing club dedicated to competition. Leading the club's organization were Ernestine Steppacher Bayer, Ruth Adams Robinhold, Gladys Hauser Lux, and Lovey Farrell. With no other competitive women's crew teams anywhere in the country, PGRC women for decades raced only one another.

Sedgeley

#15 Boathouse Row

Sedgeley is a woman's social club, not a rowing club, that started out in 1897, at a time when men monopolized the Row. A group of women asked Fairmount Park for a place on the river where they could relax after exercising in the park. Initially turned down, the women used political connections to win permission for their own house, designed by Arthur H. Brockie and built in 1902, adjacent to the lighthouse. The club's non-profit foundation, the Friends of Historic Sedgeley, dating from 1912, seeks to maintain and preserve the boathouse and to educate the public on the history of Sedgeley and the lighthouse and their place in Philadelphia history.

At the northern end of Boathouse Row is "The Viking." He is not Leif Eriksson—the first European to arrive in North America. He is Thorfinn Karlsefni, an Icelander who married Leif's sister and with her led an expedition from Greenland to eastern Canada. Their son, born about 1005, is reportedly the first European born in North America.

Sedgeley is a women's social club, not a rowing club, started in 1897. Its building, completed in 1902, stands adjacent to the lighthouse, which once lit the way for boats returning to the Row at night, typically after a trip to the Falls of Schuylkill for a dinner of catfish, waffles and mint juleps.

The Viking

The statue of Thorfinn Karlsefni was created by Icelandic artist Einar Jonsson in 1920 as a more accurate portrayal of the first Viking story in North America. The work was commissioned by local historian J. Bunford Samuel, whose wife, Ellen Phillips Samuel, died in 1913, leaving a bequest for sculpture along Boathouse Row meant to be "emblematic of the history of America."

Courtesy of Susan E. Cohen.

Going Upriver

With the historic boathouses now shoulder to shoulder on Boathouse Row and unable to further expand, a burgeoning numbers of high school, collegiate, and masters rowers have migrated upriver.

The **Gillin Boat Club**, home to crews from St. Joseph's University and St. Joseph's Prep, opened in 2002 just below the Strawberry Mansion Bridge. With capacity for 42 eights plus smaller boats, it is home to one of the area's strongest collegiate teams, routinely near the top in the annual Dad Vail Regatta. Its high school crew excels in the Stotesbury.

Temple University Boathouse

After nearly losing its rowing program in 2013 because of university budget cuts, Temple University's crew program received a large donation from philanthropist H. F. "Gerry" Lenfest, as well as city funds to rebuild its home in the crumbling East Park Canoe House, built in 1914. It was under construction at the time of this photo in December 2015.

April Saul.

Hines Rowing Center

Two Philadelphians who devoted their lives to rowing stand in the cavernous Hines Rowing Center, which they built on the edge of Conshohocken to serve growing numbers of high school and collegiate rowers. George Hines was a former coach at La Salle College High School, and his wife, Lois Trench-Hines, was in the cadre of competitive women rowers who emerged in the early 1960s. The couple also built a nearby boathouse for the all-women's Catholic prep school, Mount Saint Joseph Academy.

Temple University's boathouse, the East Park Canoe House, dating from 1914, was condemned in 2008, and the university briefly cut its program in 2013, due in part to the cost of repairs. With grants from the city and philanthropist H. F. "Gerry" Lenfest, Temple's crew program was rescued, and the facility was being rebuilt in 2015–2016.

In Conshohocken, a flat stretch of the Schuylkill River is proving a congenial site for crew. Starting in 2005, Lois Trench-Hines, an early competitive rower with PGRC, and George Hines, who raced for La Salle College and coached for 13 years at La Salle College High School, purchased and outfitted the **Hines Rowing Center**. The growing campus for crew includes a boathouse for Mount Saint Joseph Academy and a massive 17,000-square-foot facility that is used by Bryn Mawr College, Cabrini College, and Philadelphia University, as well as high school programs from Archbishop Carroll, Germantown Academy, Lower Merion, and Radnor High girls. It is also home to the Whitemarsh Boat Club. The Hines Rowing Center plans three additional boathouses, which include a new facility for Villanova University.

The **Conshohocken Rowing Center**, which opened in 2015, is home to Malvern Prep and the Haverford School crews. It is also available to residents of the Borough of Conshohocken. Further upstream is the Trinsey Boathouse in Bridgeport, operated by Upper Merion Township and serving the Upper Merion High School crew and the Upper Merion Boat Club.

Across the Delaware River from Philadelphia, **Cooper River Park** is a growing venue for rowing. Among other regattas, it hosts the Scholastic Rowing Association of America.

ACKNOWLEDGMENTS

So many, many people helped me with this book—historians, architects, archivists, rowers, photographers, friends—but the person I must thank first is my dear neighbor Ellen Carver. Early one morning years ago, I saw her come home sweaty and glowing. She had taken up rowing, and envious of her latest passion, I followed in her wake, took lessons, and joined the Vesper Boat Club. Having led me to the river, she enthusiastically cheered me on through this three-year regatta of research and writing. She never tired of hearing the stories I was discovering in century-old minute books or from the rowers she sent my way. And she read each chapter draft with the same rigor with which she ran the Head of the Schuylkill Regatta.

I am grateful to Micah Kleit, then executive editor at Temple University Press, for seeking me out to write a history of Boathouse Row, a project I had never contemplated. Thanks, Micah, for giving me creative rein to pursue my own vision for the book—one that focuses on the social currents that swirl around this architectural icon as much as the sport of rowing itself. Micah would never have approached me had it not been for the recommendation of two Temple Press authors—former *Philadelphia Inquirer* colleague Murray Dubin (*Tasting Freedom*) and Tenement Museum Director Morris Vogel (*Still Philadelphia*).

As the scope of the project grew, philanthropist H. F. "Gerry" Lenfest, who has rescued so many Philadelphia treasures and regards rowing as integral to the city's identity, stepped in to support Temple's production of this book with a generous grant.

James Hill of the Undine Barge Club shared with me not only his stupendous library of 19th-century rowing books but also his extraordinary knowledge of Boathouse Row. Henry Hauptfuhrer, another history aficionado, shared the antique minute books and photos of the Bachelors Barge Club. Other clubhouse historians spent hours with me, including Chris Doyle of the Pennsylvania Barge Club; Fred Duling and Rick Stehlik of the Malta Boat Club; John Basinski and Bruce LaLonde of University Barge Club; Joe Sweeney of the Penn Athletic Association; and Michael Murphy of the Fairmount Rowing Association. Margaret Meigs and Paul Horvat, commodores of the Schuylkill Navy, helped me fathom the Navy's long past and ongoing challenges. Architectural historians Michael J. Lewis of Williams College and Tom Beischer of Stanford, as well as Philadelphia lighting architect Ray Grenald, tutored me in the Row's structural nuances.

Many of the pioneering oarswomen who struggled for decades to break into the Row and then international competition candidly shared their tales of trials and triumphs. They include Tina Bayer, whose mother was a founder of the Philadelphia Girls' Rowing Club; Vesper Boat Club president Joanne Wright Iverson, who fought to open the Olympics to women rowers; Anita DeFrantz, who broke through ceilings both as a woman and an African American, and early trailblazers Karin Constant and Diane Braceland Vreugdenhil.

J. B. Kelly, scion of two great Olympians, shared photos and unpublished memoirs of his father John B. Kelly Jr. and grandfather, John B. Kelly Sr.

The colorful Vesper Olympic Eight, who against all odds won gold in 1964, broke from their 50th reunion weekend to reminisce with me. In particular, I thank Boyce Budd and Emory Clark, who allowed me to use several photos from *Olympic Odyssey*, his own book about that journey.

Longtime La Salle College High School coach George Hines and rowing suffragist Lois Trench-Hines opened my eyes to the upper Schuylkill, where the couple has invested millions of dollars to create expansive modern boathouses for high school and collegiate rowers, now too numerous for Boathouse Row.

Bill Lamb, who coached at St. Joseph's Preparatory, helped elucidate the complicated roots of high school rowing in Philadelphia, while Philadelphia City Rowing's founder, Tony Schneider, and Director Terry Dougherty, explained its complicated present.

The photography for this book rests on the shoulders of many as well. Pulitzer Prize winner April Saul, a colleague during our years at the *Philadelphia Inquirer*, offered to turn her discerning eye to the river for me. The *Inquirer*'s photo editor, Michael Mercanti, was instrumental in researching its archive for contemporary photos shot by its talented staff. Older photographs came from individual boathouses, whose walls are covered in history, and from Philadelphia's fine archives: Josue Hurtado of Temple University's Special Collections Research Center provided me with many images, most from the long-gone *Philadelphia Evening Bulletin*. Nicole Joniec of the Library Company was particularly helpful, as were the staffs of the Historical Society of Pennsylvania, the Independence Seaport Museum, the Free Library of Philadelphia, the archives of the University of Pennsylvania and its athletic department, and the Fairmount Park Commission, as well as the Philadelphia Museum of Art and the Pennsylvania Academy of the Fine Arts. National rowing historian Bill Miller donated some rare photographs, while the descendants of several people prominent in the book dug through scrapbooks and labored to transmit high-resolution photographs.

Anchoring the efforts of all of us through the final stretch were the dedicated staff of Temple University Press, including Kate Nichols, Nikki Miller, Gary Kramer, Dave Wilson, Ann-Marie Anderson, Joan Vidal, Irene Imperio, and Mary Rose Mucie, and capped by the exceptional project management of Debbie Masi at Westchester Publishing Services.

Finally, I want to thank my son-in-law Brendan Fernald for his ever-available legal counsel and technical wizardry; my niece, Kati Kovacs, who patiently let me babble on during our weekly rows on the Schuylkill, my friends Jean Clemons, Irv Shapiro, and Phil Goldsmith for their careful critiques, and most especially my husband, Larry Brown, whose tough-love editing I so value.

NOTES

Chapter 1: Before Boathouse Row

1   **rowed a blue shell:** J. Thomas Scharf and Westcott Thompson, *History of Philadelphia, 1609–1884*, vol. 1 (Philadelphia: L. H. Everts, 1884), 646.

4   **astounding $1,000 purse (about $25,000 today):** Throughout this book, conversions of costs to 2015 dollars are based on Robert C. Sahr's Oregon State University Inflation Conversion Factors website, available at http://liberalarts .oregonstate.edu/spp/polisci/research/inflation-conversion-factors.

4   **without viewing Westminster Abbey:** Russell F. Weigley, ed., *Philadelphia: A 300-Year History* (New York: W. W. Norton, 1982), 230.

4   **Its constitution reveals:** *Constitution of the Falcon Barge Club of Philadelphia* (Philadelphia: 1835), housed at the Historical Society of Pennsylvania. The conclusion that members were largely merchants and professionals comes from an analysis of Falcon membership from 1834 to 1839 in city directories: see Stuart M. Blumin, *The Emergence of the Middle Class: Social Experience in the American City, 1760–1900* (New York: Cambridge University Press, 1989), 368.

4   **"No personal reflections":** *Constitution of the Falcon Barge Club of Philadelphia.*

6   **"convenient sewer":** Jane Mork Gibson, "The Fairmount Water Works," *Bulletin, Philadelphia Museum of Art* 84, nos. 360/361 (1988): 28, available at http://www.phillyh2o.org/backpages/PMA_TEXT.htm.

Chapter 2: Thomas Eakins

9   **fourth largest in the world:** Edwin Wolf II, *Philadelphia, Portrait of an American City: A Bicentennial History* (Harrisburg: Stackpole Books, 1975), 207.

9   **with 260 factories:** Russell F. Weigley, ed., *Philadelphia: A 300-Year History* (New York: W. W. Norton, 1982), 326.

9   **helped to catapult:** Ibid., 309.

10   **"promote peaceful coexistence":** Elizabeth Milroy, "Assembling Fairmount Park," in *Philadelphia's Cultural Landscape, The Sartain Family Legacy*," eds. Katherine Martinez and Page Talbott (Philadelphia: Temple University Press, 2000), 76.

13   **"to oversee people walking":** Jean Barth Toll and Mildred S. Gillam, eds., *Invisible Philadelphia, Community through Voluntary Organizations* (Philadelphia: Atwater Kent Museum, 1995), 1141.

13   **"If you get a chance":** Letter from Thomas Eakins to Benjamin Eakins, February 1868, housed in the Charles Bregler Collection, Pennsylvania Academy of the Fine Arts, Philadelphia.

13   **many hours away:** Philadelphians traveled to Cape May by boat or horse-drawn carriage until a train line was built in 1854. A train from Camden to Atlantic City, taking 2½ hours, also started in 1854, when Atlantic City had one hotel.

13   **before the rise of baseball:** An early version of baseball emerged in Philadelphia in 1833, but the game with modern rules began with the Minerva Baseball Club in 1857, the Keystones in 1859, and the Athletics in 1860. See Wolf, *Philadelphia*, 203.

13   **"desirous of promoting":** "Preamble," *Constitution, Bachelors Barge Club*, 1858, 1, housed at the Library Company of Philadelphia.

14   **"with the object of healthful exercise":** *Minutes Book*, Undine Barge Club records, 1856–1986, Independence Seaport Museum Archives, Philadelphia, May 9, 1856.

16   **He graduated with a 92.8:** William S. McFeely, *Portrait: The Life of Thomas Eakins* (New York: W. W. Norton, 2007), 22.

17   **Billy's sister, Emily Sartain:** From 1866 to 1919, Emily Sartain, an artist in her own right and friend of Mary Cassatt, was principal of the Philadelphia School of Design for Women, now the Moore College of Art.

17   **born in Bavaria:** U.S. Census, 1870.

17   **Dr. Samuel Gross:** McFeely, *Portrait*, 27.

20   **"I think he liked these guys":** Chris Doyle, interview with author, April 15, 2015. Other evidence of Eakins' social ties to the rowing clubs is his presence at the Undine Barge Club's Castle Ringstetten on October 31, 1878, according to the Castle's social logbook.

20   **No records prove:** McFeely, *Portrait*, 75, citing Elizabeth Milroy, "Thomas Eakins' Artistic Training" (Ph.D. diss., University of Pennsylvania, 1986).

20   **"I had been rowing with Max":** Letter from Thomas Eakins to Carolyn Eakins, October 1, 1866, McFeely, *Portrait*, 31.

21   **"I go to the Gymnasium":** Letter from Thomas Eakins to Benjamin Eakins, March 21, 1867, Bregler Collection.

22   **"beautiful in its simplicity":** Letter from Thomas Eakins to Benjamin Eakins, November 9, 1867, Bregler Collection.

22   **facing financial problems:** *Minutes of Vesper Boat Club*, unpublished, housed at Vesper Boat Club, November 14, 1881.

22   **29 cycling clubs:** Toll and Gillam, *Invisible Philadelphia*, 9.

23   **"In active exertion":** Donald Walker, *Walker's Manly Exercises and Rural Sports*, 9th ed. (London: H. G. Bohn, 1855), 2–5.

23   **"kept in the rooms":** *Minutes Book*, Undine Barge Club, February 4, 1871.

23   **"Health to be won":** Robert B. Johnson, *A History of Rowing in America* (Milwaukee: Corbitt & Johnson, 1871), 19, available at https://books.google.com/books?id=RNI9AAAAYAAJ&printsec=frontcover&source=gbs_ge_summary_r&cad=0#v=onepage&q&f=false.

23   **"take a walk to Fairmount":** Letter from Thomas Eakins to Benjamin Eakins, November 13, 1867, *Thomas Eakins Letters, 1866–1934*, Archives of American Art, Smithsonian Institution.

24   **"to improve one's health":** Ibid., 1140.

24   **clubs "which played the game":** Ibid., 1138.

24   **those from "the meanest boy's gang":** Samuel Bass Winter Jr., quoted in Toll and Gillam, *Invisible Philadelphia*, xxxiv.

27 **"The names were for camaraderie":** Henry Hauptfuhrer, interview with author, January 21, 2015.

27 **"run with the Independence":** *University Barge Club of Philadelphia, Centennial, 1854–1954*, 2, housed at Historical Society of Pennsylvania.

27 **a "white shirt":** Ibid.

27 **"was comprised of gentlemen":** John B. Thayer, "The Early Years of the University Barge Club of Philadelphia," *The Pennsylvania Magazine of History and Biography* 29, no. 3 (1905): 285.

28 **"tired of the monotony":** The entire account of the Linda's voyage is from a letter written by its crew, *150 Years History of the Bachelors Barge Club, 1853–2003*, eds. Walter H. Pflaumer et al. (n.p.: "Trick" and "Mede," 2006), 12–16.

30 **Eakins returned to Philadelphia in July 1870:** Also creating turbulence in Philadelphia at the time of Eakins' return was the passage, on February 3, 1870, of the 15th Amendment, granting African American men the right to vote. The riots that followed in 1871 led to the death of Octavius Catto, one of the best-known educators in that community.

30 **"I'm looking out for news":** Thomas Eakins letter to Fanny Eakins, July 2, 1869, Bregler Collection.

30 **"I am glad he beat":** Thomas Eakins letter to Fanny Eakins, July 8, 1969, Archives of American Art.

34 **"he has never spent an evening":** Sidney D. Kirkpatrick, *The Revenge of Thomas Eakins* (New Haven, CT: Yale University Press, 2006), 132.

34 **750,000 pedestrians:** Weigley, *Philadelphia*, 427.

34 **10 clubs, 67 boats:** Charles S. Keyser, *Fairmount Park, Sketches of Its Scenery, Waters, and History* (Philadelphia: Claxton, Remsen, and Haffelfinger, 1872), 19–20.

34 **The *Times* of London carped:** Eric Halladay, *Rowing in England: A Social History* (Manchester and New York: Manchester University Press, 1990), 79.

36 **Those seeking to join:** *Minutes of Vesper Boat Club, August 1891–May 1900*, unpublished, housed at the Vesper Boat Club.

36 **"Despite a somewhat scattered":** "Art: Third Reception of the Union League," *Philadelphia Inquirer*, April 27, 1871, 4.

37 **"paltry sum of $200":** John Wilmerding, ed. *Thomas Eakins* (Washington, DC: Smithsonian Institutions Press, 1993), 80.

37 **"America's greatest, most uncompromising":** H. Barbara Weinberg, "Thomas Eakins (1844–1916): Painting," in *Heilbrunn Timeline of Art History* (New York: The Metropolitan Museum of Art, 2000–), available at http://www.metmuseum.org/toah/hd/eapa/hd_eapa.htm (accessed November 19, 2015).

37 **"I envy you your drive":** Letter from Thomas Eakins to Emily Sartain, November 16, 1866, Bregler Collection.

37 **"key pictures":** Albert Ten Eyck Gardener, "Metropolitan Americana," *The Metropolitan Museum of Art Bulletin*, Summer 1957, 1.

Chapter 3: Frank Furness

39 **"I can't see him suffer":** Michael J. Lewis, *Frank Furness, Architecture and the Violent Mind* (New York: W. W. Norton, 2001), 48.

41 **"should be remodeled":** James Sidney and Andrew Adams, *Description of Plan for the Improvement of Fairmount Park* (Philadelphia: Merrihew and Thompson, 1859), 13, available at https://archive.org/stream/descriptionof plaoosidn#page/12/mode/2up (accessed May 22, 2016).

41 **most age 30 and older:** Charles A. Peverelly, *The Book of American Pastimes* (New York: Charles A. Peverley, 1866), 206.

44 **demolition order from the city:** *Minutes Book*, Undine Barge Club records, November 7, 1859, housed at Independence Seaport Museum.

44 **"a good array of chicken salad":** Ibid., December 20, 1860.

44 **"architecturally neat and attractive":** J. Thomas Scharf and Thompson Wescott, *History of Philadelphia, 1609–1884*, vol. 3 (Philadelphia: I. H. Everts, 1854), available at http://archive.org/stream/historyofphilade03scha/historyofphilade03scha _djvu.txt.

44 **popular at the time:** Thomas G. Beischer, "Control and Competition: The Architecture of Boathouse Row," *Pennsylvania Magazine of History and Biography* 130, no. 3 (July 2006): 309.

46 **It had cost Skating Club members:** John Frederick Lewis, "Skating and the Philadelphia Skating Club," speech to Skating Club, Philadelphia, January 9, 1895, 38, available at https://play.google.com/books/reader?id=tbk6kjEaJS8C &printsec=frontcover&output=reader&authuser=0&hl=en&pg=GBS.PA1 (accessed November. 17, 2015).

46 **"one-story brick building":** John B. Thayer, "The Early Years of the University Barge Club," *Pennsylvania Magazine of History and Biography* 29, no. 3 (1905): 6.

46 **exiting their dock:** Ibid., 286–287.

46 **"Much to our disappointment":** *Minutes Book*, Undine Barge Club records, September 21, 1861.

47 **A frequent visitor:** Lewis, *Frank Furness*, 14.

47 **"so thoroughly":** Ibid., 22.

48 **"you acquire a certain idea":** Ibid.

48 **backing Furness was engraver John Sartain:** In addition to Fairman Rogers, John Sartain was among a number of other prominent friends of Frank Furness' father, the Rev. William Furness, who helped Frank win architectural commissions. His father's childhood friend Samuel Bradford was treasurer and director of the Philadelphia and Reading RR from 1838–1884; Frank became its chief architect, designing 130 train stations and industrial buildings. Frank's commission for Rodeph Shalom synagogue likely resulted from his father's close friendship with Rebecca Gratz. See George E. Thomas, "Frank Furness: The Flowering of American Architecture," in *Frank Furness, The Complete Works*, eds. George E. Thomas, Michael J. Lewis, and Jeffrey A. Cohen (New York: Princeton Architectural Press, 1991), 63–68.

48 **The building "percolated":** Lewis, *Frank Furness*, 98.

48 **"without regard to architectural adornment":** Beischer, "Control and Competition," 312.

49 **One Crescent innovation:** Ibid., 313.

49 **The intention might have been:** Kathryn Elizabeth Brown, "Assessment and Evaluation of Consolidation Methods on Serpentine Stone" (master's thesis, University of Pennsylvania, 2013), 30.

49 **"The house is all that could be desired":** Beischer, "Control and Competition," 317, citing *University Magazine*, University of Pennsylvania, 1876 ed.

49 **decorated by Gimbel Brothers:** *Papers 1870–1912, Malta Boat Club*, November 14, 1899, housed at Historical Society of Pennsylvania.

49 **"They'd have a manufacturer":** Fred Duling, interview with author, February 9, 2015.

50 **"frequent use":** *Minutes of Vesper Boat Club*, April 24, 1878.

50 **At a special meeting:** Ibid., August 12, 1878.

51 **"and there strip off our uniforms":** Thayer, "Early Years of the University Barge Club," 282–295.

51 **"not more than twelve hundred":** *Minutes Book*, Undine Barge Club, August 7, 1875.

51   **"Sullivan, I'm sorry":** Louis H. Sullivan, "Reminiscences of Frank Furness," in Thomas et al., *Frank Furness*, 360.

52   **"It shows Furness":** Michael J. Lewis (Eakins scholar and professor of art history, Williams College), email to author, July 3, 2014.

52   **"properly framed and put together":** Contract between Undine Barge Club and J. C. Bozworth, *Minutes Book*, Undine Barge Club, October 2, 1875.

52   **a location that became impractical:** Rowers arriving upriver on the west side of the Schuylkill River would carry their oars up the hill to the Lilacs, a walk that was cut off by the Schuylkill Expressway in 1956. A sign for the Lilacs, which in 2015 was rented to Outward Bound, can be found on the west side of I-76 off West Ford Road. The charming cottages of the Button and Castle Ringstetten are visible from Kelly Drive, just above the East Falls Bridge, separated by a nondescript white building.

52   **"One or two parties":** *Minutes Book*, Undine Barge Club records, April 3 and May 1, 1875.

54   **"Objection [by Skating Club]":** Lewis, "Skating and the Philadelphia Skating Club," 40.

54   **"were looked upon":** Ibid., 46.

56   **"the prominent gentlemen:** Details of the fundraising effort are in the *Minutes Book*, West Philadelphia Boat Club records of March 7 and April 4, 1876. Its $2 monthly dues totaled $500 a year in today's dollars, about what the clubs of Boathouse Row now charge. The brief doubling of the dues from February through May 1874 was indeed a dire step.

56   **"If we can't build":** Ibid., March 5, 1878.

56   **It was a "social change":** Beischer, "Control and Competition," 319.

56   **"A design without action":** Frank Furness, "Hints to Designers," *Lippincott's Magazine* 21 (May 1878), in Thomas et al., *Frank Furness*, 349.

56   **"The boathouse evoked":** Beischer, "Control and Competition," 324–325.

56   **He creatively employed:** George E. Thomas, "The Happy Employment of Means to Ends," *Pennsylvania Magazine of History and Biography* 126, no. 2 (April 2008): 262. Furness used the same technique of a separate stair tower in his Furness Library, now Fisher Fine Arts Library, at the University of Pennsylvania.

58   **"delight of the eye":** Furness, "Hints to Designers," 347–349.

58   **"a place of festive pageantry":** Michael J. Lewis, email to author, July 3, 2014.

58   **Furness' firm received $560:** "Report of the Building Committee," *Minutes Book*, Undine Barge Club, April 1882.

58   **And with more and more boat bays:** Unchecked expansion in the late 20th century, according to University of Pennsylvania Professor George Thomas, "has marred the gracious punctuation of separate structures to produce an effect uncomfortably like an unzoned Mediterranean beach" (Joseph G. Brin, "How to Read Your State," HiddenCity Philadelphia, January 23, 2012, available at http://hiddencityphila.org/2012/01/how-to-read-a-state/ [accessed December 28, 2015]).

58   **"elaborate woodwork, high chimneys":** Brown, "Assessment and Evaluation," 17.

61   **"a play of the symmetrical":** Beischer, "Control and Competition," 327.

61   **"With three porches":** Ibid., 329.

61   **By the 1960s:** Among the Furness buildings still standing are the Bryn Mawr Hotel, now a part of the Baldwin School; the Gravers Line SEPTA station; the First Unitarian Church, 2125 Chestnut St.; and the Merion Cricket Club.

62   **"It was simple to do":** Ray Grenald, interview with author, August 21, 2015.

64   **"When your first outline":** Furness, "Hints to Designers," 349.

70 **among the tens of thousands:** The Census of 1850 counted 72,000 Irish in Philadelphia.

70 **27 percent of the city's population:** Russell F. Weigley, ed., *Philadelphia: A 300-Year History* (New York: W. W. Norton, 1982), 422.

70 **The Kellys had migrated:** Much of the information on John B. Kelly's early years comes from an undated, untitled 34-page memoir by John B. Kelly Sr., in the private collection of John B. Kelly III (hereafter cited as John B. Kelly Sr., undated memoir).

71 **"No Irish need apply":** Jay P. Dolan, *The Irish Americans, A History* (New York: Bloomsbury Press, 2008), 96.

72 **"most popular employee of the year":** Daniel J. Boyne, *Kelly: A Father a Son, an American Quest* (Guilford, CT: Lyons Press, 2012), 26.

72 **"I had to walk and climb":** John B. Kelly Sr., undated memoir, 5.

72 **"My hopes were high":** Ibid.

74 **Among them were William Carr:** Biographical data on Vesper's 1900 Olympic crew is from the U.S. Census of 1900.

74 **He would be out:** John B. Kelly Sr., undated memoir, 6.

74 **"Vesper proved a big surprise":** Louis Heiland, *The Schuylkill Navy of Philadelphia, 1858–1937* (Philadelphia: Drake Press, 1938), 261.

75 **"There will be no beating":** Arthur H. Lewis, *Those Philadelphia Kellys, with a Touch of Grace* (New York: Morrow, 1977), 149.

75 **He was undefeated:** Ibid., 152.

75 **"I would rather row":** "Kelly May Enter Diamond Sculls," *New York Times*, April 28, 1920.

77 **Over the course of:** Stephen Longstreet, *Win or Lose: A Social History of Gambling in America* (Indianapolis: Bobbs-Merrill, 1977), 51.

77 **"an officer of Her Majesty's Army":** Eric Halladay, *Rowing in England: A Social History* (Manchester: Manchester University Press, 1990), 79.

78 **"mechanic, artisan or labourer":** Ibid., 81.

78 **In 1881, the stroke:** Samuel Crowther and Arthur Ruhl, *Rowing and Track Athletics* (New York: Macmillan, 1905), 76.

78 **"No entry from the Vesper":** Patrick R. Redmond, *The Irish and the Making of American Sport, 1835–1920* (Jefferson, NC: McFarland, 1965), 379.

78 **"and that they'd be happy":** Arthur Daley, "Recital of Facts," *New York Times*, September 24, 1956, 32, available at http://query.nytimes.com/gst/abstract.html?res=9E01E7DD1631E333A05757C2A96F9C946792D6CF (accessed August 5, 2015).

78 **Some 20,000 people:** John B. Kelly Sr., in an interview with the *Philadelphia Evening Bulletin* on January 27, 1933, said that 50,000 people watched his race with Dibble.

79 **"Never since the firing":** Robert F. Kelley, *American Rowing: Its Background and Traditions* (New York: G. P. Putnam's, 1932), 40.

81 **"This I Believe":** John B. Kelly Sr., "This I Believe," undated essay in the private collection of John B. Kelly III.

81 **"Beresford tried to set":** *Philadelphia Evening Bulletin*, January 27, 1933.

81 **"Kelly was slightly exhausted":** *Philadelphia Inquirer*, August 30, 1920.

82 **"that American crews and rowers":** Kelley, *American Rowing*, 193.

82 **In Philadelphia, a crowd:** Boyne, *Kelly*, 161.

82   **"My grandfather was very serious":** John B. (J. B.) Kelly III, interview with author, November 1, 2014. Subsequent quotes from J. B. are also from interview.

86   **Using his influence:** Peter Mallory, *The Sport of Rowing: Two Centuries of Competition*, vol. 2 (Henley-on-Thames: River and Rowing Museum, 2011), 1039.

86   **"He wasn't out with the kids":** Lewis, *Those Philadelphia Kellys*, 207.

91   **"Sports were my most important priority":** Lewis, *Those Philadelphia Kellys*, 227. "Everything"—emphasis in original.

Chapter 5: Tom Curran and Joe Burk

93   **One frigid Philadelphia day:** Kathryn McCaffrey, interview with author, February 10, 2015.

93   **"a hail of gunfire":** *Philadelphia Inquirer*, August 11, 1955, 17.

97   **"New crews were being formed":** Peter Mallory, *The Sport of Rowing* (Henley-on-Thames: River and Rowing Museum, 2011), 312.

97   **"the vicious short dig":** Ibid., 313.

97   **Nonetheless, Penn's four-oared boat:** "More on Rowing at Penn in the 19th Century," Archives, University of Pennsylvania, 65, available at http://www.archives.upenn.edu/primdocs/ups/ups80_20r78pp63to101.pdf (accessed November. 22, 2015).

97   **Ward developed the "Pennsylvania stroke":** Thomas C. Mendenhall, *A Short History of American Rowing* (Boston: Charles River Books, 1981), 20.

98   **Census records prove:** U.S. Census, 1860.

101   **"Penn left Henley":** "Rowing at Penn, the Early Years, 1854–1901," Archives of the University of Pennsylvania, available at http://www.archives.upenn.edu/histy/features/sports/crew/1800s/histy_henley.html (accessed February 17, 2015).

101   **Penn's crew "could not have been refused":** Eric Halladay, *Rowing in England: A Social History* (Manchester: Manchester University Press, 1990), 114.

104   **FISA world rowing championships:** FISA is the governing body of the sport of rowing, an acronym of the French, Fédération Internationale des Sociétés d'Aviron.

107   **the strongest and heaviest man:** Art Morrow, "No More Worlds Left to Conquer, Sculling Champion Quits Sport," *Philadelphia Inquirer*, August 9, 1940, Spt. 2.

108   **The "athletic budget is not of sufficient strength":** *The Record, Class of 1934*, University of Pennsylvania, 155.

108   **"To keep in shape":** Barry Jordan, "Man among Men," *Daily Pennsylvanian*, March 21, 1968, 12, available at http://www.library.upenn.edu/docs/kislak/dp/1968/1968_03_21.pdf (accessed December. 1, 2015).

108   **"The New York Athletic Club:"** Daniel James Brown, *The Boys in the Boat: Nine Americans and Their Quest for Gold at the 1936 Berlin Olympics* (New York, Penguin Books, 2013), 281–282.

110   **"Crew takes a lot of time":** Jordan, "Man among Men," 12.

111   **"Herein lies the essential difference":** Joe Burk, "Burk Tells How He Rows," *Philadelphia Inquirer–Public Ledger*, September 10, 1939, Spt. 2.

113   **Burk credited his wins:** "Joe Burk Feted at Penn AC Party," *Philadelphia Inquirer*, July 17, 1938, Spt. 3.

113   **"the world's greatest sculler":** Cy Peterman, "Burk's Farewell to Oars," *Philadelphia Inquirer–Public Ledger,* August 11, 1940, Spt. 1.

114 **private clubhouses withered:** The Crescent Boat Club rented to La Salle College and La Salle College High School crews; the Pennsylvania Barge Club rented to the Schuylkill Navy, the National Association of Amateur Oarsmen and other groups. Both clubs are now again active as rowing organizations.

115 **"We were it. Just him and us":** George Hines, interview with author, March 4, 2015.

118 **"He had the biggest paws":** Gavin White, interview with author, March 24, 2015.

118 **Discipline was also critical:** David Halberstam, *The Amateurs, The Story of Four Young Men and Their Quest for Gold* (New York: Ballantine Books, 1996), 92.

119 **"A boy needs to have some physical strain":** Jordan, "Man among Men," 12.

119 **"In my four years at Penn":** Mallory, *Sport of Rowing*, 1179.

119 **"He did not seek 'perfection'":** McCaffrey, interview.

119 **Using a deck of cards,** "Dealer's Choice," *Daily Pennsylvanian*, April 18, 1969, 10, available at http://www.library.upenn .edu/docs/kislak/dp/1969/1969_04_18.pdf (accessed November 22, 2015).

119 **"Using his system":** Ibid.

124 **"To European observers, Penn seemed to defy":** Mallory, *Sport of Rowing*, 685.

124 **Penn four would be the last:** Ibid., 1233.

124 **Starting in 1963:** Susan Saint Sing, *The Eight: A Season in the Tradition of Harvard Crew* (New York: St. Martin's Press, 2010), 77.

125 **"The Bear taught me":** White, interview.

125 **"I couldn't believe that Temple":** H. F. "Gerry" Lenfest, interview with author, March 27, 2015.

Chapter 6: Ernestine Bayer

127 **In 1870, Lottie McAlice:** John J. Kudlik, "You Couldn't Keep an Iron Man Down: Rowing in Nineteenth Century Pittsburgh," *Pittsburgh History* 73, no. 2 (Summer 1990): 58.

127 **On New York City's East River:** "Novel Aquatic Experience," *New York Times*, September 7, 1870, available at http:// query.nytimes.com/mem/archive-free/pdf?res=9B01E6DD113DE53BBC4F53DFBF66838B669FDE (accessed September 8, 2015).

129 **In 1888, in Newport, Kentucky:** Thomas C. Mendenhall, *A Short History of American Rowing* (Boston: Charles River Books, 1981), 40.

129 **"two mile race for stakes":** Carolyn Thomasson (member of ZLAC), interview with author, September 7, 2015.

129 **"Women have but one task:"** Pierre de Coubertin, "Les femmes aux Jeux Olympiques," *Revue Olympique*, July 1912, 109–111.

129 **"an ideal suit for cycling":** "History of Women in Sports Timeline," available at http://stlawrence.aauw-nys.org /timeline.htm (accessed November 24, 2015).

131 **"The bicycle has done more":** Ibid.

131 **"a trifle advanced":** Jean S. Thayer, *The Light on Turtle Rock, 1897–1985: A Diary of the Sedgeley Club* (St. Peters, PA: Springbrook Printing, 1978), 28.

131 **"purely social":** Ibid., 36

131 **Her earliest memory:** Tina Bayer, interview with author, July 29, 2014. Subsequent quotes from Tina are also from interview.

133 **"secretaries, saleswomen, nurses":** Lew Cuyler, *Ernestine Bayer: Mother of U.S. Women's Rowing* (Amazon Book-Surge, 2006), 47.

133 **"lighted electric headsets":** George M. Mawhiney, "250,000 View River Pageant," *Philadelphia Inquirer–Public Ledger*, June 30, 1938, 1.

135 **"women took over man's":** Joanne Wright Iverson, *An Obsession with Rings* (Atlanta: Bookhouse Group, 2009), 17.

137 **"I was 18 or 19":** Ibid., 4.

137 **"we were either guy crazy":** Ibid., 18.

139 **"All I wanted to do":** Joanne Wright Iverson, interview with author, July 24, 2014.

139 **As Nash was flying to Rome:** Iverson, *Obsession with Rings*, 25.

139 **"You just stop":** Ted Nash confirmed the two incidents and the officials' quotes in an email to author, June 17, 2015.

141 **"Building Character and Manhood":** "Official Programme," *79th Annual Royal Canadian Henley Regatta, 1961*, 3, available at http://henley.stcatharines.library.on.ca:1967/Programs/1961.pdf (accessed November 27, 2015).

141 **"a cute little girl,":** Iverson, interview.

141 **On July 3, 1963:** Numerous sources state that 1962 was the year that the National Women's Rowing Association was first conceived, but Iverson says that is an error stemming from an incorrect press release and that the actual year was 1963.

141 **fearing that the city could revoke:** Cuyler, *Ernestine Bayer*, 59.

141–142 **"was really good for publicizing":** Iverson, interview.

142 **"He said, 'No'":** Bayer, interview.

144 **Davenport candidly confessed:** Ibid.

145 **"Here comes this little guy":** Karin Constant, interview with author, October 27, 2014. Subsequent quotes are from interview.

146 **"I really didn't know anything":** Diane Vreugdenhil, interview with author, July 13, 2014. Subsequent quotes are from interview.

146 **"the rowers, especially the guys":** Diane Pucin, "Women Are Now Members of Crew," *Philadelphia Inquirer*, June 23, 1989, available at http://articles.philly.com/1989–06–23/sports/26105843_1_rowing-olympics-meters (accessed November 25, 2015).

147 **"We'd see seats out of boats":** Chuck Patterson, interview with author, July 22, 2015.

149 **She had learned determination:** Anita DeFrantz, interview with author, August 31, 2014. Subsequent quotes are from interview.

150 **Anita trained three times a day:** Henry Louis Gates and Evelyn Brooks Higginbotham, eds., *African American Lives* (New York: Oxford University Press, 2004), 222.

154 **"'Well, we don't have a toilet'":** Lois Trench-Hines, interview with author, January 31, 2015.

Chapter 7: The "Vesper Eight"

161 **But the worst defeat:** Emory Clark, interview with author, January 25, 2014.

161 **"Despair. A broken heart":** Emory Clark, *Olympic Odyssey* (Lapeer, MI: Taylor Butterfield, 2014), 1.

161 **A "Clydesdale," he called himself:** Boyce Budd, interview with author, January 25, 2014.

161 **"He was too big, too rough, too strong":** Clark, interview.

161 **"Dear Em":** Clark, *Odyssey*, 7–9.

161 **"team up in a pair":** A "pair" is a boat for two oarsmen, each with one oar. In a "double scull" each of the two oarsmen has two oars.

163 **"Come at 5":** Clark, interview.

163 **"I'd never heard of":** Emory Clark, "Lucy's Log," undated, unpublished memoir.

163 **They had largely been victorious:** The Ratzeburg Club of Germany, which won the eight-oared race in the 1960 Olympics, adopted the strength-training technique of America's star rower of the 1930s, Joe Burk, who later coached the University of Pennsylvania crew to many victories.

166 **much like a "last hurrah":** William A. Stowe, *All Together, The Formidable Journey to the Gold with the 1964 Olympic Crew* (Lincoln, NE: iUniverse, 2005), 16.

167 **"that put us on the map."** Joe Amlong, interview with author, February 4, 2014. The United States Military Academy at West Point, which Joe Amlong attended in the early 1960s, had no varsity crew until 1986. Subsequent quotes from Joe Amlong are from interview.

168 **"One of the reasons":** Clark, *Odyssey*, 37.

168 **those Ivy "pussies":** Clark, interview.

168 **"As soon as we returned":** "Two Guys from Tokyo," *La Salle* 9, no. 3 (Spring 1965): 10.

169 **"encouraged me to drop":** Stan Cwiklinski, interview with author, March 3, 2014.

170 **"His genius was in providing":** Peter Mallory, *The Sport of Rowing: Two Centuries of Competition*, vol. 2 (Henley-on-Thames: River and Rowing Museum, 2011), 1371.

170 **"I had a uniform":** Dietrich Rose, interview with author, February 27, 2014. Subsequent quotes from Rose are from interview.

171 **"You had Rosenberg":** Clark, interview.

171 **"wobbly and on port":** Clark, *Odyssey*, 18.

171 **"I became sweaty":** Ibid., 21. Description of the winter of 1964 continues to page 40.

172 **"As a non-athlete":** Stowe, *All Together*, 57. All subsequent quotes from Stowe are from his book.

173 **"Who the hell":** Ibid., 63.

173 **"Bill pulled as much":** Clark, *Odyssey*, 35.

173 **"an oarsman's nightmare":** Ibid., 49.

173 **Tony Johnson and Jim Edmonds:** The two went on to the 1964 Tokyo Olympics, where they came in tenth in the coxless pair.

173 **"We didn't care":** Clark, *Odyssey*, 49.

175 **'You can't row":** Amlong, interview.

175 **"They were short":** Clark, *Odyssey*, 19–20.

175 **"At my age":** Cwiklinski, interview.

175 **"There were times":** Mallory, *Sport of Rowing*, 1375.

176 **"We rowed six days":** Stowe, *All Together*, 70.

176 **"There seemed to be a pent-up":** Ibid., 94.

176 **Worse, Vesper was told:** Ibid., 93.

176 **They "took special pains":** Clark, *Odyssey*, 57–58.

176 **"We dressed in rags":** Stowe, *All Together*, 91.

176 **Harvard got off to its best start:** Tom Brody, "Anything That Boys Can Do," *Sports Illustrated*, July 20, 1964, 14.

177 **"made me mad":** Clark, *Odyssey*, 62.

177 **"The destruction of Harvard":** Ibid., 64.

177   **"A boatload of men":** Brody, "Anything That Boys Can Do," 14.

180   **"If we were to lose":** Clark, *Odyssey*, 138.

180   **"were lying on the dock":** Stowe, *All Together*, 146.

180   **"With the exception":** Clark, *Odyssey,* 53.

182   **"What am I doing?":** Stowe, *All Together*, 157.

182   **"Vee are in third place":** Ibid.

182   **"slapped a wave":** Clark, *Odyssey*. Clark's account of his rowing error is on pages 154–155.

185   **"Fortunately I did not stop":** Stowe, *All Together*, 160.

185   **"Let's go boyz!!":** Ibid.

Chapter 8: Edward T. Stotesbury

191   **"I never experienced anything":** Daekwon Smith, interview with author, April 16, 2015.

194   **By 1882, Episcopal Academy:** "History of the Episcopal Academy," Episcopal Academy: Celebrating 225 Years, 1785–2010, available at http://inside.episcopalacademy.org/drum/webmanager/0910/ea_225/history/history.html.

194   **"advanced instruction":** David F. Labaree, *The Making of an American High School: The Credentials Market and the Central High School of Philadelphia, 1838–1939* (New Haven, CT: Yale University Press, 1988), 32.

194   **"Our mission is to empower":** Terry Dougherty, interview with author, October 16, 2014.

196   **"Last spring the Bachelor club":** "Amateur-Sport," *Harper's Weekly* 41 (September 4, 1897): 889, available at https://babel.hathitrust.org/cgi/pt?id=pst.000020241124;view=1up;seq=249.

196   **"wealthy man in the class":** Robert Pruter, *The Rise of American High School Sports and the Search for Control, 1880–1930* (Syracuse, NY: Syracuse University Press, 2013), 140.

196   **That year, too:** *Public Ledger Almanac, 1900*, 115, available at https://play.google.com/books/reader?id=iFAWAAAAYAAJ&printsec=frontcover&output=reader&hl=en&pg=GBS.RA1-PA115.

196   **"long and severe training":** Franklin Spencer Edmonds, *History of the Central High School of Philadelphia* (Philadelphia.: J. B. Lippincott Co., 1902), 259.

196   **underscored by its defeat:** *The World Almanac and Encyclopedia, 1915* (New York: Press Publishing, 1914), 330, available at https://books.google.com/books?id=-GQ3AAAAMAAJ&pg=PA363&lpg=PA363&dq=brown+preparatory+school+philadelphia+location&source=bl&ots=FYYSKGjjuj&sig=j6NYwgaw8nyjuidcyfUBzOpBR3w&hl=en&sa=X&ei=-xiwVKi-JM-1sQS540L4CA&ved=0CEEQ6AEwBQ#v=onepage&q=brown%20preparatory%20school%20philadelphia%20location&f=false.

197   **"Philadelphia's first citizen":** "All Phila. Mourns Stotesbury Death," *Philadelphia Inquirer*, May 17, 1938, 6.

197   **"Versailles of America":** Charles G. and Edward C. Zwicker, with the Springfield Township Historical Society, *Whitemarsh Hall, the Estate of Edward T. Stotesbury* (Charleston SC: Acadia Publishing, 2004), 7.

198   **"the problems and pleasures of farming":** *Minutes of the Farmers' Club, of Pennsylvania: A Record of Seventy Years 1849–1919* (Philadelphia: J. B. Lippincott, 1920), vi, available at http://books.google.com/books?id=xUI9AQAAMAAJ&pg=PA345&dq=Effingham+morris+edward+stotesbury&hl=en&sa=X&ei=-QmBVKjjbcWbyATL8IGQBQ&ved=0CCQQ6AEwAQ#v=onepage&q=Effingham%20morris%20edward%20stotesbury&f=false (accessed December 26, 2015).

200   **"fairly definitely not an Old Philadelphian":** Nathaniel Burt, *The Perennial Philadelphians: The Anatomy of an American Aristocracy* (Boston: Little, Brown, 1963), 162.

200 **decided to join the Bachelors:** E. Digby Baltzell, "Upper Class Clubs and Associations in Philadelphia," in *Invisible Philadelphia: Community through Voluntary Organizations*, eds. Jean Barth Toll and Mildred S. Gillam (Philadelphia: Atwater Kent Museum, 1995), 1138. Digby Baltzell, quoted here on the importance of club membership to Philadelphia society, said that a large number, "particularly those who joined exclusive cricket and country clubs, never participated at all. They sought status, or at the very least, the protection of their current position in Philadelphia society."

200 **"all covered with slime":** "The Old Family Toothbrush," available at http://stotesbury.com/media/OldFamilyToothbrush.html.

200 **"Once you walked in":** Henry Hauptfuhrer, interview with author, March 4, 2015.

204 **"They had tremendous work ethic":** Bill Lamb, interview with author, December 4, 2014. Subsequent quotes are from interview.

204 **They were a parallel universe:** Pruter, *Rise of American High School Sports*, 224.

205 **"very, very supportive":** Lamb, interview.

206 **"I was not athletic":** Tony Schneider, interview with author, October 22, 2014.

207 **"under education of urban youth":** Ibid.

207 **"upper-class Ivy League image":** Brother Tim Ahern, interview with author, January 12, 2015.

207 **"a chance for the kids":** Paul Horvat, commodore of the Schuylkill Navy, interview with author, January 4, 2016.

208 **"Parents started to see opportunities":** Lamb, interview.

208 **Not only were the clubs struggling:** Ray Grenald, the lighting architect who installed lights on the Row in 1979, was shocked when he inspected the houses. "They were in deplorable condition," he said, with old electrical panel boards running hot from overloaded circuits. "It was just a matter of time until all the houses went up in flames." (Grenald, interview with author, August 21, 2015.)

208 **"And that's before we ever":** Lamb, interview.

209 **"I kept seeing it as the back of the bus":** Robert B. Coleman, interview with author, October 10, 2015.

209 **"There was no road map":** Schneider, interview.

214 **"Winning medals in races":** Ibid.

214 **"I find myself able":** Smith, interview.

The Schuylkill Navy and the Clubs of Boathouse Row

219 **"stake," or "admission money":** "Constitution, By-laws and Rules of the Schuylkill Navy of Philadelphia," Philadelphia, 1876, available at https://archive.org/stream/constitutionbyla00schu/constitutionbyla00schu_djvu.txt ARTICLE II.

228 **"the dawn of organized athletics":** John B. Thayer, "The Early Years of the University Barge Club of Philadelphia," *The Pennsylvania Magazine of History and Biography* 29, no. 3 (1905): 284.

229 **"a congenial environment":** Bart Isdaner, email to author, December 4, 2015.

235 **"healthful exercise, relaxation":** "Minutes Undine Barge Club," May 9, 1856, housed at the Independence Seaport Museum.

BIBLIOGRAPHY

A Note about Sources

Among the most fascinating and detailed accounts of Boathouse Row's history come from the minutes of those clubs, especially those of the 19th century. They reveal an era when rules of comportment were paramount—from Sunday rowing bans to elaborate uniforms that varied by season, to strictures on drinking, smoking, and entertaining women—with significant fines for violations. There is no single repository for these minutes. Some clubs have given their flaking leather-bound ledgers to the Independence Seaport Museum, the Library Company of Philadelphia or the Historical Society of Pennsylvania. But many are stashed in corners of boathouses or in the homes of club officers. Hopefully, those clubs will find the means to maintain these treasures. The Special Collections Research Center at Temple University Libraries holds an irreplaceable trove of photographs from the former *Philadelphia Evening Bulletin* and *Public Ledger* as well as the *Philadelphia Inquirer*; it is a historical treasure for the city. At the archives of the Pennsylvania Academy of the Fine Arts are the letters of Thomas Eakins, written home from Paris. I still tingle at the memory of holding these fragile documents in my hands. The Van Pelt Library at the University of Pennsylvania and the Philadelphia Free Library hold century-old books on rowing and the history of Central High School, offering insights into the crew culture of the time. And at Van Pelt, too, I was able to browse through every class yearbook since the advent of Penn crew. Information on many rowers' occupational status comes from U.S. Census records. The Fairmount Park Commission archives hold letters, news stories and park commission documents that reveal the bureaucratic side of Boathouse Row developments. Some sources here are not cited in the notes but were particularly helpful in providing background, context, and confirmation of facts.

The more recent history of the Row comes largely through interviews, generously granted by oarsmen and oarswomen who have lived it, and by club members who have chosen to study their organization's past. (Please see the Acknowledgments.)

Adams, Henry. *Eakins Revealed, The Secret Life of an American Artist.* Oxford: Oxford University Press, 2001.

Beischer, Thomas G. "Control and Competition: The Architecture of Boathouse Row." *Pennsylvania Magazine of History and Biography* 130, no. 3 (July 2006).

Blumin, Stuart M. *The Emergence of the Middle Class: Social Experience in the American City, 1760–1900.* New York: Cambridge University Press, 1989.

Boyne, Daniel J. *Kelly: A Father, a Son, an American Quest.* Guildford, CT: Lyons Press, 2012.

Bradley, U. T. "The Dad Vail Story." Rollins College Press, undated, about 1961.

Brin, Joseph G. "How to Read Your State," HiddenCity Philadelphia, January 23, 2012. Available at http://hiddencityphila.org/2012/01/how-to-read-a-state/. Accessed December 28, 2015.

Brown, Daniel James. *The Boys in the Boat: Nine Americans and Their Quest for Gold at the 1936 Berlin Olympics.* London: Penguin Books, 2013.

Brown, Kathryn Elizabeth. "Assessment and Evaluation of Consolidation Methods on Serpentine Stone at the 19th Street Baptist Church, Philadelphia, PA." Master's thesis, University of Pennsylvania, 2013.

Burt, Nathaniel. *The Perennial Philadelphians: The Anatomy of an American Aristocracy.* Boston: Little, Brown, 1963.

Clark, Dennis. *The Irish in Philadelphia: Ten Generations of Urban Experience.* Philadelphia: Temple University Press, 1982.

Clark, Emory. *Olympic Odyssey.* Lapeer, MI: Taylor Butterfield, 2014. (Self-published.)

Cooper, Helen. *Thomas Eakins: The Rowing Pictures.* New Haven, CT: Yale University Art Gallery, Yale University Press, 1996.

Crowther, Samuel, and Arthur Ruhl. *Rowing and Track Athletics.* New York: Macmillan, 1905.

Cuyler, Lew. *Ernestine Bayer: Mother of U.S. Women's Rowing.* Amazon BookSurge, 2006. (Self-published.)

Darby, Mrs. D. Weston, Jr. *The Light on Turtle Rock, 1897–1985: A Diary of the Sedgeley Club.* St. Peters, PA: Springbrook Printing, circa 1978.

"Description of Plan for the Improvement of Fairmount Park by Sidney & Adams." Philadelphia: Merrihew and Thompson, 1859. Available at https://archive.org/stream/descriptionofpla00sidn#page/12/mode/2up.

Dolan, Jay P. *The Irish Americans: A History.* New York: Bloomsbury Press, 2008.

Eakins, Thomas. *Letters of Thomas Eakins.* Archives, the Charles Bregler Collection. Pennsylvania Academy of the Fine Arts, 1866–1870.

———. *Letters of Thomas Eakins.* Archives of American Art. Smithsonian Institution. Available at http://www.aaa.si.edu/collections/container/viewer/Letters-to-Family—199030.

Edmonds, Franklin Spencer. *History of the Central High School of Philadelphia.* Philadelphia: J. B. Lippincott, 1902.

Foster, Kathleen A. *Thomas Eakins Rediscovered.* New Haven, CT: Yale University Press, 1997.

Gardner, Albert Ten Eyck. "Metropolitan Americana." *Metropolitan Museum of Art Bulletin.* New York: Metropolitan Museum of Art, 1957.

Gates, Henry Louis, and Evelyn Brooks Higginbotham, eds. *African American Lives.* Oxford: Oxford University Press, 2004.

Gibson, Jane Mork. "The Fairmount Water Works." *Philadelphia Museum of Art Bulletin* 84, nos. 360/361 (1988). Available at http://www.phillyh2o.org/backpages/PMA_TEXT.htm.

Goodrich, Lloyd. *Thomas Eakins.* Vols. 1 and 2. Cambridge, MA: Harvard University Press, 1982.

Halberstam, David. *The Amateurs: The Story of Four Young Men and Their Quest for Gold.* London: Hodder and Stoughton, 1985.

Halladay, Eric. *Rowing in England: A Social History.* Manchester: Manchester University Press, 1990.

Heiland, Louis. *The Schuylkill Navy of Philadelphia, 1858–1937.* Philadelphia: The Drake Press, 1938.

———. *The Undine Barge Club of Philadelphia.* Philadelphia: Wm. F. Fell, 1925.

"History of the Episcopal Academy." Episcopal Academy: Celebrating 225 Years, 1785–2010. Available at http://inside.episcopalacademy .org/drum/webmanager/0910/ea_225/history/history.html. Accessed November. 27, 2015.

"History of Women in Sports Timeline." Available at http://stlawrence.aauw-nys.org/timeline.htm. Accessed November 24, 2015.

Iverson, Joanne Wright. *An Obsession with Rings.* Atlanta: Bookhouse Group, 2009. (Self-published.)

Janssen, Frederick William. *History of American Amateur Athletics.* New York: Charles R. Bourne, 1885. Reprint, Provo, UT: Repressed Publishing, 2013.

Johns, Elizabeth. *Thomas Eakins: The Heroism of Modern Life.* Princeton, NJ: Princeton University Press, 1983.

Johnson, Robert B. *A History of Rowing in America.* Milwaukee: Corbitt and Johnson, 1871.

Kain, Charles F., ed. *The Schuylkill Navy of Philadelphia, 1938–1958.* Philadelphia: Franklin Printing, 1960.

Kelley, Robert F. *American Rowing: Its Background and Traditions.* New York: G. P. Putnam's Sons, 1932.

Kelly, John B., Sr. "This I Believe." Unpublished, undated essay. Personal papers of John B. Kelly III.

———. Untitled, undated memoir. Personal papers of John B. Kelly III.

Keyser, Charles S. *Fairmount Park, Sketches of Its Scenery, Waters, and History.* Philadelphia: Claxton, Remsen, and Haffelfinger, 1872.

Kirkpatrick, Sidney D. *The Revenge of Thomas Eakins.* New Haven, CT: Yale University Press, 2006.

Kudlik, John J. "You Couldn't Keep an Iron Man Down: Rowing in Nineteenth Century Pittsburgh." *Pittsburgh History* 73, no. 2 (Summer 1990): 51–63.

Labaree, David F. *The Making of an American High School: The Credentials Market and the Central High School of Philadelphia, 1838–1939.* New Haven, CT: Yale University Press, 1988.

Lewis, Arthur H. *Those Philadelphia Kellys, with a Touch of Grace.* New York: Morrow, 1977.

Lewis, John Frederick. *Skating and the Philadelphia Skating Club.* Speech to Skating Club, Philadelphia. January 9, 1895. Available at https://play.google.com/books/reader?id=tbk6kjEaJS8C&printsec=frontcover&output=reader&authuser=0&hl=en&pg=GBS .PA1. Accessed November 17, 2015.

Lewis, Michael J., "The First Design for Fairmount Park," *Pennsylvania Magazine of History and Biography* 130, no. 3 (July 2006). Available at http://www.jstor.org/stable/20093870. Accessed June 25, 2015.

———. *Frank Furness, Architecture and the Violent Mind.* New York: W. W. Norton, 2001.

Longstreet, Stephen. *Win or Lose: A Social History of Gambling in America.* Indianapolis: Bobbs-Merrill, 1977.

Maher, James T. *The Twilight of Splendor.* Boston: Little, Brown, 1975.

Mallory, Peter. *The Sport of Rowing: Two Centuries of Competition.* Vol. 2. Henley-on-Thames: River and Rowing Museum, 2011.

Martinez, Katherine, and Page Talbott, eds. *Philadelphia's Cultural Landscape, the Sartain Family Legacy.* Philadelphia: Temple University Press, 2000.

McFeely, William S. *Portrait: The Life of Thomas Eakins.* New York: Norton Paperback, 2007.

Mendenhall, Thomas C. *A Short History of American Rowing.* Boston: Charles River Books, 1981.

Milroy, Elizabeth. *Thomas Eakins's Artistic Training, 1860–1870.* Ph.D. dissertation, Philadelphia, University of Pennsylvania, 1986.

Minutes of the Farmers' Club of Pennsylvania: A Record of Seventy Years, 1849–1919. Philadelphia: J. B. Lippincott, 1920. Available at http://books.google.com/books?id=xUI9AQAAMAAJ&pg=PA345&dq=Effingham+morris+edward+stotesbury&hl=en&sa=X

&ei=-QmBVKjjBcWbyATL8IGQBQ&ved=0CCQQ6AEwAQ#v=onepage&q=Effingham%20morris%20edward%20stotes-bury&f=false. Accessed December 26, 2015.

Moak, Jefferson M. "Boathouse Row," *National Register of Historic Places Inventory—Nomination Form*. United States Department of Interior, National Park Service, 1983. Available at http://focus.nps.gov/pdfhost/docs/NHLS/Text/87000821.pdf. Accessed January 4, 2016.

"Official Programme." *79th Annual Royal Canadian Henley Regatta, 1961*. Available at http://henley.stcatharines.library.on.ca:1967/Programs/1961.pdf. Accessed November 27, 2015.

O'Gorman, James F. *The Architecture of Frank Furness*. Philadelphia: Philadelphia Museum of Art, 1973.

Palchikoff, Jan. "The Development of Women's Rowing in the United States," December 21, 1978. Available at http://www.usrowing.org/docs/default-source/resource-library/26E.pdf?sfvrsn=0. Accessed December 15, 2015.

Peverelly, Charles A. *The Book of American Pastimes*. New York: Self-published, 1866.

Pflaumer, Walter H., George F. Joly, William D. Myers, Jonathan Dyer, and James A. Meadowcroft. *150 Years: History of the Bachelors Barge Club, 1853–2003*. Philadelphia: Bachelors Barge Club, 2006.

Pruter, Robert. *The Rise of American High School Sports and the Search for Control, 1880–1930*. Syracuse, NY: Syracuse University Press, 2013.

Pucin, Diane. "Women Are Now Members of Crew." *Philadelphia Inquirer*, June 23, 1989. Available at http://articles.philly.com/1989-06-23/sports/26105843_1_rowing-olympics-meters. Accessed November 25, 2015.

Redmond, Patrick R. *The Irish and the Making of American Sport, 1835–1920*. Jefferson, NC: McFarland, 1965.

Saint Sing, Susan. *The Eight: A Season in the Tradition of Harvard Crew*. New York: St. Martin's Press, 2010.

Scharf, J. Thomas, and Thompson Westcott. *History of Philadelphia, 1609–1884*. Vol. 1. Philadelphia: L. H. Everts, 1884. Available at https://books.google.com/books?id=Qh4UAwAAQBAJ&dq=blue+devil+and+imp&q=blue+devil#v=onepage&q&f=false. Accessed March 15, 2015.

The Schuylkill Navy of Philadelphia: Her History and Records. Philadelphia: Press of Security Bank Note Company, Committee of the Schuylkill Navy, 1899.

"Sixth Report of the Commissioners of Fairmount Park," December 31, 1899.

Smith, Lissa. *Nike Is a Goddess: The History of Women in Sports*. New York: Atlantic Monthly Press, 1999.

Stillner, Anna. "The Philadelphia Girls' Rowing Club: An Incremental Historic Structure Report." Master's thesis, University of Pennsylvania, 2005. Available at http://repository.upenn.edu/cgi/viewcontent.cgi?article=1041&context=hp_theses. Accessed July 25, 2016.

Stowe, William A. *All Together, The Formidable Journey to the Gold with the 1964 Olympic Crew*. New York: iUniverse: 2005. (Self-published).

Sweeney, Joe. "A Saga of a Philadelphia Rowing Club." History of Pennsylvania Athletic Club. Available at http://pennac.org/about-us/history/. Accessed August 15, 2013.

Thayer, Jean S. "The Light on Turtle Rock, 1897–1985: A Diary of the Sedgeley Club." St. Peters, PA: Springbrook Printing, 1978.

Thayer, John B. "The Early Years of the University Barge Club of Philadelphia." *Pennsylvania Magazine of History and Biography* 29, no. 3 (1905).

Thomas, George E. "The Happy Employment of Means to Ends: Frank Furness's Library of the University of Pennsylvania and the Industrial Culture of Philadelphia." *Pennsylvania Magazine of History and Biography* 126, no. 2 (April 2002).

Thomas, George E., Jeffrey A. Cohen, and Michael J. Lewis. *Frank Furness: The Complete Works*. New York: Princeton Architectural Press, 1991.

Toll, Jean Barth, and Mildred S. Gillam, eds. *Invisible Philadelphia: Community through Voluntary Organizations*. Philadelphia: Atwater Kent Museum, 1995.

Walker, Donald. *Walker's Manly Exercises and Rural Sports*. 9th ed. London: H. G. Bohn, 1855. Available at https://play.google.com/books/reader?printsec=frontcover&output=reader&id=xezSAAAAMAAJ&pg=GBS.PR7. Accessed July 15, 2014.

Weigley, Russell F., ed. *Philadelphia: A 300-Year History*. New York: W. W. Norton, 1982.

Weinberg, H. Barbara. "Thomas Eakins (1844–1916): Painting." In *Heilbrunn Timeline of Art History*. New York: The Metropolitan Museum of Art, 2000– . Available at http://www.metmuseum.org/toah/hd/eapa/hd_eapa.htm. Accessed November 13, 2015.

Wilmerding, John, ed. *Thomas Eakins*. Washington, DC: Smithsonian Institution Press, 1993.

Wolf, Edwin, II. *Philadelphia: Portrait of an American City: A Bicentennial History*. Harrisburg: Stackpole Books, 1975.

The World Almanac and Encyclopedia, 1915. New York: Press Publishing, 1914. Available at https://books.google.com/books?id=-GQ3AAAAMAAJ&pg=PA363&lpg=PA363&dq=brown+preparatory+school+philadelphia+location&source=bl&ots=FYYSKGjjuj&sig=j6NYwgaw8nyjuidcyfUBzOpBR3w&hl=en&sa=X&ei=-xiwVKi-JM-1sQS540L4CA&ved=oCEEQ6AEwBQ#v=onepage&q=brown%20preparatory%20school%20philadelphia%20location&f=false.

Zwicker, Charles G., and Edward C. *Whitemarsh Hall, the Estate of Edward T. Stotesbury*. Charleston, SC: Acadia Publishing, 2004.

Newspapers, Magazines, and Online Archives

Below are sources that I heavily used; full citations for individual articles cited in the book are provided in the Notes.

archives.upenn.edu (University of Pennsylvania)

Boathouserow.org

Dadvail.org

Daily Pennsylvanian (University of Pennsylvania)

The Explorer (La Salle College High School)

Harper's Weekly

Hear the boat sing.blogspot.com (Bill Miller blog)

La Salle (La Salle University)

La Salle Magazine (La Salle University)

NAAO yearbooks and rowing guides

New York Times

Philadelphia Evening Bulletin

Philadelphia Inquirer

Public Ledger

Public Ledger Almanacs, 1870–1873, https://play.google.com/books/reader?id=iFAWAAAAYAAJ&printsec=frontcover&output=reader&hl=en&pg=GBS.PA4

Row2k.com

Rowinghistory.net

ScholarshipStats.com
The Scholium (Episcopal Academy)
Sports Illustrated
Sports-reference.com
Stotesbury.com
USrowing.org

Club Minutes, Records, and Websites

In addition to the following sites, websites of the individual boat clubs were accessed.

Annual Report of the Secretary of the Undine Barge Club, 1867, Philadelphia. Philadelphia: Henry B. Ashmead, 1868.
Bachelors 150th Anniversary book
Constitution and Bylaws Bachelor's Barge Club, 1853
Constitution of the Falcon Barge Club of Philadelphia. Philadelphia, 1835.
Fairmount Rowing Association Minutes
Papers 1870–1912. Malta Boat Club. November 14, 1899.
Malta Boat Club Manual, 1985
Malta Boat Club Minutes
The Record (undergraduate yearbook of University of Pennsylvania)
Schuylkill Navy Administrative Minutes, 1900–1910
Undine Barge Club Minute Book, 1856–1885
University Barge Club of Philadelphia, 1854–1926, Charter By-laws Membership. Philadelphia: Thomson Printing, 1926.
University Barge Club of Philadelphia, Centennial, 1854–1954. Philadelphia, 1954.
Vesper Boat Club Minutes, 1870–1891
West Philadelphia Boat Club Minutes, 1873–1879

INDEX

Photos and illustrations are indicated by the number in italics.

Dotty Brown is a former reporter and editor at the *Philadelphia Inquirer*. During her newspaper career, she edited numerous prize-winning projects, including one that won a Pulitzer Prize. She is also a member of the Vesper Boat Club. Visit her online at www.BoathouseRowTheBook.com.